JEWISH HUMOR

Classics in Communication and Mass Culture Series

Arthur Asa Berger, Series Editor

JEWISH HUMOR

EDITED BY

AVNER ZIV

With a New Introduction
by the Editor

Transaction Publishers
New Brunswick (U.S.A.) and London (U.K.)

New material this edition copyright © 1998 by Transaction Publishers, New Brunswick, New Jersey. Originally published in 1986 by Papyrus Publishing House at Tel Aviv University.

This book is printed on acid-free paper that meets the American National Standard for Permanence of Paper for Printed Library Materials.

Library of Congress Catalog Number: 97-27107
ISBN: 1-56000-991-8
Printed in the United States of America

Library of Congress Cataloging-in-Publication Data

Jewish humor / edited by Avner Ziv ; with a new introduction by the editor.
  p. cm. — (Classics in communication and mass culture series)
  Originally published: Tel Aviv : Papyrus Pub. House at Tel-Aviv University, c1986.
  Includes bibliographical references and index.
  ISBN 1-56000-991-8 (paper : alk. paper)
  1. Jewish wit and humor. I. Ziv, Avner. II. Series.
PN6231.J5J463   1997
808.88'2'089924—dc21   97-27107
                                                                CIP

Contents

> *A clown may be the first in the kingdom of heaven ,*
> *if he has helped lessen the sadness of human life.*
> — Rabbi Baroka in Talmud

Three Jews are sentenced to death. They are put in front of a firing
squad. The officer turns to the first condemned man:
"Do you want a blindfold?"
"Yes, sir."
He asks the second one the same question.
"Yes, sir."
He asks the third.
"No, I don't want anything from you."
The second man turns to the third, and says to him in a worried voice:
"Moshe, don't make trouble now."

How would this same joke sound with slight changes? If instead of "three Jews," there were "three Frenchmen"? And then if the punchline were: "Jacques, don't make trouble now"?

In a research project I conducted in France the two versions (Moshe and Jacques) were given to groups of Jewish and non-Jewish students. Some had the "Jewish" version, others the "French" one. They were asked to rate this joke (among many others) on a "funniness" scale from 1 (not funny at all) to 10 (very funny). The "Jewish" version was presented to certain groups of subjects, and the "French" one to other groups. All students rated the Jewish version as significantly funnier that the non-Jewish one. When talking to the students afterwards, it appeared that most of them considered the Jewish version as more "appropriate." There seems to be a better understanding of the comment of the second man who turns to the third asking him not to make waves, if he is Jewish. The perception of Jews includes a stereotype in which they are supposed to be more worried and try to avoid confrontation in every kind of situation, even when they face death.

This is one example among many others, showing that there is a form of humor which can be considered Jewish. However, when the same study was replicated with Israeli students the results were even more interesting. In the study done here the names were not changed. Only the beginning of the story: in one version it began with "three Jews"; the other started with "three Israelis." Here also, the "three Jews" version was considered as funnier and more appropriate. It seems that Israelis perceive some essential quality of Jewishness, which transcends their own identification with the Jewish people. They perceive the difference created by themselves between Jews in general and Israeli Jews. They came to Israel not only to be free and independent and to create a new state of their own. They wanted also to bring into being a "new Jew," different from those living in the Diaspora: proud, not afraid by confrontations and able to do everything other nations do. They changed many things: for instance, Jews all around the world are known for their business abilities and not very famous for their military or agricultural talents. In fact, they created an extremely efficient army and did a very good job in agriculture. Their business talent is only so-so. However, many characteristics remained: they are skeptic, doubting, inquisitive and love humor. The love of humor is a constant and consistent attribute of Jews all over the world.

But what is Jewish humor? There are heated debates on this question among scholars in different areas of research in many disciplines. Does such a concept exist at all? What is Jewish humor and in what ways can it be differentiated from other types of humor?

Of course, we cannot limit ourselves to such simple "Talmudic" questions. We are also called upon to answer the question: What is humor? With this question we already encounter quite a few difficulties. Nearly 30 years ago, no less than 80 definitions were put forth in the professional literature (Bergler, 1956) and since then about another 30 have been added. And isn't it worthwhile asking what is (or who is) a Jew? As we all know this question also has a number of answers. Quite a bit of intellectual pleasure is derived from grappling with such questions. Attempts to define the concepts, to present reasons, counter-reasons and counter-counter-reasons, create schools, quarrels, criticism, and, all in all, a real academic ball. Experts in theology, in Jewish history and tradition, in philosophy, literature, in anthropology and folklore (among others) express a wide variety of views on the essence of Jewish humor.

I shall restrict myself here to two examples from the field of folklore. In 1973, Dan Ben Amos of the University of Pennsylvania wrote an article entitled "The Myth of Jewish Humor." In 1983, Oring wrote one called "The People of the Joke: On the Conceptualization of Jewish Humor." The former claims, of course, that there is no such thing as Jewish humor, and he gives reasons for this view. The latter takes the opposite view and bases his arguments on reasons that sound no less persuasive.

As a psychologist, I am glad to state that not many arguments on this subject take place among my professional colleagues. This is for a very simple reason: very few psychologists have taken any interest in the subject. One notable exception was Sigmund Freud who loved Jewish jokes and he began work on a collection of them, but unfortunately never completed it. In his important work, published in 1905, "Jokes and Their Relation to the Unconscious," he wrote: "I do not know whether there are many other instances of a people making fun to such a degree of its own character" (p. 112). In this sentence, Freud for the first time gave expression to one of the better known characteristics of Jewish humor: self-disparagement. This is humor in which the person employing it takes himself (or the group to which he belongs) as the object of laughter. In his book, Freud employs many examples of Jewish humor. Shadchens (marriage brokers), nudniks and schnorrers (beggars) fill the pages of this book, which was intended — let us not forget — for the European scientific community. Apparently, these characters were familiar to and understood by Christians as well. In my view, this proves to a certain extent how well-known Jewish humor was to both Jews and non-Jews. In addition to Freud, several other psychologists, from the psychoanalytical school (within which there are various factions that are very reminiscent of modern Jewry: orthodox, reform, and others), have related to Jewish humor. Thus, Reik wrote a brilliant book about Jewish humor (1962) and Grotjahn also wrote several articles on the subject. By the way, Grotjahn is not Jewish, but proudly declares himself to be an "honorary Jew" (1970). Without going into details, psychoanalysts link the concept of Jewish humor with the notion of masochism. Masochism is a psychological phenomenon which is the underlying factor in behavior that derives pleasure from humiliation and self-abuse. The reason for the self-hate that motivates such behavior is connected with deep and basic guilt feelings. The source of the guilt is the Jewish religion. The religion of the Jews which preserved them and allowed them to survive over so many generations despite their great suffering, created in them, at the same time, extremely strong feelings of guilt. The suffering of the Jews is after all, like everything else in the world, an outcome of God's will. Since man cannot be angry at God and show aggression towards him, this aggression is directed inward, that is, towards ourselves.

Masochism operates as a mechanism that causes a man to forego his strength and self-dignity in order to gain love and forgiveness for aggressive impulses that he cannot express outwardly. Since God is always right and since he never stops punishing the Jews, then we can only conclude that we must be doing terrible things. The masochistic self-hate of the Jews, one of the expressions of which is Jewish humor, developed from this subconscious view.

This masochistic explanation is not accepted by those psychologists who do not have a psychoanalytical orientation. They regard Jewish humor as a particular expression of humor, which is a result of the special experiences and trials of the Jewish people throughout its development. As with any other people, humor fills various important functions that satisfy central psychological needs. It is possible that in the case of the Jews, these functions, or some of them, filled more important needs in the process of their survival as a people, and this may explain the special characteristics of Jewish humor.

Before going into discussing the essence of humor in general and Jewish humor in particular, I would like to share the way which lead me to start doing research on this topic. The special conditions which led me to it are typically Israeli, relating to the strong connection of Jewish humor with anxiety.

My love affair with humor research (I had a long flirt with humor since childhood) started more than a quarter-century ago. As it happened rather frequently in the short history of Israel, a conflict with our neighbors was expressed not only in belligerent word exchanges. The Syrians were shelling the northern part of Israel, and all settlements close to the border were under bombardment nearly every night. Children were taken down to the shelters and after the bombing brought back to their apartments. This went on for a long period. The Syrians continued their shelling and started doing it not only at night, but also during the day. Children were taken from their classrooms to shelters and back again, until it was decided to transform many shelters into classrooms. So, for a long duration children spent most of their days and nights in shelters.

At that time, my topic of research was stress and anxiety, and of course the situation in the North of the country created a great deal of stress for the children there, as well as for adults. A team of psychologists and counselors from Tel Aviv University decided to go to the settlements which were under bombardments and find ways to help children cope with the very stressful situation. We went from one kibbutz to another, to small villages and settlements which were under frequent shelling and we talked to parents, children and teachers, giving the children many psychological tests measuring anxiety and many other variables. We took all the material we gathered back to the university and fed them into computers. Rapidly we had a huge amount of data which we analyzed and used to prepare intervention ways geared toward helping children to cope as best as possible with the situation. During our work with the data we brought in, we stumbled upon a result for which we had no explanation: in two kibbutzim, the anxiety level of the children was significantly lower than in all other places we have been. Looking and analyzing again and again the data did not bring us any closer to understanding the cause of differences in anxiety between these two kibbutzim and all the others. While working again on the data, one of my assistants said: remember that in those two kibbutzim we saw the "magnets"? The "magnets" were a phenomenon we saw many times in these two kibbutzim. Frequently, during stressful situations, like having to run down to the shelters or when shelling was heard, many children gathered around one teenager, who seemed to attract them. Sawing this, one of us gave the name "magnet" to the recurring happening. We did not have any good explanation to the possible relation between the magnets and the lowering of anxiety and therefore we decided to go back and observe. And there it was.

Imagine children playing in the playground and sirens start wailing. Everybody is running down to the shelters and we follow the children. As soon as they are down, the "magnet" starts functioning: about thirty children gather around him (a boy aged about 13). What we saw and heard when we approached was rather astonishing: the magnet did one thing: he made others laugh. This was a somewhat surrealistic picture: children laughing while shelling was heard.

Approaching the group of children around the magnet I asked them to explain to me what was going on. And they told me in many ways which can be summed up by "when you are frightened and something or somebody makes you laugh, for a while, you are less frightened." One kid added that it "is like going alone during the night in a strange place. What you do is you start whistling to yourself — it gives you a bit of courage." It all seemed so plausible. Why didn't I think about it?

Theories relevant to stress and anxiety are more than abundant in the professional literature, but none relate to the effect of humor or laughter. Since the children's explanation seemed so credible, at least on a face-value level, I started thinking about ways to validate their intuitive observation about the stress-reducing effects of humor. The first step of course was to read and learn. I rushed to the university's well-stacked library to find all the research published on the topic. To my surprise, I quickly discovered that there was almost nothing. Except the theoretical writing of many philosophers (from Plato and Aristotle to Kierkegaard and Bergson) no psychologist seemed to pay attention or do research on laugher and humor. Of course Freud is an exception; he wrote about humor. But of course this is no wonder; he wrote about almost everything related to the human psyche. Where were the others? While reflecting on the topic I recalled that during all my studies at the university, from the first year of my undergraduate studies till the end of my doctorate, I never heard a single reference to research on humor and/or laughter. And my studies were in psychology, the science aimed at understanding human thoughts, emotions and behavior. How come that psychologist did not pay attention to the fact that humor is an everyday occurrence, and most people laugh rather frequently? Even psychologists laugh, and they should have asked a long time ago: why do people laugh, what kind of function humor has, and how does it influence human behavior, feelings and interactions? This especially in the light of the fact that laughter is a universal reaction and humor exists in every known human society. The strange fact is that even today, in most textbooks on psychology, a perusal of the indexes shows that the topic of humor does not exist. Depression, anxiety, aggression and many other forms of negative feelings appear in much detail.

There and then I decided to follow the children's intuition and start doing research on humor. If what they told me was right, I felt that I was on the frontier of great discoveries, and in my fantasies I saw somewhere in the distance a Nobel prize. How does one start doing research on humor? In order to do research one needs, in addition to a good theory, an empirical definition (what is humor) and some measuring instruments. An empirical definition of humor is not as easy as it might seem. Although we all know how to differentiate between those of our friends who have a good sense of humor and those who don't, we cannot define with any precision what we mean by it. As for instruments to measure humor, there were none. My first step in humor research was to understand what is humor.

What is Humor?

Humor is a form of communication with an intent to amuse, including special cognitive and emotional characteristics, that causes a physiological reaction. We will discuss each element of this definition, dealing with the last one first.

9

The *physiological* reaction to humor known to all of us is laughter (or, at least, a smile). It is easier to relate to laughter than to humor because it can be seen and heard, whereas humor is merely a theoretical concept. Laughter, as a daily phenomenon of a physiological nature, can be precisely described. Dearborn described it in 1900 in the following manner:

> *There occur in laughter and more or less in smiling, clinic spasms of the diaphragm — ordinarily about 18 in number, and contraction of most of the muscles of the face. The upper side of the mouth and its corners are drawn upward. The upper eyelid is elevated, as are also, to some extent, the brows, the skin over the glabella, and the upper lip while the skin at the outer canthi of the eyes is characteristically puckered. The nostrils are moderately dilated and drawn upward, the tongue slightly extended, and the cheeks distended and drawn somewhat upward...The lower jaw vibrates or is somewhat withdrawn (doubtless to afford all possible air to the distending lungs) and the head, in extreme laughter, is thrown backward; the trunk is straightened even to the beginning of bending backward, until (and this usually happens soon) fatigue-pain in the diaphragm and accessory abdominal muscles causes s marked proper flexion of the trunk for its relief. The whole arterial vascular system is dilated, with consequent blushing from the effect on the dermal capillaries of the face and neck, and at times the scalp and hands. From this same cause, the eyes often slightly bulge forwards and the lachrymal gland becomes active, ordinarily to a degree only to cause a "brightening" of the eyes, but often to such an extent that the tears overflow entirely their proper channels* (Dearborn, 1900, p. 853).

This massive physiological phenomenon is a reaction to humor, but not only to humor. It can also be caused by physiological stimuli, the best known of which is tickling. We all know the "technique" of tickling: you move your fingers quickly and lightly over humorogenic areas of the body. Parents know that tickling their children is a sure way to get them to laugh.

But here the *social factor* intervenes. Tickling, a simple activity in itself, which links a physiological stimulus with a physiological reaction, does not in actual fact work only on this level. The simple proof of this fact is that a person who tickles himself does not laugh. A somewhat more complicated (and dangerous) way of proving this is to try to walk down the street and start tickling a stranger. It is very doubtful if his reaction will be one of laughter. Laughter as a result of tickling requires a special relationship between the tickler and the ticklee: a social relationship of mutual confidence. Small children laugh when their parents tickle them — but not when strangers do the same thing. The importance of the social relationship is also very evident in activity directly connected with humor. Many researches point to the fact that we laugh more when we are with friends than when we are with strangers (Goldstein and McGhee, 1974). Since humor is a social message, it contributes to *gray* social processes such as the reinforcement of group cohesiveness, the reduction of tension within a group and the creation of a positive atmosphere (Ziv, 1984). In our definition of humor, a stress was laid on a social message with an intent to amuse. In other words, whoever sends such a message wants to amuse his listeners. Therefore, funny things that people do unintentionally are not considered humor. Take, for example, a politician who talks seriously about various issues but unknowingly causes some people to laugh at what he says. He is not aware that he makes people laugh; therefore this should not be considered as humor.

In addition to the social aspect, there is an *emotional element* in all humor. Since humor causes pleasure and since laughter is the behavioral expression of pleasure, it creates positive emotions. A person laughing, or even smiling is "telling" us that he is happy, in a good mood, Just as weeping is a sign of sadness and the emotional message in it is very clear.

Finally, in all humor there is an important *cognitive component*. Freud, in the book we cited above, stresses that the main element of all humor lies in technique. By technique, he meant the conscious and unconscious cognitive processes that turn a story into a joke. Elements such as surprise, a short time span, incongruity, and so forth, create a sort of puzzle which the person hearing the joke has to "solve." Setting up a problem, grappling with logical and illogical elements in the joke, call for a process similar to that involved in the creation of a problem (by the creator of the joke) and its solution (by the listener). The creation and solution of a problem call for intellectual processes, and these processes are activated in every humoristic interaction. We cannot go into the complexities of the cognitive processes of humor here, but what is involved is a special logic called local-logic (Ziv, 1984).

These four components in humor (cognitive, social, emotional and physiological) are also the basis elements in the definition of psychology. Psychology, as is known, is the science that investigates the intellectual, social and emotional processes of human beings and their physiological adjuncts. In our attempt to understand humor lies perhaps a spark of hope that from this understanding there may spring a better understanding of psychology, and even more important, of people. As for *Jewish Humor*, research may help us understand the Jews during the course of their special development as a people.

Jewish Humor

While it is relatively easy for me to define humor, I find it much more difficult to define what is (or who is) a Jew. This is mainly because I am not an expert in the field of Judaism and I will have to leave the resolution of this problem to those more competent than I to cope with it. From my standpoint, a Jew is a man who considers himself Jewish and identifies with the Jewish people.

Thus, Jewish humor can be defined as humor created by Jews and reflecting special aspects of Jewish life. This is a very broad definition which contains within it the humor collected by folklorists which flourish among people as well as humor created by professionals. Therefore, Shalom Aleichem's writings, Neil Simon's plays, and Woody Allen's films are all examples of Jewish humor. Naturally, Jewish humor changes as a result of important changes that take place in the life of the Jewish people. Thus, one can speak of Eastern European Jewish humor, Moroccan Jewish humor, American Jewish humor or Israeli Jewish humor. Nevertheless, what is identified in worldwide professional literature as Jewish humor originated in nineteenth-century Eastern Europe. There Jews lived under special and extremely harsh conditions confronted with a real danger to their lives. In these conditions a humor developed which had particular characteristics that helped the Jews cope with their terrible ordeals. This humor, the language of which was mainly Yiddish, over time moved throughout Europe and later with the mass immigrations also moved to the United States. The humor of a minority, it kept its special characteristics for nearly one hundred years. It became well known because of these characteristics and made a considerable contribution to the image of Jews as a people with a sense of humor. The special characteristics of Jewish humor are discussed in greater detail in my article in this book.

There is no doubt that Sephardic Jewry also had a special humor that developed under the influence of the Jewish experience in the various countries. Possibly due to the living conditions of this Jewry, which were not as bad as those of Eastern European Jewry, it did not develop the same characteristics of Jewish humor. But the truth is that we do not know very much about Jewish humor in the Islamic countries. Despite many efforts, I was unsuccessful in finding someone to lecture on the humor of Sephardic Jewry for the First International Conference on Jewish Humor. That is why there is no article in this book dealing with this special aspect of our subject. I hope that at future International Conferences on Jewish Humor, material will be presented that also reflects this aspect of the heritage of our people's humor.

In Israel, from a minority, the Jews became a majority. Yiddish, a language which had never been used by people in positions of power, control and in government, was replaced by Hebrew, which had been revived and renewed. In Yiddish, no compulsory economic orders had ever been issued; no police force had ever operated in this language; no orders for the movement of tanks or bombing of targets had ever been given in Yiddish. The only power this language possessed was that of its intellectual force. It served very well as a means of communication for a people that had always been a minority in a hostile environment. Thus, it also served as a means of expression for the Jewish humor that developed under these conditions. In Israel, where the Jews are a powerful majority that runs the establishment, Yiddish has almost disappeared. Those same characteristics of Jewish humor that served the Jews of the Diaspora as a way of coping with the wretched conditions of an oppressed minority no longer fill important functions. Israeli humor has no more than a fragmentary and indirect link with the Jewish humor that developed in Eastern Europe. I shall also discuss this humor and its psychological traits in my article.

Thirteen Attributes for Expounding Jewish Humor

There are thirteen articles in this book which represent the best lectures given at the First International Conference on Jewish Humor. The conference, held in June 1984 at Tel-Aviv University, has a brief history.

The idea of holding the conference was conceived by me after many meetings with people engaged in humor-related research. In most of these conversations, the researchers, Jews and non-Jews alike characterized Jewish humor as a rich and extraordinary phenomenon. In this way, I discovered that there are people who take an interest in Jewish humor and engage in research related to this field in different parts of the world. To my surprise, it turned out that although there are many books in different languages that contain collections of Jewish jokes and humoresques, no book exists that approaches research on Jewish humor from the standpoint of different disciplines. I then decided to take advantage of the fact that the Fourth International Conference on Humor was being held in Israel, and to add to it two days devoted to Jewish humor. I thought this would be an opportunity to develop international channels of communication for scientists from different disciplines who are engaged in research on Jewish humor. When we sent out a call for papers in this field, I thought we would receive 6–10 proposals for lectures. To my surprise, and joy, 56 arrived. Out of these, during the two days of the conference, 46 lectures were presented, and after an examination of all the material, the articles included in this book were selected.

It may not be a coincidence that the number of articles is 13. Although I did not plan to reach this number, after the book had been set up I thought that probably this fact would bring a smile to the lips of those conversant with Jewish tradition. Thirteen articles representing the work of scientists from different fields, all trying to understand different aspects of Jewish humor, will certainly evoke associations, of a local-logical nature, with Jewish tradition. Those engaged in humor-related research recognize local-logic as one of the important elements in any humor.

The thirteen articles in the book reflect the first interdisciplinary approach to Jewish humor. The authors are scientists from the areas of literature, linguistics, sociology, psychology, history, communications, the theater and Jewish studies.

They were joined by the cartoonist who created the character identified with Israel and who accompanied the development of Israel with his graphic work and humor. This is Kariel Gardosh, so well known to us as Dosh, who also made a written contribution to this book.

The articles have been arranged in four parts: three deal with Jewish humor in the Diaspora and one is devoted to humor in Israel. The first part relates to humor as a way of coping with Jewish identity. Dorinson's article underscores the dilemma facing Jewish comedians in the United States. These comics, who are recognized as having made very important contributions to American humor, try to assimilate into this culture, but without giving up their Jewish identity. Their assimilation is not total and they stress this in their humoristic way. In my article, I try to show what are the main psychological functions filled by humor in Jewish life in the Diaspora. In Israel, due to the different conditions of life, humor fills other functions, and one can speak about a different Jewish humor in the Diaspora and in Israel. In Adler's article, which analyzes a famous story by Shalom Aleichem, she discusses the approach of Jewish humor to authority but it also has a universal message.

The second part deals with a central function of humor: aggression. Davies in his analysis, makes a clear distinction between jokes that present the Jew as a victim of anti-Semitic attacks and those in which the approach is not aggressive. His work also discusses the fact that humor is perceived by non-Jews as a Jewish trait regardless of whether they relate to them positively or negatively.

In her article on gallows humor, Kauffman relates to the special revenge of a Jewish comedian on the Nazi who murdered him. Romain Gary's book "The Dance of Genghis Cohn" is full of examples of bitter, sometimes cruel, humor that all the same evokes a smile, and sometimes even laughter. Gallows humor is considered by several researchers of Jewish humor as one of its typical characteristics. Kauffman, in analyzing Gary's book, gives many examples of this special humor.

Fuchs' article relates to a different function of humor: the sexual function. Although sexual humor is not a particular characteristic of Jewish humor, it is of course also represented in it. In her approach, Fuchs tries to show that the aggressiveness of the Jews often chooses a convenient target that is close at hand — the woman. Fuchs sees anti-feminist aggression in certain aspects of Jewish humor.

Humor in the Jewish tradition is the focus of the third part. Mintz writes about jokes involving Jewish and Christian clergymen. Through the characteristics of these jokes, he stresses the approach of Jewish humor and the views it holds on rabbis and priests. Friedlander describes Jewish satire in the nineteenth century. Opposing stands on questions of Jewish tradition created groups that waged "ideological" warfare among themselves. The aggression between the adversaries found a humoristic expression as well. Jewish satire of that period was very caustic and played an important role in the "Jewish wars" about questions of tradition. Rivlin also concentrates on an approach to tradition, in analyzing the humoristic expressions in Shalom Aleichem's work "Tevie the Milkman." Tevie talks to God, complains about his fate, a Jewish fate, and copes with his difficult life, with courage and humor.

The last part of the book deals with humor in Israel. This is an area on which relatively little research has been done thus far, although many researchers have been preoccupied with the question of what happened to Jewish humor in Israel. In the first article in this part, David Alexander writes about the development of satire in Israel. In relation to this form of humor, he suggests an explanation that links the forms of satire developed in Israel with the development of the idea of Zionism and its realization in Israel. The researchers of the media, Nir and Roeh, analyzed news

14

broadcasts on Israeli radio. As one might expect, there is not much humor to be found in this serious medium. Nevo investigates one of the best-known characteristics of Jewish humor in the Diaspora — self-disparaging humor. The results of her research show that the Jews in Israel have lost this trait, which is apparently connected with the minority status of the Jews. Nevo found in her research that Israeli Arabs are more capable than their Jewish compatriots of enjoying laughter at their own expense. Finally, Dosh describes the development of caricature in Israel as a reflection of the country's development.

The thirteen articles, each in its own way, paves the way for an understanding of the different aspects of Jewish humor. There are undoubtedly many other ways to approach research on this subject, and it is my hope that this first book will encourage other researchers to contribute to a further understanding of the humor of our people.

In producing the book, I thought at first that I would present the bibliographical appendices of the different articles in a uniform format. Psychologists arrange their bibliographies differently than those engaged in the field of literature. Historians also have their own way of doing so, and this holds true for representatives of the other disciplines. I finally decided to leave each bibliography in the form in which it was submitted by the author, in accordance with the method accepted in his field of work. This approach underscores the heterogeneity of the book which is intended for all those interested in the different aspects of research related to Jewish humor.

A few words before I conclude. In my own article in the book, concerning humor in Israel, the division of Israel's history by the wars should include another war: Desert Storm. Israel had one war in each decade since it has existed as an independent Sate, and I hope we can rest a few years — we already had a war this decade. The humor, as I predicted in the article, has become less political and there is more absurd and even sexual humor. Israeli television has numerous comedy programs and the situation continues to be tense, which produces, it seems, more humor.

Since the First International Conference on Jewish Humor, we had two more. One was held in New York. The main papers were published in the journal dedicated to humor research (*Humor: International Journal of Humor Research*), a new addition to the field. I had the honor of being the guest editor of the special issue (Ziv, 1987). The third conference was held in Tel Aviv, and the best articles were published in a book (Ziv and Zajdman, 1993).

In conclusion, I would like to thank all of the authors who cooperated with me in this work. Their patience and their willingness to hear my comments and to make changes (sometimes several times) in their articles were very helpful to me. Their remarks also enriched my understanding of Jewish humor from the viewpoint of disciplines in which I am not proficient.

My thanks to Chaya Naor for her beautiful translation of the articles that were originally in Hebrew.

Avner Ziv

References

Ben Amos D. (1977) The myth of Jewish humor. *Western Folklore*, 32, 112–131.

Bergler E. (1956) *Laughter and the sense of humor.* N.Y., International Medical Books.

Dearborn G. V. (1900) The nature of the smile and laughter. *Science*, 9, 851–856.

Freud S. (1916) *Jokes and their relation to the unconscious.* N.Y., Marow.

Goldstein J. and McGhee P. (1972) *The psychology of humor.* N.Y., Academic Press.

Grotjahn M. (1970) Jewish jokes and their relations to masochism. In Mendel W. M. (Ed.) *A celebration of laughter.* Mara Books.

Reik, W. (1962) *Jewish Humor.* London: Prescot.

Ziv A. (1984) *Personality and sense of humor.* N.Y., Springer.

Ziv A. (1987) Jewish humor. *Humor: International Journal of Humor Research* (special issue).

Ziv A. and Zajdman A. (1993) (Eds.) *Semites and stereotypes: studies in Jewish Humor.* N.Y., Greenwood.

R. Adler
SHALOM ALEICHEM'S
"ON ACCOUNT OF A HAT"

Ruth Adler
Yeshiva University, USA

SHALOM ALEICHEM'S "ON ACCOUNT OF A HAT"
Universal and Jewish Applications

The notion "Jewish humor" immediately evokes the name of Shalom Aleichem. This great narratist is the representative of the humor of the Jewish village, the shtetl. Finishing a story by Shalom Aleichem, the reader feels a sense of closeness-in-understanding toward the characters whom the narratist has presented to him. Shalom Aleichem had a talent for giving his characters vitality and credibility. Were we, totally by chance, to meet a character like Tevye or Menachem-Mendel in the street, we would experience a feeling of *déjà vu*; we would almost want to reach out and greet him, as though we had come across an old friend.

Jewish humor is unique in its ability to find a jest amongst the tears and make tragic situations tolerable. Shalom Aleichem, the champion of capsulated Jewish humor, was blessed with the virtue of seeing the light within even the most tragic of human events. The toil of labor, persecution, pogroms, conversion, even death — all were slices of life in which Shalom Aleichem could still find humor. The cloud of tragedy engulfing such situations did not distract his discriminating eye from their human elements: weakness, stubbornness, naiveté, arrogance.

Although these experiences are described from the point of view of the shtetl in typical Jewish terms, nonetheless, the feelings, the fears, and the motivations are universally human in the widest meaning of the term. An Italian, an Irishman or someone from the East who found himself in the kind of situation that Sholem Shachnah finds himself in, someone who bumps into a meticulously dressed government clerk lying spread-eagled on a bench in a railway station waiting room might respond with the same sense of anxiety and with the same accompanying humoristic component as the response of the Jew. And indeed, the stories of Shalom Aleichem have been translated into many languages and are read with pleasure even in the Far East.

Shalom Aleichem does not write as a distant cut-off observer; he weaves into his stories experiences from his own life. It is enough to read the memoirs of his daughter, Mary Weiff-Goldberg or those of his son-in-law Y.D. Berkowitz, to discover the many personal experiences of the author that are interpolated into his stories. The subjects which reoccur in them are like the financial distress, the anti-Semitism and the breach of trust which he experienced in his private life. Presumably, the authenticity of his stories originates to a large extent from the fact that fatherly Tevie and the good-for-nothing Menachem-Mendel are different aspects of his own personality.

Shalom Aleichem's story "On Account of a Hat"[1] at first glance stretches the reader's credulity. It appears farfetched and remote from the modern reader's experience. Yet, on closer reading, it is at one and the same time universally applicable and quintessentially Jewish. The story addresses such wide-ranging issues as strategies for coping under stress, relationship to authority, paranoia, wish-fulfillment and identity crisis. All of these are triggered by the dilemma confronting a shlemiel in his attempt to reach home on the eve of Passover.

Shalom Aleichem's story "On Account of a Hat"[1] at first glance stretches modest business success in a far-off province and plans a trip home for the Passover holiday. But he commits the unpardonable sin of dispatching a telegram to his wife which reads: "Arriving home Passover without fail." This pretension to infallibility is duly punished. The railway timetable forces him to wait several hours in the town of Zlodievka which he reaches after two exhausting and sleepless days of travel. The station is filthy, and the only free seat is at the corner of a bench occupied by the sprawling figure of an official whose red-banded visored cap indicates a definite yet unspecified importance. Despite misgivings, Sholem decides to avail himself of the space; but before doing so, he pays a porter, Yeremei, to wake him once the train arrives. Congratulating himself on such foresight, he falls into a deep sleep and dreams that he is being driven home in a wagon by a thievish peasant whose horses "barely drag along." Seized by impatience, Sholem urges the driver, Ivan, to whip them, and when he does so, Sholem loses his hat. Frightened by the mad gallop and disoriented by the loss of his hat — "How will he be able to enter the shtetl without it? — Sholem begs Ivan to slow down. The race continues until suddenly, without warning, Ivan brings the horses to a dead stop in the middle of a field, saying "Get up! Time to get up!" Confused, Sholem opens his eyes to find that the peasant is really Yeremei, the porter, and that if this is the case, he must hurry to the ticket office. But the hat which he had placed on his carpetbag is missing. Spurred by his anxiety not to miss the train, he finds a hat under the bench and reflexively places it on his head and rushes off. Approaching the crowded ticket office, he is amazed when people make way for him and the usually dismissive and superior clerks address him as "Your Excellency." He allows a conductor to disregard his third class ticket and lead him to a spacious and comfortable first-class compartment. While passing down a corridor he chances to see himself in a mirror and, in a state of shock at recognizing the official's red-banded cap on his head, realizes that all that has taken place has, in fact, not involved him — Sholem Shachnah — at all, but rather the official whom the porter had mistakenly roused. He himself must obviously still be sleeping in the station. He rushes from the train to wake himself on the bench. The train pulls off and Sholem is forced to spend a miserable Passover with strangers in Zlodievka. By the time he eventually reaches home, the details of his mishap are known to the people of Kasrilevke. He is assailed by his wife who attacks his presumptuousness in using the phrase "without fail" and by the townspeople who mockingly ask, "How does it feel to wear a cap with a red band and visor?" and "What's it like to travel first-class?"

Shalom Aleichem has created a universal character here. Sholem Shachnah is an Everyman of a sort, whose incompetence marks him as the classic ne'er-do-well. The deal which symbolizes his professional success cannot really be attributed to his skill, it has been worked out by others and it is only after "a holler and an outcry" that they give in "to shut him up." Sholem Shachnah is aware of this and feels his success to be undeserved. As a response to this illusory success, he sends a telegram whose contents insinuate that his long career of failure is in great measure connected to his own masochistic character, indicating what Theodore Reik has referred to as "a masochist's strong unconscious will to fail and to spoil his chances."[2] Indeed, Sholem's fear of success is a central feature of his personality. In sending his shrewish wife a telegram claiming the impossible, arrival "without fail," he is, in a sense, tempting misadventure and delay. He cannot deal with his unaccustomed victory over competitors and feels a reluctance to return to someone who has long been a witness to his inadequacy and who probably, on account of that, mistrusts his every effort to break that pattern. Consequently, he sets himself up for failure in order to destroy the very change which threatens his familiar and comfortable identity. We sense that the full sentence of the telegram might well read, "Without fail, I will fail."

The world is not a kindly place for a Sholem Shachnah. His own feelings are reflected in the description of the station in Zlodievka — "It was dark, it was terrible" with soot on the walls and spit on the floor. And, of course, he arrives in it already tired, fatigued by the struggle for survival — "He was half dead" after two nights without sleep and with the prospect of another. There is no real place for him in the station and if he is to make one, it will only be on the edge of things. Indeed, it is only after an extensive internal monologue that he persuades himself that he is within his rights in occupying a corner of the official's bench. For the figure of the official is the personification of the power of the system. He is, as Sholem Shachnah imagines, one of the powerful who drive up to the station with a ringing of bells, are full of meat and drink, and treat the world as if it is theirs to do with as they please. They have the badges of authority, uniforms with buttons and red-banded visored caps which declare to others that power resides with

21

them. The red-banded cap and the multitude of shiny buttons is the most visible, and hence most important, part of the official's uniform. A uniform proclaims status and power and tends to intimidate its beholder. It is surely no accident that the only description given of the official is in fact of his uniform. Shalom Aleichem was perfectly aware that this would be all that Sholem would notice, and hence be able to communicate. The official is otherwise faceless, an anonymous agent rather than a particular individual. The cap has special significance. It tells Sholem that "Buttons" is no "dime a dozen official." The color of the band — red — is also noteworthy. That color has always been associated not only with the life-giving but also with the dangerous. The fact that the hat has a visor, a sharp assertive extension, rather than a soft brim, transfers it into a veritable instrument of control. Subsequently, when Sholem Shachnah wears the cap it endows him too with authority. Both Sholem's reaction to the sleeping official and that of people to Sholem's cap very much resemble the results of an experiment carried out, in which subjects, confronted by strangers wearing even totally unfamiliar uniforms, accorded them significantly more respect and obedience than they granted to those wearing civilian clothes.[3]

In describing Sholem's passage from fear through rationalization to a coming to terms with the official, Shalom Aleichem has given us a remarkably incisive account of the thought processes involved. At first, overcome by the presence of the official, Sholem Shachnah begins, step by step, to exaggerate his importance, to inflate the official's rank from "district inspector" to "provincial commander," thus justifying his fear to himself; indeed, perhaps the uniformed man on the bench is Purishkevitz, the most notorious of anti-Semites. Then, so as to counteract, ease and contradict this fear, he begins to diminish the official's importance and make claims for his own worth. He rages to himself, "Who the hell is Buttons? Don't I pay my fare the same as Purishkevitz? So why should he have all the comforts of life and I none?" This accordion-like process of inflation and deflation is an exercise of the tottering ego attempting to bolster itself, attempting to turn disadvantage into, at least, equality. So Sholem eventually does take his place on the edge of the bench; but even after this skillful game of self-manipulation, he concedes the official's preeminence by claiming that it is just "to snooze" rather than actually to sleep. At this point, filled with anxiety, he has a sudden inspiration. In order to guard against oversleeping he will pay the peasant-porter, Yeremei, to wake him once his train arrives. And by way of assuaging his sense of violation, for he understands that his fear of the official is demeaning, he abuses Yeremei by calling him a "goyisher kop." The pejorative reestablishes his sense of self-esteem. He has found someone weaker than himself, someone who, like himself, must swallow humiliation. This catharsis enables him to fall asleep triumphant.

22

He has not only found a seat but has also taken precautions against missing his train; and he has seemingly assured himself that he will arrive "without fail."

But his dream belies this superficial sense of well-being. In the nightmare, the hat (a symbol of identity and power) is lost by a town-dwelling trader on his way back home. The catalysts behind this loss are the thundering horses (which can be seen in Freudian terms as the irrepressible demands of the pleasure centers and, in non-Freudian terms, as unrestrained elements which easily lead passengers off the track as opposed to the train which always stays on the track) and a thievish peasant (a brutish yet normal man). When faced by the unrestrained wild gallop of the horses, the trader's hat falls off and he panics; faced by their unchecked energy, he imagines that in another minute he will have lost God knows what. What he stands to lose might be interpreted as his masculinity, or simply his ability to reestablish his proper status with his family. Interestingly, when he is on the train heading home with the official's cap on his head, and with the opportunity thus presented to him to regain control of his life and reassert his manhood, he is unable to utilize the opportunity, for he is too accustomed to the role of a shlemiel. Sholem's failure to exploit his new-found privileges is attributable to his failure, at every stage, to see himself in the guise of the advantaged. As psychologists tell us, self-images are difficult to change despite external transformations. The internalization of an image is a deep and multi-layered phenomenon. Thus, people who have been fat may continue to see themselves as fat long after they have actually ceased to be so. In Sholem's case, one may say that the porter aroused the fantasy, wish-fulfilling part of his personality, and allowed the unaspiring, reality-bound self to continue sleeping on the bench. And so Sholem rushes to awake that sleeping part of him which is so resistant to change.

These aspects of the story — Sholem Shachnah's nonrecognition of himself in his new hat, his nonacceptance of his new appearance and his rush back to the bench — are all the aspects which lend it a certain lack of credibility. They also make the task of conveying the story's essence to a modern audience more difficult. Such an audience often tends to reject the story as too fanciful, reflecting no reality with which it can identify. Having personally experienced these difficulties in teaching it, I undertook some experiments to help students grasp the universal relevance of the story. Before reading the story students were asked to close their eyes and conjure up the following situation. Upon returning to their locker in a gym, they discover that their clothes are missing and in their place are the kind of clothes they would "not be seen dead in." They were then asked to imagine themselves donning these clothes and making their way home with them. They were then to convey the feelings they had experienced in this imaginary situation. Sholem's situation no longer seemed fanciful to them and they were quite able to identify with his reluctance to enter the shtetl with the official's hat.[4]

The importance of this story is not due to its universal aspects alone. No less striking are the insights regarding the Jewish condition in Czarist Russia. The Jew, of course, was a member of a persecuted minority whereas the official represented the institutionalized form of the oppressive majority. Survival for the Jew lay in placation — let the sleeping official enjoy the comfort of the entire bench so long as the Jew could surreptitiously snooze on the edge. Seen from this perspective, Sholem is the archetypal Jew caught between the twin threats of the Russian bureaucracy, agent of the imperial and landowning classes, and the serfs or peasantry. Discriminated against by educational quotas, unable to own land and confined to the Pale of Settlement, Jews were forced into the most marginal, least productive and most precarious forms of economic life. They were largely traders or middlemen and small-time speculators. Jews often had personal contacts with Ivans and Yeremeis whom they feared and patronized at once. Shalom Aleichem indicates the way in which the Jew as a member of an oppressed minority can escape his status as a Jew. The observant Jew in the shtetl did not dare to appear bareheaded. In losing his hat, Sholem is freed of his Jewishness and able to move in society as a free agent. Baptism was an entrance ticket to European civilization, as Heine pointed out. When he wears the red cap, Sholem's past identity is obscured and observers view him only as a member of the powerful bureaucratic apparatus. In a play "Hard to Be a Jew" Shalom Aleichem addressed the same issue, having a Jew and a Russian change places for a year. Disavowing one's Jewishness was a constant temptation for those who sought personal advancement and liberation. Shalom Aleichem was aware of this and referred to it in many of his works. In his own life he was refused admission to university because of a numerus clausus barring Jews. But loss of the hat as symbol of the observant Jew also troubles Sholem. In his nightmare he covers his head with his hands for how can he drive into town bareheaded? Just as the train which is to take him home is about to pull out of the station Sholem sabotages his attempt to immerse himself in gentile society.

The story reflects an ambivalence keenly felt by Shalom Aleichem and by an entire generation. This generation, affected by the Haskala, broke from the influence of Jewish religious values but was unable totally to embrace the values of gentile society.[5] In presenting "On Account of a Hat" Shalom Aleichem revealed that, although he considered absorption into the non-Jewish world possible, he did not believe it to be a practical solution. The Tevye stories also illustrate this theme of Shalom Aleichem's. They are concerned with the shtetl in transition, with the breakdown of tradition, and the difficulty for the Jew to adjust to new realities. Each of Tevye's daughters represents an option. The path taken by Chava, conversion, prompts his bitterest agonies, and it is the Jew rather than the father in him which dominates. Tevye refuses to see her. So Sholem struggles with his Jewishness. "It is not such a bad life to be a gentile," he thinks. Yet when given the option of being a gentile, he rejects it. Nevertheless, the way back to orthodoxy and religious observance was also closed for Sholem. He does not arrive home in time to celebrate Passover, the holiday of freedom. He celebrates it elsewhere. On a symbolic level, "home" no longer exists. The world of the shtetl was disintegrating and what, indeed, awaited Sholem should he have succeeded in reaching Kasrilevke in time for the holiday — a shrewish wife, namely, a hostile and claustrophobic life-style from which he was already alienated. This, then, is the matrix of the story — the dilemma of enlightened Jews who could neither return to old traditions nor embrace the outside world.[6]

In giving the main character his own name, Shalom Aleichem was revealing the strong autobiographical element in the story. He was himself embroiled with a shrewish mother-in-law as well as a carping stepmother; and his financial position was always precarious (he lost money inherited from his father-in-law). His identity crisis can be surmised from the fact that in the course of his literary career he used no fewer than twenty-three pseudonyms. As someone who had a profound regard for the positive aspects of Jewish culture, Shalom Aleichem had no wish to leave his "hat" in the station; but as someone who was acutely aware of the terrible price attached to being Jewish in an anti-Semitic environment, he expressed the unconscious desire to escape these limitations on personal freedom by walking off with the official's cap. This represents the understandable unconscious desire of members of any persecuted minority. Thus, the Jewish aspects of Shalom Aleichem's story also bear a universal imprint.

On the universal level Sholem Aleichem has presented the "fool" in each of us, struggling with our identities, unwilling to leave old ones behind or don new ones completely, trying vainly to merge both. Shalom Aleichem has also made an important statement about the Jew in Russia and the world.

NOTES

1. The English translations of the story are from Isaac Rosenfeld's translation in *A Treasury of Yiddish Stories* ed. I. Howe and E. Greenberg (New York, 1954).
2. T. Reik, *Jewish Wit* (New York, 1968), p. 4.
3. See L. Bickman, "Social Roles and Uniform: Clothes make the Person," *Psychology Today,* (April 1974): 48–54.
4. To help the students understand the accordion-like process of inflation and deflation that Sholem experienced in his encounter with the official, they were asked to picture themselves being interviewed by an important and powerful personage. They were to relate what they would do to ease their anxiety in that situation. The reactions they came up with were strikingly similar to those Shalom Aleichem describes — they would go through a process such as "This V.I.P. is really an S.O.B." etc.
5. S. Halkin describes this trend in Haskala and post-Haskala Hebrew literature in *Modern Hebrew Literature from the Enlightenment to the Birth of the State of Israel: Trends and Values* (New York, 1970), pp. 34–99.
6. Agnon's story "A Whole Loaf" [*Elu ve'Elu* (Tel Aviv, 1966) pp. 209–223] bears a strong resemblance to Shalom Aleichem's "On Account of a Hat." In Agnon's story, the narrator — shlemiel does not get to his destination, the Post Office, in time. He is deterred from getting there by a driver whose carriage and horses go out of control and turn over. Like in Shalom Aleichem's story, the protagonist neither gets to his destination in time nor succeeds in satisfying his pleasure instinct, i.e. getting "a whole loaf." For a full interpretation of Agnon's story see B. Kurzweil, *Masot al Sipurav Shel Shay Agnon,* (Tel Aviv, 1970), pp. 216–229.

J. Dorinson

THE JEW AS COMIC: LENNY BRUCE, MEL BROOKS, WOODY ALLEN

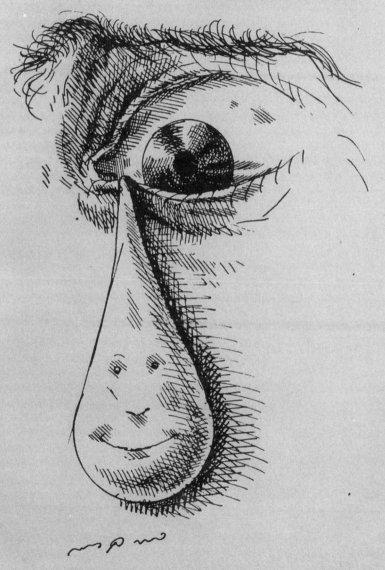

JOSEPH DORINSON
Long Island University, USA

THE JEW AS COMIC
Lenny Bruce, Mel Brooks, Woody Allen

Jewish comics enjoy a high profile in American culture. As Samuel Janus has shown, many — indeed the vast majority of them — emerged from poverty and pain.[1] In their pursuit of fortune and bliss, they have travelled from vaudeville to television. In releasing their stored-up aggression they not only provide comic relief but also help to reinforce social controls as well as to reshape group fantasy. Thus, while diverting mainstream Americans with crude stereotypes, dialect jokes, and ethnic caricature, Jewish comedians have made lots of money. Laughing all the way to the treasury, they fulfill the fantasies of Harold Price's Tevye, if not Sholem Aleichem's.

Generating laughter at the expense of one's group allegedly constitutes a staple of traditional Jewish humor. Although there is never enough respect, the work, as the messiah-watcher in Chelm learns, is steady. Vaudeville-radio comedians avoided overt tribal connections by design. Others, like George Burns, married gentile girls (as opposed to the pejorative *shiksa*). Jack Benny preferrred a middle-American image to win friends and induce laughs. In the 1960s a dramatic reversal witnessed, as Wallace Markfield phrased it, "the Yiddishization of American humor." A primary mover in this new direction was Lenny Bruce. Mel Brooks and Woody Allen also served as catalytic converters as they follow in Lenny's wake. Their comic engines generated both light and laughter.

Before I trace their comedic odysseys in the Babylon that is America, some observations on the nature of Jewish humor are in order. Jewish humor is a pervasive skepticism, so observed Sigmund Freud who also listed among its salient traits: sharp self-criticism of one's own people, democratic i.e. deflationary mode of thought, social principles underlying Judaism, revolt against religion and reflections on the miserable lot of the Jewish masses (clearly inappropriate to the current American scene). Freud's disciple, Theodore Reik, wrote a fine survey of Jewish wit in which he noted four singular traits: intimacy, antithetical thought, unmerry laughter, and explosive truths. Jewish wit shifts from paranoia to masochism; when released, aggression targets social institutions rather than persons. According to Albert Memmi, a French-writing Algerian Jew, the Jewish joke is a plea for love. Rooted in deep feelings of guilt sparked by periodic rebellions against God and his laws, this kind of humor offers a "sacrifice in order to

29

survive." In this confession, we confront the underlying identity process which informs Jewish humor.[3] Even at the grimmest moments of oppression, this gallows humor provided a last line of defense. In happier times, I contend, Jewish humor goes on the offensive. A two-sided weapon, it provides a cutting edge for historical change and social commentary.

On the surface, it appears that Jews are comfortable in America. Nevertheless insecurity gnaws at one's complacency. Certain residues have survived the journey from *shtetl* to suburbia. Is assimilation viable? Many who think not are returning to orthodoxy. Others are moving to Israel's West Bank. Yet many Jews continue to marry outside the faith. For the vast majority, slouching to Bethlehem provides no sound alternative. Remaining in limbo, therefore, the Jew turns to wit as both shield and identification tag. As Elliot Oring reminds us, we are "the people of the joke."[4]

The contemporary Jewish comedians started in the local candy store. Nervous, restless, boisterous, they learned to *shpritz*. They specialized in self-mockery to be sure; but they also showed considerable skill in directing the needle trades outward. As professionals, they lampooned culture, breeding, and power. Witness the Marx Brothers and their legion — emitic not Roman — of imitators. The Ritz Brothers, the Three Stooges, et al., (especially et al.) plunged into "gleeful nihilism" as noodniks rather than narodniks. Fortified with Perelman scripts, they assaulted all American institutions with ruthless Jewish deflation. Groucho quipped: "When I came to this country I didn't have a nickel in my pocket. Now I have a nickel in my pocket."[5] Later Saul Bellow scored with one liners à la Herzog. "Lead me not into Penn Station..." or "how I rose from humble origins to complete disaster."[6] Sharply resistant to *la dolce vita,* Jewish humor preserves the tradition of biting satire and moral outrage.

Lenny Bruce was possessed by a fierce sense of moral outrage which he expressed with caustic wit. He developed an arsenal of cogent social commentary that shocked more than it amused. Born Leonard Alfred Schneider on October 13, 1925 in Mineola Long Island, he was the only child of an odd couple. His father, Albert Goldman contends, was a Jewish mother in disguise while his mother, née Sadie Kitchenburg, harbored illusions about a career in show business.[7] Only five when his parents separated, Lenny shifted from one family to another. Denied a bar mitzvah or a secular Jewish education, Bruce became an *amharetz* (ignoramus). Lacking ethnic pride or cultural underpinnings, Bruce's sense of self was fragile at best as he attended school in a German neighborhood — the only Jew in his class. One can imagine the vast supply of rage that he stored for subsequent release.

A high school drop-out, Bruce's education was mediated through radio and movies which offered fantasy and escape from a less than blissful childhood.[8] Bereft of moorings, Lenny went to sea figuratively and literally. He joined the Navy in 1942 and departed four years later by posing as a homosexual. Upon liberation, he intermittently worked odd jobs, returned to the sea, and studied drama. Eventually, he followed his mother, now a pal, into the fringes of show biz. Starting in Brooklyn, he introduced strip acts and performed mindless *shtick*. The big break occurred on Arthur Godfrey's Talent Scouts program where, introduced by his mother as the talent scout, he impersonated Edward G. Robinson and Peter Lorre and James Cagney in a bizarre German accent. He won. This victory led to better bookings. While on the road, he met a twice-divorced, once-arrested, bi-sexual stripper, Honey Marlowe. After another stint as a merchant seaman, he married her. Playing Pygmalion to her Galatea, he tried to convert her into a *chanteuse*. A near fatal car wreck ended that experiment. To hustle additional money, Lenny impersonated a priest. A living fantasy, he emerged as Father Mathias, the head of a foundation, to raise money for an African leper colony: "Hello young lepers wherever you are..." Ultimately exposed, Lenny received a stern judicial rebuke but no prison sentence.[9] He returned to the legitimate theatre.

Success, the big time, the gaudy glitter of making it arrived in the late 1950s. Lenny gained a large following at Enrico Balducci's Hungry I in San Fransisco. In 1960 he earned more than $3,000 per week and had sold 190,000 records. Yet, Lenny as quarry continues to elude our critical faculties. Neither happily assimilated nor proudly Jewish, Bruce remained in a permanent state of purgatory. He oscillated between a wish for sainthood and an inescapable sense of his own corruption. He confessed: "I can't get worked up about politics. I grew up in New York and I was hip as a kind that I was corrupt and the mayor was corrupt. I have no illusions."[10] Lenny essayed many roles — hipster, underground man, counter-culture hero, hustler, junkie, gadfly, victim, litigant, satirist, priest, Jew — before he self destructed on a toilet in his California dream house. In the earlier "bits," Lenny projected the hustler as the ultimate villain who sparks derisive laughter. Hustlers in advertising, he advised, should make it "hip" to have cancer in order to sell more cigarettes. The biggest hustle was organized religion. The Pope, Billy Graham, Oral Roberts, Stephen Wise, all were cited for contempt of authenticity. Pickled in Jewish brine, these bits conveyed what Freud called "tendency wit." Such wit unlooses inhibitions which are primarily sexual and aggressive. John Cohen's *The Essential Lenny Bruce* yields a barrel of tendency wit in a section entitled "Jews."[11] British accented rabbis are...

> *so reformed, they're ashamed they're Jewish. This Sabbath we discuss Is roy el. Where is Is roy el? Quench yon flaming yortsite*

31

candle. Alas, Alas poor Yosel ... Today on Chin uka with Rosh-hashona approaching ... someone had the chutz-pah to ask me, "Tell me something, Doctor of law, is there a God or not?" What cheek! To ask this in a temple! We're not here to talk of God — we're here to sell bonds for Israel. ... A pox upon you Christ and Moses! Go among them and kiss your empty mezzuzahs.

Moses is depressed. "The *shules* are gone." Except for a "joint" the mezzuzahs are empty. And they are made in Japan.

On the high holidays, Bruce reveals, Jews actually celebrate the killing of Christ. From an unexpected source — his friend, Morty — he obtains the confession: "We killed him." Why? There are several variations on this theme. Because he didn't want to become a doctor or lawyer. Because of the crimes that would be committed in his name. Consistent with Reik's analysis, Bruce's bits combine aggression and guilt.

Lenny observed that a Jewish mother's liberalism dissolves in tears when her daughter brings home a Filipino groom with a gold tooth and long black foreskin. He recalled that Mema, his aunt, a Jewish seagull, crowed in lamentation because of Lenny's tatooed arm. Jewish law precludes the burial of tatoos (graven images) in sacred ground. So he offered to bury a hand elsewhere. Lenny shpritzed overprotective Jewish mothers with onion breath (now a status symbol re: Dick Gregory), assimilated Jewish college kids, Jews intimidated by violence, afraid of "duking," and Jews lacking identity.

As I wrote this, our television transmitted *The Greatest Story Ever Told*. During Easter week especially, Christ was everywhere in the person of Max Von Sydow. Bruce noted the presence of Christ on rocks, bank buildings, museums, cars, movies, musicals, crucifixes. It's a story that you can follow, instant identification. Where is the Jewish God?[12]

He's on a little box nailed to a door jamb. In a mezuzah, there he is, in there. He's standing on a slant, God ... I told the super don't paint God ... Gevult! They stashed a joint!

For Lenny all residents of the big cities were Jewish. "If you live in Butte, Montana, you're going to be goyish even if you're Jewish." Bruce embraced Italians, Dylan Thomas, Count Basie, Eugene O'Neill, converted Irishmen, mouths, bosoms, rye bread, chocolate, children's tushy kissers as Jewish. He defined as goyish: evaporated milk, spam, George Jessel, Danny Thomas, baton-twirling, fudge, and gold star mothers.[13]

Lenny probed the motives for Jack Ruby's act. Living in Texas, he had to prove his virility. He had a Jewish Billy the Kid complex. He wanted the national TV audience to know that this Jew had *cohones*. But he gave himself away with that two-handed [= Jewish] shot. As for the great number of Jews in show business, Lenny had an ingenious explanation. During the Egyptian captivity before Charleton Heston liberated them, Jews wanted out of that back-breaking, ball-busting pyramid construction. So they turned on the charm, working to perfect their show. Eventually, the Egyptians began to smile.

> *Egyptian: These Jews got bullshit that don't quit! I mean it's an art with them. C'mon let's go watch a Jew be charming. We know you're bullshitting, but you do it so good we get a kick out of it. Do it for us, will ya please?*

Now, Jews dominate the show business scene. So (unless Laurence Olivier does a high class Shylock), you never see a Jewish bad guy in the movies. Who are the bad guys? The goyim — the Irish. "And you see a lot of pictures about Christ — a ton of religious pictures, in the most respectful position. And that is, I'm sure, it's the way the Jew's saying 'I'm sorry.' That's where it's at."[14]

Early in his career, Bruce created a character called Superjew. Upon hearing anti-Semitic remarks at a bar, he would don an imaginary costume and cape and like the Golem of Prague would seek to redress wrongs. Unfortunately, this Superjew would get the hell kicked out of him. Reality bested fantasy; the modern Superjew, bloody and battered, was laid to rest. Lenny tried to illustrate Jewish aversion to violence in this bit; in others he dealt with sexuality. In our tribe there is no merit badge for abstaining: in fact, rabbis are notoriously big *shtuppers*. Bruce explained: "...perhaps that's why words come freer to me."[15]

What is a Jew?[16]

> *A Jew. In the dictionary, a Jew is one who is descended from the ancient tribe of Judea, but ... you and I know what a Jew is: one who killed our Lord ... We did it about two thousands years ago, and there should be a statute of limitations for that crime ... and those who pose as Christians ... still make the Jews pay their dues.*

If these bits contained obvious ambiguities including a strong dose of self-hatred, they also seem to confirm those canons re: Jewish humor as formulated by Reik, Freud, and Landmann. In his private life he broke with Jewish stereotypes, he married a *shiksa*. He experimented with sex and drugs. Fascinated by violence, he valued those *shtarkers* who could "duke" in much the same way that Issac Babel related to cossacks. In a sense Bruce epitomized Norman Mailer's "White Negro" for he found that hip, cool, underground culture more compelling than his own.

As gadfly and shaman (Goldman's designation), Lenny Bruce confirmed

33

Freud's model. Animated by a democratic mode of thought, he deflated the pompous and powerful while he identified with the outcasts and the losers. Lenny belligerently used Yiddish phrases, hip-argot, and obscene language in order to shock white Christians into an awareness of their deeply buried feelings about foreigners, Blacks and Jews.[17] Profoundly Jewish in terms of ethics as well as humor, Bruce punctured the shibboleths and questioned what C. Wright Mills used to call "crackpot realism." He tried, unsuccessfully perhaps, to penetrate that thin veneer of civilization with its tinsel, subterfuge, and camouflage which masks us. From the best and the brightest to the insulted and the injured, Lenny believed in common, corruptible, humanity. As witchdoctor or, if you prefer, Jewish exorcist, Lenny tried to purge the demons that plague us.

Humor, Dwight MacDonald once observed, is like guerilla warfare. Success (and we might add survival) depends on travelling light, striking unexpectedly, and getting away fast.[18] Bruce violated this prescription; he went too far. There are countless comedians of Jewish origin who know the limits. Take Don Rickles, the "merchant of venom," for example. On the surface, he seems to be reckless to a fault. Aggression in staccato bursts issues from his mouth. These insults have become status symbols. Unencumbered by thought, Rickles travels light. Basically a clown, his humor in fact bothers no one, especially no one in power. Others, like Bruce's friend, Buddy Hackett, continue to poke fun at themselves consistent with the canons of Jewish humor.

Why couldn't Lenny Bruce do the same? Perhaps he was neither smart nor Jewish enough. Painfully ill-educated, Bruce was egged on by *Village Voice* intellectuals to do their fighting against repression. Unsuited either mentally or emotionally for his heavy role, Bruce succumbed to self indulgence. As he grew flabby from too many candy bars, and cokes, not to mention drugs, his mind went slack. Frank Kofsky, a Bruce enthusiast, claims that Lenny was hounded to death by the establishment including the CIA.[19] If Jewishness carries with it a penchant for survival then Lenny was incurably assimilated. Despite personal failure, Lenny Bruce served as an agent of the emergent counter-culture. He challenged obscenity laws. He brought pervasive group fantasies under the comic microscope and beckoned to younger comedians to chart new comic territory.

If Lenny Bruce epitomized the mad *maggid,* Mel Brooks represents the *meshuginer* (crazy) who descends from a long line of *naronim* (fools). This coarse type *(grober yung)* was refined in the Borscht Belt. Born Melvin Kaminsky on June 28, 1926, he was the youngest of four boys. His father, an immigrant from Danzig, died young. Orphaned at age two, Melvin was smother-loved: the adored youngest son. At P. S. 19 in the Williamsburg section of Brooklyn Mel excelled as class clown. By wit alone he kept the bullies at bay. "If they're laughing, how can they bludgeon you to death?"[20]

At the movies, particularly on the Sabbath, Melvin discovered the uses of enchantment. He parodied current films with a speciality in putting on the Ritz as a lumbering Frankenstein. After a brief interlude in Brighton Beach where Melvin befriended a drummer, Bernard Rich, his family returned to Williamsburg. During the summers, Mel followed Buddy Rich to the Catskills. There he honed his comedic skills and banged the drums slowly. His wildest bit featured a fake suicide. Fully dressed with satchel in hand, he ascended the high diving board, screamed: "Business is terrible, I can't go on," and jumped off. Here in the Catskills, he met a wild saxophone player named Sid Caesar. Inspired by actual events, Brooks bellowed: *"Loz mir arois!"* ("Let me out!") This cry derived from a panic-stricken chambermaid who had been locked in a linen closet. If life was a linen closet, Melvin was a young Jewish talent yearning to bust loose. His theme song goes to the heart of *unzer shtick* (our tradition). Listen:[21]

> *Here I am, I'm Mel Brooks*
> *I've come to stop the show*
> *Just a ham who's minus looks*
> *But in your heart I'll grow*
> *I'll tell you gags, I'll sing you songs*
> *Just happy little songs that roll along.*
> *Out of my mind, won't you be kind?*
> *And please love Mel Brooks.*

Upon graduation from high school in 1944, Mel entered the Army and saw little action abroad, i.e. in combat. By his own admission and according to the Jewish comic tradition, he put survival above bravery. Back in the U.S.A., Brooks tried to make it as a salesman, college student, stage hand, summer stocker, and writer. As a college student he lasted one day; as a writer he hit paydirt with Sid Caesar on television. His first sketch for *Your Show of Shows* in 1950 featured Caesar as Tarzan, Jr. roaming the streets of New York clad in lion skin and being interviewed by a roving reporter. Brooks also created the pedantic but stupid German professor known variously as Kurt von Stuffer, Siegfried von Sedative, Rudolf von Rudder and Heinrich von Heartburn. Thus, continued Brooks's career-long obsession with Germans as objects of fear and subjects of ridicule. He confessed:[22]

> *Me? Not like the Germans? Why should I not like the Germans? Just because they're arrogant and have fat necks and do anything they're told so long as it's cruel, and killed millions of Jews in concentration camps and made soap out of their bodies and lamp shades out of their skins? Is that any reason to hate their fucking guts?*

35

For Brooks, Jews and Germans represent opposite sides of the same coin.

As a writer in Caesar's stable, he soared from $50 a week to $5,000. Fear of flying that high, however, precipitated a breakdown and led to six years of intensive analysis. Shrinkage brought lasting benefits: "... because 'I'm less inhibited and more in touch with unconscious realities ... If it did nothing but crush my societally taught sense of shame ... that was enough; that was plenty to free me.'"[23] Married in 1952 to dancer Florence Baum, Brooks was freed by divorce in 1962. Separation from the thorough-bred writers — Neil and Danny Simon, Carl Reiner, Lucille Kallen, Mel Tolkin and a runty redhead named Woody Allen — who created for Sid Caesar also spelled a new freedom. Such freedom proved expensive. Not until Mel Brooks teamed up with Carl Reiner did he finish in the money.

Psychoanalysis yielded funny stuff. After a period of blockage, Brooks began to swing with Reiner. The best of their material bears the stamp of Jewish humor. A master of comic deflation, Brooks assaulted the major authority figures — the heroes in history.

Interviewed by Reiner, Brooks took Freud's measure with material that was as wild as it was deflationary. As Kenneth Tynan remembers the exchange:[24]

> *Q.: I gather, sir, that you are a famous psychoanalyst?*
> *A.: That is correct.*
> *Q.: May I ask where you studied psychiatry?*
> *A.: At the Vienna School of Good Luck.*
> *Q.: Who analyzed you?*
> *A.: I was analyzed by No. 1 himself.*
> *Q.: You mean the great Sigmund Freud?*
> *A.: In person. Took me during lunchtime, charged me a nickel.*
> *Q.: What kind of man was he?*
> *A.: Lovely little fellow. I shall never forget the hours we spent
>   together, me lying on the couch, him sitting right there beside
>   me, wearing a nice off-the-shoulder dress.*

Strangely, Dr. Brooks is a prude who refuses to acknowledge the Oedipal complex. "That's the dirtiest thing I ever heard." When informed that the essential idea of a passionate desire to sleep with one's mother is Greek, not Jewish, he breathes a sigh of relief. "With a Greek, who knows? But with a Jew, you don't do a thing like that even to your wife, let alone your mother."[25] The marriage of Brooks and Reiner yielded the bountiful 2000 year old man. Fear makes the patriarch's comic pump. Thick with a Yiddish accent, the old man relates how, before God, man feared their leader Phil. They prayed to him "Ohhh, Philip. Please don't take our eyes out and don't pinch us and don't hurt us. Ooo-main!" A bolt of lightning ended Phil's hegemony and started the Lord's, also known as *Gevalt*, Yahveh, Yahway, Your-way, His-Way and Goodness. Everything in the universe is based on fear, especially transportation. The old man tries to defeat death in a Jewish accent. He prays for twenty-two minutes each day so that the ceiling will not fall and his heart will not attack him. In addition, he eats a lot of garlic to ward off the *Malechhamoves* (Angle of Death). Alternately proud and disappointed, he asserts: "I have 42,000 children and not one comes to see me. How dey forget a father?"[26]

The "dream factory" that is Hollywood beckoned to Mel Brooks. He was attracted by the dominant group fantasies generated there to be sure; but he was also driven by the desire to parody the genre and make his own mark. Brooks first movie won an Oscar. In this short film, he articulated the voice of critic, modelled after his Uncle Joe, thick with Yiddish accent, who put down the inanities of modern art (rhymes with fart) as they flashed across the screen. Thus, began the assault on high culture. Next, pickled in Jewish brine with flavorings by Will Jordan and Lenny Bruce, came *The Producers*.

The best parody of the Hollywood Western genre, *Blazing Saddles* violates all of our canons. Mercilessly, Brooks slaughters our sacred cows and parades the carcasses before our tearfilled eyes (from excessive laughter). A perfect pastiche, we are treated to a black sheriff as the hero of A Jewish Western.

Young Frankenstein (1974) continues the parody parade. The lumbering monster puts on the Ritz and drives Elizabeth (Madeline Kahn) into Victor Herbert rapture — "Ah, Sweet Mystery of Life!" — with his enormous *shvantzenstucker*.[27] In *High Anxiety* (1977), Brooks pays homage to Hitchcock. In one scene, we see the portraits of Sigmund Freud, Carl Jung, and Joyce Brothers hanging together. Better they should hang separately, especially Brothers. *History of the World: Part One* (1981) portrays Moses as a *klutz*. He drops one of God's tablets, leaving ten instead of the original fifteen. We also encounter Amicus, a stand-up Roman philosopher, a waiter at the Last Supper; Torquemada — the Grand Inquisitor (né Isidor?). With nuns in an Esther Williams synchronized swim, Torquemada sings:[28]

> *We hava a mission to convert the Jews*
> *We're gonna teach them wrong from right*
> *We're gonna help them see the light*
> *And make them an offer they can't refuse.*

Brooks believes that God designated him "to be crazy and amuse the breast beaters." What is the source of Brooks's comedy? He admits:[29]

> *It comes from not being kissed by a girl until you are sixteen. It*
> *comes from the feeling that, as a Jew and a person, you don't fit*

into the mainstream of American society. It comes from the realization that even though you're better and smarter, you'll never belong.

Resentment, rage, ethnicity, dependency, fear, and laughter fuse in the comedy of Mel Brooks.

Woody Allen is also a short, insecure, Brooklyn, Jewish comedian, writer, and film maker. By looking at life through the prism of irony (the phrase and much that follows is lifted from Schechner; I took the idea and ran with it), Woody Allen crafted a self-image. Basically a *shtick* that is worn like a comic mask, Woody becomes a schlemiel.[30] An emotional stutterer — at least prior to *Annie Hall* (1977) — he personifies vulnerability. And the schlemiel, Howard Stein reminds us, is easy prey for the gentiles. He functions, in the concept coined by Erik Erikson, as a "negative identity." The debasement of this type in Jewish humor functions as a necessary social control. Each joke reminds the listener that "this is the sort of fellow you don't become."[31]

Before he became Woody Allen, Alan Stewart Konigsberg was born on December 1, 1935. Although much of his private life is deliberately veiled in obscurity, Eric Lax among other writers fascinated by Allen provides a few important facts. We know, for example, that Konigsberg did not like school. He played a lot of hookey. He ignored homework assignments in favor of card tricks and magic shops. Contrary to his self-styled comic image, he played baseball with skill; the clarinet with fluency. He even tried boxing in the Golden Gloves. Parental disapproval, however, aborted his career as pugilist. Nothing could stifle his love for Willie Mays or his passion for the New York Giants.[32] Despite a few fitful subsequent attempts at college, Woody ended his formal education at age eighteen. He turned to gag-writing. His gag-bag includes many goodies spun from the Brooklyn-Jewish environment that was his matrix.

From 1953 to 1962, Woody served his apprenticeship writing jokes for others; watching Mort Sahl perform inspired Woody to try center-stage too.[33] Prior to Sahl, comedians were essentially visual clowns dressed in tuxedos who put down their mothers-in-law while supported by chorus girls ("tits and ass' in the argot of Lenny Bruce) in big dance numbers. Not only was Sahl subversive in content, he was also an innovator in presentation. Attired in sweater and slacks, he affected a casual Joe College image. Strictly a verbal comedian, Sahl relied on subtlety, ideas, and wit. Woody decided to come on as the sad-faced, alienated, urban Jew. One can trace his progress as a comic pilgrim through his one liners.[34]

I was breast fed through falsies. My parents worshipped old-world values: God and carpeting. We were too poor to own a dog; so my parents went to a damaged pet store and bought me *an ant. My neighborhood was so tough, that the kids stole hubcaps from moving cars. They broke my violin and left it embedded in my body. I went to school for emotionally disturbed teachers. I stole second when playing softball. Guilty, I returned to first. I went with a girl who had a child by a future marriage. My first wife was so immature; she sank my boats in the bathtub. My cousin was very successful, a lawyer. He insured his wife with Mutual of Omaha for orgasms. If he failed to deliver, she collected. I spent $1,000 to have my nose fixed. Now, my brain won't work. My apartment was robbed so often, I put up a sign: "We gave already." I moved to a safer apartment with a doorman. Two weeks later I was mugged — by the doorman. Not only is there no God, try getting a plumber on weekend.*

Laughter provides distance and protection against an oppressive world. As with Lenny Bruce and Mel Brooks, wit functions in the world of Woody Allen as a defense mechanism as well as a cry of defiance. When he became a film-maker, Woody brought to his new vocation the venerable cultural baggage of Jewish humor. For example in his first film, *What's Up Tiger Lily* (1966) some Japanese characters speak Yiddish. *Bananas* (1971) poked fun at Jews who send money, UJA money, to dictator Vargas and Christians who pitch New Testament cigarettes. "You switch to . . . and all is forgiven." *Play It Again, Sam* (1972) plays the warm generous Jew, Alan Felix against the cold, vacuous Christian, Dick Christie. *Sleeper* (1973) shows the Jew as outsider in 2173 who stirs excitement and makes trouble in a robotized Orwellian world. *Annie Hall* (1977) concludes with a Jewish joke. 'My brother thinks he's a chicken," a client tells his shrink. "Why not have him committed?" He responds: "Because we need the eggs." Alvy Singer, a Jewish comedian looks at life through bifocals. Like the food in a Catskill Hotel, life is terrible. Nevertheless, he wants a bigger portion. Pearl is the life-affirming, Jewish earth-mother in a serious film, *Interiors* (1978).[35] In *Manhattan* (1979), Isaac Davis is a Jewish television writer, lost in the stars, who is dumped by a lesbian wife, abandoned by his girl friends, one a seventeen year old nymphet, no Litvak Lolita. So what else is new? In *Stardust Memories* (1980), Woody Allen has shed the schlemiel skin and is transformed into Sandy Bates: love object. *Zelig* (1983), however, signals a severe regression; the chameleon in search of authenticity.

Woody Allen shares a drive for upward mobility with other Jewish comedians. As a direct result, Mark Schechner argues, comedy plays second fiddle to Woody's clarinet. When Allen lets go in the manner of Philip Roth, he combines self-irony and external aggression.[36] Taking it on the chin (masochism) and countering with the left-hook of paranoia and the right-cross of revenge creates a devastating one-two punch enabling Woody to box with God. Yom Kippur, in Allen's exegesis, is the "sacred holiday commemorating God's reneging on every promise." In *Love and Death* (1975) Allen's Boris jabs: "If God is testing us, why doesn't he give us a written?" The virtuous man, he knows, will "dwell in the house of the Lord for six months with an option to buy." He demands proof of God's existence through a miracle such as the parting of the seas or impelling Uncle Sasha to pick up a check. "If Christ was a carpenter, I wonder what he charged for bookshelves."[37] Nor are rabbis spared verbal blows. Rabbi Henry Sharpstein alias Little Tony is singled out for "the transportation of a large whitefish across the state line for immoral purposes." In *Everything You Always Wanted...* (1972) the winning contestant on *What's My Perversion* is a tied-up rabbi whose favorite fantasy involves a beautiful girl who whips him while his wife eats pork at his feet. When B'nai B'rith protested, Woody Allen confessed: "I've never considered rabbis sacred as I've never considered any organized religion sacred. I find them all silly. Costumed and bearded just like popes, to me it's all absolutely absurd."[38]

Absurd or not, comic fantasies invite serious study. What Bion and deMause[39] have formulated with regard to group process leader-delegates should be applied to exemplary humorists. Clearly, vast amounts of energy collect in the group fantasy ready for action. Unless the "healthy" ego rechannels this pent-up psychic energy, it can lead to massive destruction. Creative role-play is necessary to dissipate the poison and diffuse the fear. Comic figures cut in the pattern of Lenny Bruce, Mel Brooks and Woody Allen serve at least two vital functions. First, they help us to define the national group fantasy. Second, through their wit, they pave the way to alternative national styles by releasing aggression through the healing process of laughter.

Our Jewish trinity all confronted media-nurtured American fantasies. Of the three, Lenny Bruce swings the most: from creative risk to self-immolation. Lenny broadened the range of humorous possibility. He held up the comic spotlight and flashed it into the dark corridors of our psyches.[39]

Success, status, high culture, Christian women all tempt the Jewish comedian. Woody Allen and Mel Brooks crave love and fear death. Listen to Woody:[40]

> *Life is a concentration camp. You're stuck here and there's no way out, and you can only rage impotently against your persecutors.*
> *It's not that I'm afraid to die, I just don't want to be there when it happens.*
> *Death is an acquired trait.*

Death . . . is one of the worst things that can happen to a Cosa Nostra member and many prefer simply to pay a fine.
It is impossible to experience one's own death objectively and still carry a tune.
Death is one of the few things that can be done as easily lying down.
The thing to remember is that each time of life has its appropriate rewards, whereas when you're dead it's hard to find a light switch.
I do not believe in an afterlife, although I am bringing a change of underwear.
History will dissolve me.
Why are our days numbered instead of lettered?
Yea, I shall run through the valley of the shadow of death.

Mel Brooks also wants to live forever. His 2,000 year old man is very Jewish and therefore highly vulnerable to "hostile man . . . nature and God." 5,000 years of Jewish life poured through him. "Death," he realizes, "is a greater enemy than a German soldier." Young Frankenstein tries to defeat death. Highly anxious, Brooks prefers to "swing, shout and make noise!" In his psychic arsenal, humor is "another defense against the universe." "Let's not mimic death before our time comes!"

Which of our three subjects ranks first among equals? Such a question could fuel as much heated debate as the old hot stove league when New York City had three baseball teams. Each comic has earned his share of criticism. Woody Allen charges that even God is a chronic underachiever. With that admonition in mind, we can now praise famous men, especially Jewish comics. There is a method in their madness. They enable us to accept honesty over fabrication without abandoning ancient imperatives or sacrificing child's play. They celebrate life in the face of death.

REFERENCES

1. Samual Janus, "The Great Comedians: Personality and Other Factors," *The American Journal of Psychoanalysis,* 35:2 (1975), 169–174; also see "Analyzing Jewish Comics," *Time,* October 2, 1978, 76.

2. Wallace Markfield, "The Yiddishization of American Humor," *Esquire* 64 (October 1965), 114. For the many facets of Jewish humor see Earl Rovit, "Jewish Humor and American Life," *American Scholar* 36:2 (Spring 1967), 237–244; the dual function of this genre is canvassed in Joseph Dorinson, "Jewish Humor: Mechanism for Defense, Weapon for Cultural Affirmation," *The Journal of Psychohistory* 8:4 (Spring 1981), 447–464.

3. Sigmund Freud, *Jokes and Their Relation to the Unconscious,* translated and edited by James Strachey (New York: W.W. Norton, 1960) contains Jewish jokes and pithy comments, 33, 49–51, 55–56, 61–63, 111–155, 142. Theodore Reik, *Jewish Wit* (New York: Gamust Press, 1962), 188–216, 221–222. Albert Memmi, *The Liberation of a Jew,* translated and edited by Judy Hyun (New York: Orion Press, 1966), 43–51. Salcia Landmann, "On Jewish Humor," *Jewish Journal of Sociology* [1962] pp. 193–198.

4. Elliot Oring, "The People of the Joke: Historiography of Jewish Folklore and Ethnography," Unpublished Paper, October 1983. Citation is by permission of the author who graciously sent me a copy.

5. Jesse Bier, *The Rise and Fall of American Humor* (New York: Holt, Rinehart & Winston, 1968), 3.

6. *Ibid.,* 346.

7. Albert Goldman, *Ladies and Gentlemen — LENNY BRUCE!!* (New York: Random House, 1974), 76–79.

8. Lenny Bruce, *How to Talk Dirty and Influence People* (Chicago: Playboy Press, 1966), 2, 3, 9, 15.

9. *Ibid.,* 78–90.

10. John Cohen, ed., *The Essential Lenny Bruce* (New York: Ballantine Books 1967), 76.

11. *Ibid.,* 35–51.

12. *Ibid.,* 42.

13. *Ibid.,* 45.

14. *Ibid.,* 50–51.

15. *Ibid.,* 44:
    "Lenny Bruce at Carnegie Hall," February 4, 1961, United Artists Records, UAS 9800. Bruce equates "pride" in Judaism with "adjustment" — not "happiness."

16. Bruce, *How to . . .,* 196.

17. John D. Weaver, "The Fault, Dear Bruce . . .," *Holiday,* 44:5 (November 1968), 72.

18. Dwight McDonald, *On Movies* (Englewod Cliffs: Prentice Hall, 1969), 160–161.

19. Kofsky's bitter remarks were presented at the AHA Convention, December 30, 1971. They were tempered in his subsequent book, *Lenny Bruce: The Comedian as Social Critic & Secular Moralist* (New York: Monad Press, 1974). Kofsky claims, 87–89, that Bruce combined the traditional roles of rabbi, *maggid* and *tzaddik*.

20. Kenneth Tynan, *Show People: Profiles in Entertainment* (New York: Simon & Schuster, 1979, 207–209, 213; Will Holtzman, *Seesaw: A Dual Biography of Anne Bancroft & Mel Brooks,* (Garden City: Doubleday, 1979), 6.
21. Maurice Yacower, *In Method of Madness: The Comic Art of Mel Brooks* (New York: St. Martin's Press, 1981). 15–16, 18–20.
22. Yacower, 17; the Germanic creatures of Brooks are nicely captured by Ted Sennet, *Your Show of Shows* (New York: Collier Books, 1977), 47–55.
23. Yacower, 20.
24. Tynan, 190.
25. *Ibid.,* 191.
26. Yacower, 50–52.
27. Gerald Mast, *The Comic Mind: Comedy & the Movies,* (Chicago: Univ. of Chicago Press, 1979, second edition), 310–312.
28. Lester D. Friedman, *Hollywood's Image of the Jew* (New York: Frederick Ungar, 1982), 301.
29. Monaco, 186–187; see *Newsweek* (February 17, 1975), 57.
30. Mark Schechner, "Woody Allen: The Failure of the Therapeutic" in S. Cohen, *From Hester . . . ,* 238.
31. H. Stein, "Judaism & Group Fantasy . . . ," 164–165.
32. Eric Lax, *On Being Funny: Woody Allen & Comedy* (New York: Charterhouse, 1975), 30–33.
33. *Ibid.,* 13–17.
34. Earl Wilson, *Show Business Laid Bare* (New York: New American Library, 1974), 246–247; Maurice Yacower, *Loser Take All: The Comic Art of Woody Allen* (New York: Frederick Ungar, 1979), 20; many of these jokes are found on "Woody Allen: Stand-up Comic, 1964–1968," United Artists-LA849-J2, a wonderful two-record set. Also see Richard Schickel, "The Basic Woody Allen Joke . . . ," *New York Times Magazine,* January 7, 1973, 33.
35. In tracing Jewish themes in Allen's films I am deeply indebted to L. Friedman, *Hollywood's Image . . . ,273–281.*
36. Schechner, 231, 235–236.
37. Yacower, *Loser . . . ,* 162–163.
38. *Ibid.,* 145; Leonard Probst, *Off Camera* (New York: Stein & Day, 1975), 261 contains Allen's counter-punch to the B'nai B'rith's jab.
39. Lloyd deMause, *Foundations of Psychohistory* (New York: Creative Roots, 1982), ch. 6.
   I have tried to measure the man. See Joseph Dorinson, "Lenny Bruce, A Jewish Humorist in Babylon," *Jewish Currents* 35:2 (February 1981), 14–19, 31–32.
40. As quoted by Lax, *On Being . . . ,* 224–225; also on death consult Yacower, *Loser . . . ,* 215–216.

A.Ziv

PSYCHO-SOCIAL ASPECTS OF JEWISH HUMOR IN ISRAEL AND IN THE DIASPORA

AVNER ZIV
Tel-Aviv University, Israel

PSYCHO-SOCIAL ASPECTS OF JEWISH HUMOR IN ISRAEL AND IN THE DIASPORA

> *Irwin, a Jewish soldier in the American infantry, is a real schlemiel. In training, he always did the wrong thing; in a parade, he was never in step with the others; his gun was never clean, and on the firing range he never hit anywhere near the target.*
>
> *One of the former commanders of his battalion heard that Irwin had been awarded a medal for his courageous stand in the face of a German attack, and that he even took half a company of enemy soldiers prisoner. The commander looked up Irwin's platoon commander and asked him how he had worked this leadership miracle of turning Irwin into a hero.*
>
> *— It's very simple. The German attack was dreadful and I decided to retreat. I put a machine gun in Irwin's hand and told him: "Irwin, from now on this is your private business."*

There is no question that this joke reflects Jewish humor. It contains both self-disparaging humor and pride. It makes the listener laugh, or at least smile, and it has a moral. It sounds simple, but it is really sophisticated, because it takes thought to derive pleasure from its point. It does in fact reflect a Jewish experience, but this is a Jewish experience of the Diaspora. If that same joke was told about the IDF not only would it be pointless but it wouldn't be at all funny. The Jewish experience in Israel is different from that in the Diaspora, and therefore Israeli humor differs from Jewish humor in the Diaspora.

This article deals with the psycho-social aspects of the Jewish humor that developed in the Diaspora and in Israel. No attempt is being made here to present an overall explanation of the concept of Jewish humor, since the comprehensive interdisciplinary effort that could serve as a basis for such an explanation has not yet been completed. Scholars engaged in research related to folklore, Judaism, sociology, literature, as well as experts in other fields, all have specific knowledge and it is from their particular vantage point that they try to understand Jewish humor. In this book, several examples of these approaches are presented. My approach is that of a psychologist who naturally avails himself of the knowledge accumulated in other sciences and fields of research, but makes no pretensions to possess the expertise needed to represent this knowledge. I shall first relate to the sources of Jewish humor, and then to its

47

characteristics. Later in this paper, I will also discuss the different directions of development it has taken in the United States and in Israel.

The Origins of Jewish Humor

Many of those engaged in research related to Jewish humor point to Eastern Europe as the place where it first developed and flourished. Other researchers claim that its origins are much further removed, both in time and in place. Baumgartner, for example, in his book (1896), analysed the humoristic elements in the Bible. A similar effort was made by Lang (1962) and Knox (1963). Others, such as Landman (1962) and Friedlender (1984) are of the opinion that Jewish sources are not replete with humor. Friedlender points out that with the exception of the customs connected with the Purim holiday, the Jewish religion regards humor with suspicion. It is reasonable to assume that this is an attitude common to all religions: after all, one is expected to relate to the principles of religion with seriousness and severity, and who knows what would happen if people found reasons to laugh at sacred things? Experts among those engaged in research related to Judaism are certainly better qualified than I to reply to the question whether there are expressions of humor in the sources. Nevertheless, it is clear that there are references to laughter in the Bible. Koestler (1964) cites research done by Mitchell, who counted the number of times the word laughter appears in the Bible. He found 29 instances, 13 of which have a connotation of derision and disparagement. In the Talmud there are also references (although very few) to humor. But all in all, one cannot regard the Jewish sources as a treasury of humoristic material.

Chotzner (1905) in his book describes a less known sector of Jewish humor. He mentions the humoristic writings of Jewish authors in Western Europe during the 13th and 14th centuries. Nevertheless, very little attention was paid to Jewish humor until the end of the 19th century, so little in fact that the chief rabbi of London, Herman Adler, wrote an article (1893) in which he spoke out against the charge that Jews have no sense of humor. But these examples are exceptions. From the end of the last century, Jewish humor became widely recognized as superlative humor and is growing in renown to this very day.

During the '20s of this century, there was a flurry of books published on Jewish humor. These were collections of jokes or short stories that were becoming increasingly popular. Hundreds of such books were published, first in Europe,and later in the United States. The fact that the same jokes, with minor changes, could be found in all of them, did not detract from their success. In bibliographies that I have checked, I found no less than 86 such books that were published in Germany, France and in the United States in the last 60 years. This is an average rate of more than one book a year, and certainly the number of books on the national humor of any other nation has never reached such proportions.

During that same period, scores of books and hundreds of articles were also published by authors, psychoanalysts, by those engaged in folklore-related research, by anthropologists and experts in other fields, all trying to explain one or another aspect of Jewish humor. The overwhelming majority of these writers treat Jewish humor as a phenomenon that was born and developed mainly in the 19th century in Eastern Europe. I shall now attempt to answer the question as to why it in fact happened there and at that particular time.

19th Century Jewry of Eastern Europe: The Foundations of Jewish Humor.

During that same period, more than two-thirds of all the Jews of the world lived in Eastern Europe, mainly in Russia and Poland. Their living conditions were harsh. They were not granted any civil rights and were forced to live within certain restricted areas, in villages and towns (the famous shtetl). Despite these difficult conditions, the Jewish communities organized themselves, and ran various institutions very effectively. Religion and religious studies played a central role in these communities, and all male children attended school regularly. This was a continuation of the ancient tradition of the people of Israel that places great value on studies. The many learned people in the community earned a great deal of social prestige and usually filled its positions of leadership. As a result , most of the Jewish population had a higher level of culture and education than the surrounding ignorant populace. In addition to the knowledge they acquired through their studies, most of the Jews spoke two and often three languages: Hebrew in their sacred studies, Yiddish in their interrelations within the community, and Russian or Polish in their dealings with their environment.

This remarkable intellectual ability, which was constantly being reinforced by the society, also found its expression in complex, and frequently exaggerated, analyses — as "pilpul" (casuistry), a kind of intellectual gymnastics frequently far removed from reality. Several things happened to this world of the Jews that contributed to the creation of that humor known as Jewish humor. In order to understand this phenomenon, we will return to the components of humor (intellectual, social, and emotional) that I described in the Introduction.

Intellectual Factors

The Jewish people preserved its identity in the Diaspora thanks to its faith in its religion. The books of the Jewish religion provided a frame of reference, not only for the future and the redemption of its people, but also for their daily life. The laws of ethics, the principles of justice, and the rules of behavior found in

49

the religious books served as guides to the Jewish people. The rabbis, who were the experts authorized to interpret the sacred books, were their undisputed spiritual leaders.

Against this background, revolutions in thought took place that shocked the world of Jewish tradition. In contrast to ideological revolutions connected with religion that erupted in other cultures (revolutions accompanied by physical clashes, persecution, wars and victims), the "Jewish revolutions" were purely in the realm of thought. The Hassidic movement that was created in Poland in the 18th century constituted a threat to the traditional Jewish leadership. The Mitnaggedim movement arose to oppose it. In addition, the Haskalah (enlightenment) movement came from Western Europe to Eastern Europe in the 19th century. These were in the main different streams of thought, but there were also psycho-social elements in the conflicts between them. The Hassidic movement introduced a strong emotional element into the Jewish religion, which was in marked contrast to the rational element which until then had been the overriding one in traditional Judaism. The Mitnaggedim, who with all their might, strove to preserve the rational elements, went into battle — and let us remember that this is mainly a battle of intellectual thought and not one of violence — to defend the tradition. The Haskalah, as an innovative revolutionary element, tried to change not only the mode of thought of the Jews, but also their daily customs. The Hassidism and the Mitnagdim were able to arrive at compromises that made possible their co-existence while maintaining their differences of opinion. The Haskalah was another matter. It attracted to its ranks a considerable number of the Jewish authors of the time. How was it possible to react when irreconcilable differences arose within a community that had no political force, no police or army? After all, it was impossible to send someone to jail for having committed the sin of "erroneous" thought. It was also impossible to expel him. One possible way to deal aggressively with your opponent is through humor. The effectiveness of aggressive humor has been well known throughout history (Ziv, 1984). Examples of satire among Jews of that same period can be found in Friedlender (1981, 1983) as well as in his article in this book. Satire and counter-satire in the oppressed and closed Jewish society could of course be aggressive, but it also had to exercise caution. This was because none of the streams attacked Judaism itself nor did they propose escaping from it. Only the Haskalah in the West exerted an influence in the direction of encouraging assimilation and since there this was possible in practice, there were Jews who converted to Christianity. In Eastern Europe, this was nearly impossible. Therefore, the satirical criticism was ambivalent. The humoristic criticism of Mendel Moher Sefarim and of Shalom Aleichem did indeed attack the typical characters and values of the shtetl, but it was clear that this criticism contained a considerable measure of love for this life which they knew so well, and of identification with it (Stora Sandor 1984). The Yiddish

50

folklore of the time laughed at the casuistry of the wise men of Helem, but this was criticism that arose from a sense of identification and an understanding that this ridiculous casuistry was a part of the life of the community.

One can, therefore, discern, at the end of the last century and at the beginning of the present century, far-reaching attempts to change the mode of thought in the Jewish community of Eastern Europe. Since these attempts could not result in their instigators being expelled from the community, and since the Jews fought for internal changes within the community, humor developed as a weapon of criticising those who held differing views on what was in the community's best interests. The situation of the Jews who had lived for generations according to their ancient tradition and who suddenly saw other "better" ways of life, heightened the community's needs to search for self-identity, particularly since it was isolated from the ruling Christian community. The main weapon in the internal wars that were waged in the community, along with this search for self-identity, was the intellectual weapon, and humor was one of the forms it took.

Social Factors

Life in the shtetl did not permit the Jews to engage in professions that were open to others. Many Jews had to really exert their imaginations in order to "get by." In this way, the "luftmenschen" developed. These were people who engaged in "luftgescheften" in order to "manage" somehow. The shadchen was an important figure in the shtetl, not only because of his contribution in arranging marriages, but because he carried gossip from house to house. The schnorrers, who lived on the earnings of others, elevated chutzpa to a state of art, as the beneficiaries of the tradition of charity in the Jewish world. Since the giving of charity is a religious duty, the schnorrer often felt he was doing a "favor" to those he enabled to perform such good deeds.

Although these "professionals" were an integral part of the community, they were also a cause of frustration, and as such were a target for humor (Ziv 1981). There are numerous jokes about shadchens and schnorrers among the examples Freud gives in his book on humor (1916). The laughter directed against these targets served as a criticism of them, but it also expressed acceptance and recognition of them and their place in the community. This allusion to their closed world with its characters and customs worked as a cohesive factor. The cohesiveness of the Jewish community was based on its religious customs. Power was in the hands of the rabbis, who were accorded honor. But like anyone in a position of power they were also subjected to criticism. Humor gave expression to this criticism, and so there are innumerable jokes about rabbis. Naturally, the surrounding hostile world also was a butt of criticism. In humor directed against an outside group there are also elements that contribute to internal cohesiveness.

The accent on "us" as different (and of course better) than "them", reinforces a person's sense of belonging to his own group. And indeed the Jews used humor directed against the gentiles for this purpose of strengthening Jewish affiliation. The intellectual and moral superiority of the Jews was obvious to them. Since they had no other weapons in the war against their enemies who victimized them and shed their blood, they resorted to the intellectual weapon. Evidently this is how the classical joke type of humor was created:

> *If you tell a joke to a Russian peasant, he'll laugh three times: once when you tell the joke, the second time when you explain it to him, and the third time when he finally understands it. But if you tell a joke to a Russian landowner, he'll laugh twice, once when you tell it, and once when you explain it. Understand — he'll never understand. If you tell a joke to a Cossack, he'll only laugh once: when you tell it. He won't let you explain it, and he certainly won't understand it. And if you tell a joke to another Jew, he won't laugh at all. Before you finish the story, he'll stop you and shout: "I've already heard it! Besides, I tell it a lot better than you do."*

The stories about a "Yiddishe kopf" (a Jewish head) and a "goyishe kopf" expressed a sense of superiority, but at the same time ridiculed the Jewish community as well. For example:

> *A Jew decides to convert to Christianity. One day his wife finds him wrapped in a talit, wearing a kippa, a prayer book in his hand, and praying fervently. "What are you doing, Moishe? Did you forget you're not a Jew any more?"*
> *— "Oi," Moishe replies, striking himself on his forehead, "this goishe kopf!"*

Emotional Factors

The joys that brightened the Christian world around them were foreign to the Jews. A sense of sadness accompanied their tragic lives. From a psychological standpoint, one might expect that the Jewish people in that time, and under those living conditions, would exhibit signs of depression. Here humor acted as a defense mechanism. It is no simple matter to defend yourself against a tragic reality when you are weak and possess no weapons. One possible way is to distort reality, to see the absurd in it. Not only not to cry at what you see but to react in the opposite way — to laugh. Oring (1983) writes: "The conception of a Jewish humor derives from a conceptualization of Jewish history as a history of suffering, rejection, and despair. Given this history, the Jews have nothing to laugh about at all. That they do laugh and jest can only signal the existence of a special relationship between the Jews and humor, and suggests that the humor of the Jews must in some way be distinctive from other humors, which are not born of despair." (p. 266-7).

As I pointed out in the Introduction, psychoanalysts like Bergler (1965), Kris (1952), Reik (1954, 1962), have claimed that the origin of Jewish humor can be found in the masochistic elements that are typical of our people. Grotjahn (1966) adds to this pathological analysis, an additional component that he has discerned: paranoia! Ben Amos (1973) who rejects the concept of Jewish humor as an expression of masochism, writes that in actual fact one can see in it rather an expression of sadism. (p. 130).

Masochism, paranoia, sadism? Perhaps there is no expression of pathology in humor, but rather a healthy element of actively coping with life. When a man finds himself in a difficult situation, he can choose one of the following psychological defense mechanisms: Resignation: "This is fate, this is how things are, and I have no choice but to reconcile myself and to accept bitter reality."
This is a mechanism that can only leave one feeling sad and depressed. Another mechanism is an escape to pathology: when a man can no longer bear reality, he creates a different reality — a world only he understands which appears unreal to others — and sinks into it. This behavior is one of the mechanisms of schizophrenia (Arieti, 1948). A third way is denial: "This doesn't exist, there is no such thing, it can't be, therefore it doesn't exist."

In addition to these defense mechanisms and many others, humor can also be regarded as a defense mechanism. In contrast to other mechanisms, which are based on a passive approach, humor adopts an active approach that combines imagination and fantasy with reality. The fantasy in humor is controlled and temporary. In psychonalytical terms, humor serves as a constructive mechanism of withdrawal for the sake of the self. In this context, mention should be made of one of the more mature and complex forms of humor — irony. Irony requires formal thought and obliges both its creator and its audience to engage in complex intellectual activity. The classic work of Kierkegaard (1968, 1975) and Yankelevitz (1964) discuss the complex intellectual basis of irony. It is only natural that ironical humor should become the typical weapon of the Jews who want to alter reality at least in the world of the imagination. A good example of such irony can be found in Shalom Aleichem's writings. One of his characters writes the following letter to his relatives in the United States: "Dear Yankele, You asked me to write you a long letter, and I would do so gladly, but there is not much to write about. The rich are still rich and the poor die of hunger as always. What's new about that? As for the pogroms, thank God, we no longer have anything to fear because we already had one — in fact, we had two already. And it's not worth their while to bother about a third one...Our whole family got through the pogroms, except for Lipi who was murdered together with his two sons, Noah and Mordechai — wonderful craftsmen all three of them...You asked about Herschl. He has been out of work for more than half a year now. That's because in the prison they don't let him work...Mendel did a smart thing: he simply died. Some say from weakness, others say from hunger. I personally think he died from both. Really, I don't know what else to write, except that cholera is spreading like wildfire." (cited in Novak, Waldocks 1981).

The irony in this letter, the ability to introduce humor into such dreadful tragedies, gives a man the strength to perservere. The Jewish people, that continued all throughout its long history to stand against up the hostility of its environment, needed this strength. Despite the tragedies that befell them, the Jews nurtured an optimistic element of hope in the redemption that would come in the wake of their suffering.

"Laughter through tears", the expression that has become a sort of trademark of Jewish humor, filled an important psychological function. By merging of two opposing emotions — anxiety and laughter — man can effectively cope. There is also an element of rebellion in the decision to introduce laughter into situations that arouse anxiety. We can learn again from Shalom Aleichem: "I tell you it is an ugly and mean world, and only to spite it, we mustn't weep. If you want to know, that is the real source of my constant good spirits, of my, as it is called, 'humor'. Not to cry, out of spite. Only to laugh out of spite, only to laugh." (From a letter written in 1911, quoted in Madison 1968).

Irony can be directed towards a situation, towards another person (as a weapon of aggression) or towards oneself. This last form of irony is called in the literature of the psychology of humor, self-disparagement. Self-disparaging humor, like gallows humor, is included within the functions of humor as a defense mechanism (Ziv, 1984). Gallows humor relates to phenomena that meet anxiety with a smile. In an article that Freud wrote in 1928, he made an oblique reference to this type of humor and explains it as encouragement given by the super-ego to the ego that is coping with anxiety. Freud claims that the ability to laugh at a frightening situation helps change our attitude towards it. It is as if the super-ego were saying: "Look here, there is nothing to be afraid of. It's really not serious, it's even funny." Faced with situations of anxiety that were common occurrences in Eastern Europe at that time, gallows humor developed and flourished. It fulfilled and continues to fulfill an important funcction as a defense mechanism. It is possible that gallows humor is more prevalent among people who lead lives filled with enxieties and fears. Another form of humor in which it acts as a defense mechanism, is self-disparaging humor. In this type of humor, a man makes himself and his traits an object of lauther. In contrast to aggressive humor (which forms the main bulk of humoristic creation throughout the world) in which one laughs at others and their weaknesses, srlf-disparaging humor directs its darts at the humorist himself. A man who laughs at himself is regarded positively by his environment. This is because most people try to put forth their better attributes despite the fact that they are aware of their negative sides. An identical pattern exist on the group or national level. As Freud wrote: "I do not know whether there are many other instances of a people making fun to such a degree of its own character, as the Jews do." (Freud, 1905, p. 112).

This ability to employ self-disparaging humor derived from the efforts of Eastern European Jewry to understand itself, while still trying to change under the influence of the Haskalah. Criticism of the traditional ways of life was accompanied by love and affection, and thus self-disparaging humor provided the opportunity to combine criticism and pleasure. From the emotional standpoint, such humor can be regarded as a defense mechanism: "Don't attack me, I'm doing it myself, even better than you can." It is possible that when a person relates to his own weakness, it arouses sympathy as well. But let us not forget that self-disparaging humor also has an element of power in it: "Only someone who is really strong can see and show his weaknesses. The very fact that he refers to these weaknesses shows the greatness of a person who is capable of openly coping with them." (Weiss, 1922, p. 124). The use of self-disparaging humor — the phenomenon of Jews laughing at their foibles as Jews — was also taken up on the personal level, and Jewish humorists, like Woody Allen for example, turned their own image of a schlemiel into a superb style of humor.

The Characteristics of Jewish Humor

We have discussed the major historical reasons for the development of Jewish humor in Eastern Europe, in the 19th Century. During that period, the Jewish community differed and deviated from the surrounding majority in every possible way (language, religion, customs). The Jews were a marginal society, a target for the hatred and hostility of the ruling Christian majority. The closed Jewish world with its strong intellectual and religious tradition began to be affected by the new spirit of the Haskalah. The Haskalah endeavored to introduce far-reaching changes into the thought and customs of the Jews. The movements of the Haskalah, Hassidism and Mitnaggedism, led to sharp clashes — and let us bear in mind that these were only intellectual clashes — that called for harsh introspection which was inevitably accompanied by self-criticism. Because of the deep ties of the Jews to their community, this introspection and criticism were accompanied by strong emotions of sympathy and affection for the very same community they wanted to change. An ironic outlook and self-disparaging humor arose from these feelings, that not only helped them to cope with their vicissitudes, but also to express their faith in a better future, an unwillingness to sink into despair. Their active intellectual contest with life also found an expression in humor. Thus intellectual, social and emotional factors were merged and formed the basis for Jewish humor. It is in terms of these factors that one can understand the main characteristics of this humor, which

55

can be summarized as follows:

1. A desire to distort the tragic reality, to alter it and make it laughable (and thus — less frightening and threatening). Here lie the elements of absurd humor, which fulfills the intellectual function of humor. One also finds here the elements of gallows humor which functions as a defense mechanism and is known by the term "laughter through tears."

2. The desire to preserve internal cohesiveness, to perceive what is special about "us" in contrast to what characterises "them." This is humor that stresses the unique elements and trademarks of our society and emphasizes its contrariety (and superiority) in contrast to the hostile society surrounding it.

In addition to criticism of the surrounding society, which was directed against the strong and powerful, Jewish humor was also an attack on those holding positions of authority within the community itself. This humor mainly fulfilled a social function.

3. Self-disparaging humor that makes possible self-criticism, and enables a man to take a courageous look at his own negative aspects, and those of the group or people with which he identifies. Self-disparaging humor is a sign of maturity and of self insight. Recognition of one's own shortcomings, readiness to accept and even laugh at them, demonstrate, paradoxically enough, a sense of self-confidence. In this way, self-disparaging humor actually evokes sympathy, and staves off aggression by its listener.

Of course, these three characteristics — distortion of reality ("laughter through tears"), the contribution to cohesiveness and to preservation of identity, and the element of self-disparaging humor, are not restricted exclusively to Jewish humor. They can also be found among other peoples, just as one can find in Jewish humor other elements we have not mentioned (as for example, the element of sexual humor, which is so popular in France). But most Jewish humor is marked by these three salient features.

In a book on British humor (1982), George Mikes writes that this humor has three characteristics: self-disparaging humor, understatement, and cruelty. About self-disparaging humor, he writes: "If the English know how to smile at themselves, the Jews know how to laugh heartily at their weaknesses. A nation must have a lot of self-confidence in order to be capable to laugh at itself. These two people, the English and the Jews, know very well that they are the most wonderful people in the whole world....despite the fact that their answers to this question are not identical" (Mikes, 1982, p. 73). Although there is no doubt that both British humor and Jewish humor are characterized by self-disparagement, Jewish humor contains nothing (or nearly nothing) of the other two characteristics of British humor. Expressions of cruelty in Jewish humor are extremely rare and as for understatement, I will return to that later, when we will see that in Israeli humor one can speak rather of overstatement.

Since Jewish humor fulfilled such important functions in its development in

19th century Eastern Europe, it continued to accompany the Jewish people even after it was uprooted from this region. The contribution of humor to the survival of this people (even if it was a relatively small contribution) has not yet been accorded scientific treatment. But it is reasonable to assume that a sociological analysis would probably contribute greatly to an illumination of this aspect of our people's survival.

At the end of the 19th century and the beginning of the 20th century, many Jews left Eastern Europe. We will refer later to two segments of this people: those who chose the land of unlimited opportunity and those who decided to immigrate to the promised land. Between 1880 and World War I, several thousand Jews immigrated to Palestine. During that same period, more than a million and a half of our people immigrated to the United States (Eban, 1984). In these two countries, the Jews experienced different living conditions, problems and trends of development. Their humor reflected and continues to reflect their outlook on life in the United States and in Israel. In this paper, I will therefore relate to these two communities which form the two largest concentrations of the Jewish people.

Jewish Humor in the United States

When the Jews of Eastern Europe arrived in the United States, they found there a relatively well-established community of Jews who had escaped from Germany. The German Jews regarded the new immigrants with suspicion. They looked askance at their strange clothing and queer customs. The "newcomers" brought with them their own language — Yiddish, and a strong desire to adapt to and to exploit the unlimited opportunities of the "new country." The tradition of the "people of the book" and their strong stress on education facilitated the rapid advancement of the Jews in a world where achievement counts and a man succeeds through his efforts and not because of his origins. Without any knowledge of the English language, and despite enormous difficulties in understanding the American way of life in view of their past experience in Russia, the Jews worked with diligence and perserverance, in conditions perhaps even more difficult that those in the shtetl, but fortified by the knowledge that here there is no limit to the fruits of their labors. The pattern of the Jewish family underwent a change: the father worked long hours (the children seldom saw him) and the Jewish mother played a more central role in their education.

During the period of the first wave of immigration, the Jews from Eastern Europe organized themselves into frameworks that were familiar to them. In New York, especially, the Jews gathered into ghettos not because the authorities demanded this, as was in the case in Russia, but from a desire to find mutual support among people who spoke and thought as they did.

The Yiddish tongue, its authors and tradition found fertile soil in the new

57

Jewish community in the U.S. Many newspapers, books, and theaters in the Jewish language developed and found ready audiences. One of the newspapers was the humorist paper "Greisa Kundas" which first appeared in 1904 and was regularly published until 1927. The Yiddish theater, in which comedians met with huge success, also flourished in the "new world" and there are those who claim that the foundations of vaudeville can be found in the Jewish humor presented on the stage in those days.

The second generation of the Jews who had immigrated from Eastern Europe, did their utmost to become "real Americans." To their parents, most of whom spoke only Yiddish, the children replied in English. The customs, clothing — and of course, language — of the children were far removed from the traditions their parents had brought with them. General opportunities for advancement and the encouraging "push" they got from their parents to study and become educated (in the best Jewish tradition) rapidly created a stratum of successful second-generation Jews that contributed greatly to itself as well as to American society. It seemed to most of them that their total acceptance into the American society was possible and imminent.

The economic depression of the thirties in the United States was accompanied by an awakening of antisemitism that alarmed the Jews of the U.S. As in any economic crisis, in the search for a scapegoat the Jews were found. Father Coughlin's movement blamed the Jews for having caused America's economic fall. He was provided with an additional weapon by the rise of Nazism in Germany, and accusations that the Jews were bolsheviks and harbored anti-American sentiments created a sharp wave of anti-semitism. The Jews were fortunate in that this wave receded once the economy recovered, but the lesson they learned was not easily forgotten. The threat united and strengthened the Jewish community. It understood that it had to become integrated into American society, and yet at the same time — to preserve its Jewish identity as well. This ambivalance between a desire to assimilate into the larger society and an aspiration at the same time to preserve Jewish identity became the central problem of American Jewry. It found its expression in Jewish humor in those days as well as in our own time. Jewish comics give this subject incisive treatment in their work. They launch attacks on both American society because of its insularity, as well as on the failings and singularity of their own people through self-disparaging humor (see Dorinson's article in this book).

When the great economic depression was over, the Jews continued to prosper and adopted the custom of taking a vacation (a luxury undreamed of in Eastern Europe). They spent their vacations at Jewish hotels around New York city, where Jewish comics presented humorous acts and perfected the technique of stand up comics, a style that later became the dominant comic style on the American stage, and is now considered a specifically American style. These hotels in the Catskills which were to become so well known, had names like The

Jewish Alps and the Borscht Belt. They served as a school and testing ground for Jewish comedians who were to go on to become leading figures in American humor (the most famous one is probably Mel Brooks). These Jewish comedians — in keeping with the tradition of Jewish humor — made a laughing-stock of the hardships and strategems of the Jews trying with all their might to adjust to and be accepted into American society. In their humor, Yiddish was assigned a place of honor, and infused into English sentences. Now the use of Yiddish in American humor is so widespread that many comedians who have no connection with Judaism pepper their acts with Yiddish expressions that have become a part of American folklore. The following is an example of the "Yiddishization" of American humor:

> *Bernstein goes to a kosher Chinese restaurant. To his surprise, he discovers that while he is ordering, the Chinese waiter is answering him in fluent Yiddish. Bernstein is very pleased and when he goes over to the owner to pay his bill, he says: That's really something. How did you manage it that even the Chinese waiter speaks Yiddish? The owner replies in a whisper: Shh... not so loud. He thinks we're teaching him English.*

Of course this joke does not belong to the Borscht belt days (there were no Chinese restaurants then). But it is a good illustration of the phenomenon that Leo Rosten called the "Yiddishization of the English language" (Rosten, 1983). Rosten is the Jewish American author who described with delightful humor the struggles the Jews had in learning the English language: "The Education of Hyman Kaplan" is a classic in American comic literature (Rosten, 1947).

Unquestionably, due to its important contribution Jewish humor was accorded a place of honor in American humor. In his research work on the most successful American comics, Janus (1975) found that 80% of them are Jewish (and let's bear in mind that the Jews are only 3% of the American population). In American comic literature, some of the names figuring prominently are Philip Roth ("Portnoy's Complaint"), Joseph Heller ("Catch 22","Good as Gold"), Greenberg ("How to be a Jewish Mother"), Leo Rosten ("Silky"), and many other Jewish names. In the American theater as well, some of the foremost names are Neil Simon, Woody Allen, and Bruce G. Friedman. In the American radio comedies of the 40's and 50's, Jews were the leading pioneers of this humorist medium. In American film comedies there are the Marx Brothers, Jerry Lewis, Mel Brooks and Woody Allen, and in television, the names of Jews figure prominently as comic scriptwriters (Norman Lear — the creator of Archie Bunker, for example), and as actors. If the contribution of Jews were eradicated from American humor, not very much would remain (as is apparent from the detailed list at the end of this article).

American Jewish humor contains the same elements as are found in the

Jewish humor that developed in Eastern Europe. These elements developed with such vigor that they became the main stream in American humor, which in very large part is no more than an imitation of Jewish humor. The explanation for the continued existence of Jewish humor in the United States can be found in the conditions of life of the Jews there. In this case it is not economic conditions that are involved, but psychological conditions. The life of Jews in Eastern Europe can certainly not be compared to that in the United States. From an oppressed minority in Eastern Europe they became in the United States a successful and prosperous minority, from the social and economic standpoint. Nevertheless, they remained a minority on the fringes of a large society which is ruled by non-Jewish elements. And Jews still, to one degree or another, perceive themselves to be marginal. The Jews would like to be accepted, to be "like everyone"; on the other hand, they want to be themselves, different, and maybe even better. So the Jews are angry at American society that refuses to accept them and are also angry at themselves for not being willing to give up their singularity. Here lie the elements of the intellectual humor, that accentuates the absurd in a society that is unprepared to accept the Jews as they are. Here one also can find the elements of self-disparaging humor, in which the Jews relate to themselves and their shortcomings as they themselves see them, and as they are also known to the wider American society.

The focus of the intellectual aspect of Jewish humor in the United States is on seeing what is absurd about the values of the ruling society and in turning frustrations into funny situations (and in this way making them less painful). The Marx Brothers and Lenny Bruce slaughtered all the sacred cows of American society. Jewish humor seems to say something like: "See what a ridiculous society this is and they have the nerve to think they are better than us and won't accept us" This is a message similar to Groucho Mark's famous quip: "I wouldn't want to be a member in a club that accepts guys like me as members." The humoristic attack on the customs, beliefs and prejudices of the ruling American society, is mingled with bitterness arising from the knowledge that there is no chance of being accepting and "really" becoming one of them. Portnoy's fantasies about gentile girls seem to be fulfilled in Woody Allen's life. Can anyone imagine more "shiksa" types than Diane Keaton or Mia Farrow?

But just as in Eastern Europe, currents developed in American Jewry that tried to dictate the "right" ways of being a Jew. In the Jewish religious establishment, there are the orthodox, conservative and reform movements that are constantly contending with each other. Just as the Jews in the U.S., as part of their process of adaptation to life there, tried to escape from their religion (or at least from its external manifestations) and made the "old" customs an object of laughter, today humor is also directed against the behavior of Jews trying to shun or evade their religious identity.

Three reform rabbis are having an argument about how progressive each of their synagogues are. The first one says, we're so liberal that we have ashtrays between the seats, so that anyone who wants to can smoke, even during the service. The second one says — in our synagogue, we have a snack bar. People can pray and eat, even on Yom Kippur. The third one says: Oh, in our synagogue on Rosh HaShana and Yom Kippur, we put a big sign on the door saying: Closed for the holidays.

In Jewish humor and its intellectual approach to absurd elements in both the ruling society and the Jewish society, there is a pessimistic overtone (which is reminiscent of the "laughter through tears" of Eastern Europe). But jovial pessimism is not really depressing; it contains hope and even a spark of optimism.

The pessimistic outlook in Jewish humor goes along with a wink that says: "It's not really so bad, after all, we're laughing at it." Thus Woody Allen writes in his speech to the graduates:
"Today, more than at any other time in history, humanity stands at the crossroads. One road leads to total despair. The other — to complete annihilation. Let us pray that we will have the wisdom to choose the right way." (Allen, 1975, p. 57).

The social aspect of American Jewish humor focusses, as in the Eastern European tradition, on life in the community. This is in order to preserve its identity. With the aim of reinforcing group cohesiveness, this humor attacks those factors that endanger the community's existence and laughs at its traits and characters. The Jews in America are fortunate in that they no longer face the danger of pogroms and violent persecution. But there are new dangers, spiritual in nature, that threaten the Jewish community. The most serious is that of assimilation. As a result of intermarriage which is constantly on the uprise, many of its finest sons are leaving the Jewish community. The problem of conversion to Christianity which was more serious prior to the '60s, also still exists. There are innumerable jokes about these subjects. It is worth recalling that Heinrich Heine, the German Jewish author who converted to Christianity, once said: "I don't trust the sincerity of Jews who have converted to the religion of Jesus. No Jew can ever really believe in the sanctity of another Jew." All of the traditional roles so familiar to the Jews of Eastern Europe have almost completely disappeared from the American Jewish community. Shadchens are very rare in the United States. Schnorrers? Maybe not completely. The special link between Israel and the Jews of American recalls to mind what I wrote above about the chutzpa of the schnorrer who is certain that he is graciously affording his benefactor the opportunity to do a charitable deed, and perhaps this is the source of his strength. The schnorrer is probably better known today by the more respectable name of "fund raiser."

A tall, broad, hefty Texan is sitting in a New York bar, drinking whiskey and looking somewhat contemptuously at a short, thin, spectacled Jew, who, all hot and bothered, is ordering a martini. He adds: "But I want a few drops of lemon in it." The barman replies: "Sorry, we have no lemon." The Jew, who is infuriated, says : "I asked for lemon and you've got to find me what I want!" "I'm very sorry, sir, but we have no lemon." The Jew points to a half a dry lemon lying on the counter and asks: "What's that?" "That's an old lemon that's been lying there a long time and there's not a drop of juice in it." "Give it to me, along with a large glass." The barman does so with a smile. The Jew takes the lemon and with a quick twist of his wrist, squeezes it hard. The glass quickly fills up with juice. The Texan, who knows how to appreciate strength, turns to him in amazement, and asks: "Excuse me, sir, but I've never seen anyone who could squeeze with such force. What is your profession?" "I'm a fund raiser for Israel Bonds."

Changes that took place in the Jewish family created new comic characters. The pushing and complaining ambitious Jewish mother became such a frequent target for the arrows of Jewish humor that she is a popular figure among non-Jews as well. As Dan Greenberg wrote in his best seller How to be a Jewish Mother: "You don't have to be Jewish to be a Jewish mother." Unquestionably the Jewish mother had, and apparently still has, an important role in preserving the family. She is the driving force behind her son's progress up the American social ladder. Jokes about a mother watching her small 3 — 4 year old children playing in the park and introducing them as "Sammy, the doctor, and David, the lawyer" have become classics. The way she treats her daughters created another comic character, the "Jewish princess." This character is so familiar even in non-Jewish society that they refer to daughters that demand and get everything they want as "Jewish princesses." How "Jewish princesses" turn into Jewish mothers (a drastic change in psychological structure) is a question that can best be answered by those engaged in research on folklore.

The social function of Jewish humor is also very evident in its criticism of the Jews who have exchanged their traditional values for the materialistic values of American society.

Mrs. Goldberg, Mrs. Cohen and Mrs. Schwartz are talking about their sons during lunch. Mrs. Goldberg tells them that Sammy, a successful lawyer, makes 70,000 dollars a year. Mrs. Cohen reports that her son the doctor makes 80,000. Mrs. Schwartz who is embarrassed, keeps quiet. When her friends press her, she admits that her son David graduated from the rabbinical seminary and as the rabbi of a small community earns 10,000 dollars a year. "Oy," her friends exclaim, "What kind of a profession is that for a nice Jewish boy?"

But the most striking characteristic of American Jewish humor is self-disparagement. If we look at all the jokes in this chapter, we will find that they all have elements of self-disparaging humor: criticism of the negative aspects of the Jewish character:

The Baptist church offered 20 dollars to every Jew who converted. Two Jews, very much in need of money, decide to flip a coin to see who will convert, and they agree that they will share the money that he gets. Cohen loses and enters the church. When he comes out, his friend asks: "Well, did you get the money?" "Yes," Cohen answers. "Then give me my share." "No," Cohen answers indignantly, "You're like all the Jews, you only think about money!"

We have already discussed the psychological importance of self-disparaging humor as a defense mechanism against anxiety, and as a means for gaining sympathy and affection. Without doubt self-disparaging humor is regarded in the United States as the most prominent trait of Jewish humor, and this is the secret of its success. Americans appreciate the strength that lies in a man's ability to admit his failures, live with them and even take pride in them.

In summing up, we can say with assurance that Jewish humor is flourishing and developing in the United States. What happened to Jewish humor on its way to Israel?

Jewish Humor in Israel

"What happened to the famous Jewish sense of humor? It seems that it got lost in transit to Israel." (Mikes, 1950, p. 44). This rather severe view taken by a visitor from England is shared by many Israelis as well. Eilon (1970) writes: "Traditional Jewish humor — with its incisive self-irony — disappeared among Israelis. It remains a flourishing art only in one realm — government and politics" (Eilon, 1970, p. 298).

There is unquestionably Israeli humor and it is Jewish humor (according to the definition given in the Introduction). However, since nearly all the articles published in the world on Jewish humor were related to its various permutations in the Diaspora, the particular characteristics of Jewish humor in Israel were never given appropriate attention. The psychological functions that Jewish humor fulfilled in the Diaspora differ from those it fulfills in Israel. The development of a people is strikingly reflected in the humor that develops under changing conditions. The drastic change in the fate of the Jewish people that gained renewed independence after two thousand years of exile neccessitated a similarly drastic change in Jewish humor. The Jews in Israel are no longer an oppressed minority as they were in Eastern Europe, nor are they a prosperous and well-established minority like those in the United States. In Israel, the Jews are a majority. Under the influence of the altered circumstances of their existence, immense changes also took place in the functions humor fulfills in their lives.

Although comprehensive scientific research on Jewish humor in Israel has not yet been completed (such a project has been in progress for the last three years), we have several beginnings in our book. Alexander's research on the development of satire in Israel, Ofra Nevo's research on self-disparaging humor among Israelis, Dosh's work on political caricature in Israel, and that by Nir and Roeh on humor on Israeli radio — all of these constitute important beginnings. To the best of my knowledge, only those engaged in folklore-related research have made any attempt to delve into the history of the popular Jewish joke in Israel (among whom are Dov Sadan and Dov Noy, who are the most important scholars in this area).

In an attempt at a concise description of the development of Israeli humor, one can divide the subject into three main time periods:
1. Prior to the establishment of the State.
2. From the establishment of the State until the Six Day War.
3. From the Six Day War up to the present time.

These three periods are characterized by socio-political factors affecting all Israelis. The humor created during them can be found in written and pictorial sources, in the theater, as well as in radio broadcasts and later in television. Israeli humor has its reflection in all these communication media, as well as in daily life.

The first period, up to the establishment of the state, was arduous and imbued with ideals. The will for renewal, the elevation of physical work to an important value, the revival of the Hebrew language, and the adoption of collective goals as the highest social values, generated a different spirit and mood than that which had prevailed in the Diaspora. In Israel, the term "Diaspora Jew" gradually took on a connotation of scorn, even contempt. The aim was the creation of a "new Jew". The notion of pioneering had a completely different meaning here than it had in America where immigrants also set up a society built a country. The American pioneer put his trust in himself and his aim was to succeed as an individual. The Jewish pioneer dedicated his efforts to the general welfare of all, and regarded the aims of the "collective" as of supreme importance. We should bear in mind that the Zionist movement at its outset embraced many of the tenets of socialism. Due to the harsh living conditions and the deep involvement of most of the Jewish population in the wider overall aims, individualistists did not have an easy time of it. The leaders of the Yishuv thought and acted with the feeling that what they were doing was irrefutably right. They worked to achieve their goals with a dedication which today may seem somewhat fanatic. In psychological research related to humor a negative correlation was found between fanaticism and a sense of humor. There is no question that the leaders in that period were in no way noted for their humor (and that is an understatement). This may also result from the fact that in that period self-irony was considered a specific feature of the "Diaspora Jew", an image from which they wished to be liberated.

Despite the new attitudes fostered by the Jews in Palestine in pre-State days, the Jewish tradition of love and use of humor, brought with them by the Jews of Eastern Europe, never disappeared. Thus, for example, in 1902,there appeared in the "Hashkafa" newspaper an item written in a style that brought to mind Shalom Aleichem. It was a report of a medical finding according to which in locations where malaria germs were present, the risk of cancer was reduced. One piece of medical advice was to infect everyone with malaria. The newspaper adds: "How happy we are, the residents of Palestine, that we have thank God more than enough malaria, even without having to infect ourselves with it!"

During that same period, many humorous newspapers appeared and became very popular. In 1923, the first humoristic paper came out called: "LaYehudim" ("To the Jews"). It was published more or less regularly for about twelve years. Other humorous papers were published during the thirties and forties, some of them on the occasion of holidays. These papers contained jokes (original and translated) and many caricatures. Some worth mentioning are "HaLulyan" ("The Acrobat"), "Tashlich", "HaMiklahat" ("The Shower"), "Iton Mezupat" ("Lousy Newspaper"), "Tesha Ba'Gerev" ("Nine in a Stocking") (a satire on a popular entertainment weekly "Tesha Ba'Erev" ("Nine in the Evening") edited by Uri Kesary). The most famous was "Egel HaZahav" ("The Golden Calf") that carried the sub-title "A public platform for flogging".

Most of the humor in these newspapers was devoted to satire directed against the British, but the leaders of the Yishuv were not spared the darts of satire. The editors of these newspapers and the writers of their columns were new immigrants from Eastern Europe.

As Gardosh points out in his article, Hebrew caricature first made its appearance in the thirties, in the Saturday supplements of newspapers. Caricature was then, as it still is now in our country, an expression of political struggle. First of all, of the struggle against the British, but also, and perhaps mainly, of the internal struggles, according to the familiar paradigm of the left opposed to the right.

Satirical theater also began before the establishment of the State. "HaKumkum" ("The Kettle"), the first satiric cabaret, started out in 1927, and a year later the "Matateh" ("The Broom") opened its doors. The latter, very popular theater, continued to give performances for 26 years. In his article in this book, Alexander relates to the development of these two theaters and takes note of their somewhat strange attempt to attack society (as every satiric theater does), but without hurting it. The British naturally were an easy target for the thrusts of satire, but in relation to the Yishuv itself things were more complicated. It was very difficult to regard the Yishuv as something marvellous, as the fulfillment of the dreams of a people, and yet at the same time to see its negative and ridiculous aspects. It was because of this conflict, that the members of the "Matateh" decided to close it down. (See Alexander's article).

The second period, that began with the establishment of the State, is marked by several outstandng phenomena in the sphere of humor. The first found its expression in a native product, the "chizbats" of the Palmach. The book written by Hefer and Ben Amotz called "Yalkut Ha-Kevazim" ("Collection of Tall Tales") (1956) became a best seller. It expressed the attempt of Israelis to create humor "adapted to its locality." The Yiddish language that had permeated Diaspora humor was now replaced by Arabic words. Perhaps the attempt of the inventors of the chizbat can be regarded as a way of expressing adaptation to the Middle East and a breaking away from the "Diaspora Jew." Elliot Oring wrote an excellent piece of research on this book, which he published in 1981. This work which analyzes the period and many of the stories has a very English subtitle *The Chizbat of the Palmach.*

The chizbat had a number of original features: first of all, the hero was always a member of the Palmach known to most of the members of the group. The chizbatim were related orally to the group members in a group setting (the famous kumsitz). Unquestionably, the chizbat reflected a new and distinctively Israeli entity, because of the atmosphere that it succeeded in imparting even to those who were not in the Palmach. Oring believes that even if the patterns of performance of the chizbat, the techniques of the story, and the picturesque characters in it were all original, the contents generally were not. He writes: "The most important aspect about the chizbat's uniqueness was that the Palmach felt it was unique." (Oring, 1981, p. 30).

Possibly in the chizbat of the Palmach, one can find elements of the ideal image of the Israeli: Tough, not given to expressing feelings and trying to appear hard-hearted at all costs. Contrary to Jewish humor in Eastern Europe, where Jews dared to talk of their weaknesses and laugh at them (the famous self-disparaging humor), the Israeli was intent upon emphasizing his superiority. Their — justified — pride in their achievements: the establishment of an independent state, rapid development of agriculture and industry, organization of an excellent army, the building of the country — gave the Israelis a sense of superiority that they expressed uninhibitedly. The ideal of the "new" Jew, i.e., the Israeli, was to be tough and inflexible and his weaknesses were taboo. The

66

ability to laugh at oneself disappeared (or at least was concealed), and was replaced by the opposite psychological phenomenon — unrestrained "self-conceit".

Mikes (1950) writes with astute humor about this disposition for self-admiration: "If you want to get on with the Israelis, praise them. It is silly to praise people behind their backs, not very manly either. Tell them openly to their faces that you think they are wonderful. Have the courage to insist that they are admirable, brave, brilliant, efficient, noble and inimitable. At first I thought such statements might embarrass them. But not at all. They do not mind them. They can face the truth. They say it themselves." (Mikes, 1950, p. 31). Mikes also writes in a similar vein, in his book on British humor, one of the characteristics of which is understatement. He writes that during his visit to Israel, an Israeli friend took him to see Tel Aviv. Wherever they went, he pointed out the uniqueness, the size and the merits of each building, park, avenue, and of the people in them. Finally, his host stated that despite all of their marvellous accomplishments, the Israelis are noted for their modesty and their frequent use of understatement. Mikes responded with amazement: "But you never stopped boasting and exaggerating about everything we saw." Without any hesitation, his Israeli friend replied: "What are you talking about? That was all understatement."

An air of self-importance and an attempt to exude self-confidence are not conducive to the creation of humor. In research done on the "founding fathers", the establishers of the state, they were found to have patterns of personality, in which strong ideological approaches, perserverance, dedication to a goal were some of the more pronounced traits, along with a not inconsiderable measure of fanaticism. A sense of humor was not one of their outstanding features. There is unquestionably a connection between revolutionism and humor. Intelligent and sensitive people react in one of two main ways to a given social situation: the non-serious, humoristic way tries to present the ridiculous in the given situation in order to cope with it more effectively. There may be an expression here of disparate philosophies of life. The "serious" ones are more optimistic. They believe that by exerting efforts and fighting for a goal they can change the situation. The "non serious" are more pessimistic. They have no faith in their ability to change anything. They therefore restrict themselves to flogging the undesirable situation, as if to say "Look how ridiculous it is, it's actually funny." In their own way, they are also pointing to a need for change, even if they are not saying how this should be done. They don't deal with this aspect of it; they leave that to the revolutionaries, the politicians, and the pioneers.

During that same period, the collective zeal in establishing and building the state did not encourage expressions of humor. Such expressions inevitably have an element of criticism and scrutinize the absurd and ridiculous in these "serious" aspects of life. For this reason, humor took on forms unknown in the

67

traditional Jewish humor of Eastern Europe. It had elements of cruelty in relation to minorities. Thus for example, the expression "soap", still in widespread use in adolescent slang, has a gruesome history. When the World War II refugees arrived in Israel, the people of the Yishuv (who had heard about the concentration camps and the Holocaust and read about Jews being burned in furnaces, their remains being turned into soap) gave the derisive nickname "soaps" to those who, in their view, had allowed themselves to be victimized without putting up any resistance. Each wave of immigration brought a wave of aggressive humor towards those arriving from the various parts of the Diaspora: "Morocco the Knife", "Rumanian thieves", "Yeke (German) potz", and other similar expressions, were added to the Israeli lexicon, and were interjected into jokes that were rife with contempt and aggression.

However, while the phenomenon of Israeli "self-conceit" was taking shape and the new crude humor coming into being, traditional Jewish humor did not vanish from the scene. The new immigrants brought it along with them and adapted it to the new conditions in Israel. This period marked the high point in the careers of the "Hungarians", new immigrants who in the Diaspora had already learned the secrets of self-irony. Kishon and Lapid in the field of humoresques and theater, Zev and Dosh in the field of caricature — all of them engaged in one way or another in self-disparaging humor, in displaying the Israeli not only as a "perfect" creature with marvellous traits, but also as a human creature, with shortcomings, and sometimes (or even frequently) as a ridiculous creature.

The most outstanding creator in this group is Ephraim Kishon, who achieved prominent international standing. With his prolific and multifaceted talents, he created characters (such as Ervinke and Salah Shabati) and humoresques that are still a model for many Israeli humorists today. In the Israeli theater, that continues to develop and prosper, not many comedies are performed (and that is an understatement). Most of those that are performed were written by Kishon, who gradually became active also in the world of film. Many of Kishon's works were performed by the Nahal troupe, which produced most of the comedians who succeeded in becoming the top performers in their profession at the time, and the "Batzal Yarok" ("Green Onion") troupe, one of the famous entertainment groups of that period. Kishon's humor focusses on the day to day life of Israeli society. His social satire is mingled with love for the characters he describes, in a manner that is reminiscent of Jewish humor that laughed at the characters and leaders of the shtetl. Kishon does not remove himself from the establishment he criticizes and tries to understand. His sensitivity towards the social phenomena of the day did not relate to the establishment and its officials as "bad", "criminal" or "cruel" people, but rather to a large extent, as "shlemiels", as little "wheeler-dealers". From this standpoint, Kishon was an exceptional humorist in that period. The other creators of humor, including the

68

caricaturists, were more preoccupied with political controversies and with wars (both external and internal). This is a reflection of the seriousness with which Israelis relate to the life of the country. Humorists don't have an easy time of it when there is a national consensus about the rightfulness of the state, and about most of the things done in its name. It is worth mentioning a humorous radio program that met with unusual success during that period. "Three in a boat", supposedly a spontaneous program, had most of the population riveted to their radio sets, and the books that came out following the program (HaEzrahi, 1957, 1959) became best sellers. The "formula" employed in this program is popular to this day and radio still uses it frequently. The success of the program was due to the contributions of its brilliant participants, but regrettably none of them, with the exception of Dan Ben Amotz, later engaged in humoristic writing on a regular basis.

The third period began with the outburst of joy over the victory at the end of the Six Day War. The euphoria was as great as the anxiety felt on the eve of the war, and the celebrations went on for a long time. The sense of enormous victory even further reinforced our feelings of superiority, which in no way encouraged the development of humor. In this context, it should be pointed out that unlike our enemies who employed crude anti-Israeli caricatures, we did not succumb to the temptation to react in this manner.

After the initial euphoria, voices were heard that raised doubts in the minds of many Israelis. Those who viewed the results of the war as occupation and oppression of another people expressed views that were not at all popular. Hanoch Levin's play "The Queen of the Bathtub" had only 19 performances. It was taken off the stage because of the violent audience reaction. This reaction proved that self-irony and criticism of our behavior are not acceptable to Israeli Jews.

There were growing signs of cracks in the national consensus, and doubts about our justness and our support of the country's actions. The Yom Kippur War, the national trauma and changes in government all intensified the polarization and hostility between the camps. Right and Left, Ashkenazim and Sepharadim, religious and secular all were subjects that were now discussed with intense feeling, with sharp verbal aggression, and sometimes even with violence. Humor became almost exclusively political and satires gave vent to merciless criticism. Unlike traditional Jewish humor in which criticism was fused with love of its targets and identification with them, in this case those being criticized were perceived as enemies. The attack was no longer being launched at "shlemiel" and "wheeler-dealers" as in Kishon's feuilletons. It was directed against deceitful and brutal politicians who trampled under all ideals and justice. This time the writers were not new immigrants who had brought with them a tradition of Jewish humor, but "sabras" who had been brought up on an image of toughness and "straight from the shoulder" talk.

Caustic political satire also contributed to polarization and intolerance not only towards the "political enemy" but also towards satire itself. The popular television program "Nikui Rosh" ("A head cleaning") nearly every week caused furious debates in the Knesset and its corridors. Nonetheless, it also brought a lot of pleasure to an audience that was thirsty for humor and needed some release from tension. It was probably no coincidence that this superb program was given the name "head cleaning." In the wake of the Lebanese war, there was a clear rift in the national consensus, and political satire became even more caustic and brutal. Israeli writers, who had been blessed with one degree or another of a sense of humor, completely forgot that there were other subjects that might bring a smile to serious Israeli faces.

The "HaGashash HaHiver" ("The Pale Tracker") troupe is an exceptional phenomenon in Israeli humor. This trio, with the help of talented writers, has succeeded in relating with marvellous humor to life in Israel. Without getting into conflicts with one or another side of the political spectrum, they keep alive the spark of Jewish humor. And as a matter of fact, one can find in their humor all of the characteristics described above: intellectual aspects of both the laughable and the ridiculous in daily life, as well as of its painful facets, a social approach that attempts to crystallize an Israeli entity that blends Eastern and Western sources, and the ability to express self-irony and see both our negative and our positive sides. Lately, a radio program called "Mah Yesh?" ("What's the matter?") is being broadcast. It also does not focus on aggressive satire, but reverts to the absurd and to self-disparaging humor.

How will Israeli humor develop in the future? It is hard to say. Since humor reflects the psycho-social and general development of a people, the fate of Israeli humor is linked to the fate of the people of Israel in its land. If this development will take the direction of extremism and fanaticism, humor cannot expect a great future. Let us hope that this development will take a course that is closer to the Zionist dream and to the Jewish values that found such wonderful expression in Jewish humor in the Diaspora.

References

Adler H. (1983) Jewish wit and humor **The Nineteenth Century,** 33, 457-469
Allen W. (1924) **Without feathers,** N.Y., Rondom House
Allen W. (1975) **Side effects,** N.Y., Random House
Arieti S. (1978) Special logic of schizophrenic and other types of autistic thought **Psychiatry,** 11, 325-338
Baumgartner A.J. (1896) **L'humour dans l'ancien testament,** Laussane, Grayot

Ben Amos D. (1973) The "myth" of Jewish Humor **Western Folklore**, 32, 112-131

Ben Amotz D., Hefer H. (1956) **The bag of lies,** Tel Aviv, Kibutz Meuhad (Hebrew)

Chotzner J. (1905) **Hebrew Humor and other essays** London, Methmen

Durianov A. (1963) **The book of jokes,** Tel Aviv, Dvir (Hebrew)

Eban A. (1984) **My people: the story of the Jews** N.Y., Random House

Eilon A. (1970) **The Israelis,** Tel Aviv, Shoken (Hebrew)

Freud S. (1905) **Jokes and their relation to the unconscious,** N.Y., Marrow

Freud S. (1928) Humor in **Collected Works**

Friedlender Y. (1984) **Hebrew satire in Europe in the Nineteenth Century,** Ramat Gan, Bar Ilan University (Hebrew)

Friedlender Y. (1984) Humor in strict religious education (un published, Hebrew)

Grotjahn (1966) M. **Beyond laughter: humor and the subconscious** N.Y., Mc Graw Hill

Haezrhi I. (1957) **Three in a boat,** Tel Aviv, Dvir (Hebrew)

Janus S.S. (1975) The great comedians: personality and other factors **American Journal of Psychonalysis,** 35, 169-174

Isaac A.S. (1911) **Stories from the Rabbis,** N.Y. Mildland

Kierkegaard S. (1968) **The concept of irony** Bloomington, Indiana University Press

Kierkegaard S. (1975) Le concept d'ironie constamment rapporte a Socrates-**Oeuvres Completes,** Paris, Editions de l'Orante

Knox I. (1963) The traditional roots of Jewish humor **Judaism,** 12, 327-337

Koestler A. (1964) **The art of creation,** London, Danube

Kris E. (1952) **Psychoanalytic explorations in art,** N.Y., International University Press

Landman S. (1964) On Jewish Humor **Jewish Journal of Sociology,** 4, 193-204

Lang D. (1962) On Biblical comic **Judaism,** 11, 249-254

Madison C.A. (1968) **Yiddish literature: its scope and major writers** N.Y. Garden

Mikes G. (1950) **Milk and honey,** London, Andre Deutsch

Mikes G. (1981) **English humor for beginners** London, Unwin

Novak W., Waldoks M. (1981) **The big book of Jewish Humor,** N.Y., Harper & Row

Ofek A., Cahanman N. (1984) The language of Gahash Hahiver texts, **Criticism and explanation** (Hebrew)

Oring E. (1981) **Israeli Humor: the content and structure of the Chizbat of the Palmach,** Albany, State University of New York Press

Oring E. (1983) The people of the joke: on the conceptualization of Jewish Humor **Western Folklore,** 42, 261-271

Reik T. (1954) Freud and Jewish wit **Psychoanalysis** 2, 12-20

Reik T. (1962) **Jewish wit,** N.Y., Farrar & Strausss

Weininger A. (1953) **Sex and character,** Tel Aviv, Ktavim (Hebrew)

Ziv A. (1981) **The psychology of humor,** Tel Aviv, Yahdav (Hebrew)

Ziv A. (1984) **Personality and sense of humor,** N.Y., Springer

C. Davies

JEWISH JOKES, ANTI-SEMITIC JOKES AND HEBREDONIAN JOKES

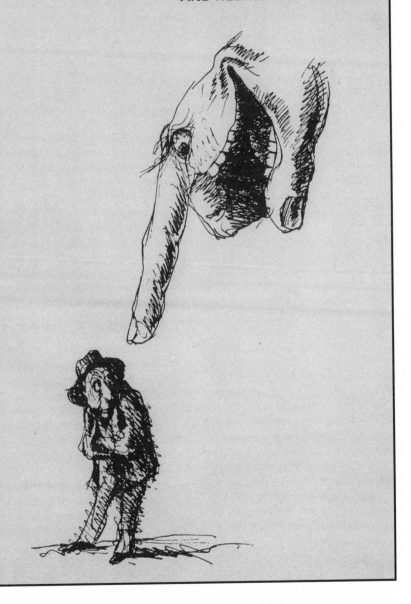

CHRISTIE DAVIES
Reading University, England

JEWISH JOKES, ANTI-SEMITIC JOKES AND HEBREDONIAN JOKES

Throughout Europe and North America Jews probably figure more frequently in jokes than any other ethnic group and there are three sources of these jokes. First there is a very rich tradition of Jewish jokes based on the diverse social experience and cultural contacts of the Jewish people, and on an intellectual tradition which values the ability to use words and concepts for its own sake. Second, there is a subterranean river of anti-Semitic jokes — Jokes that invoke a negative comic image of the Jews which is highly congruent with the beliefs and prejudices of anti-Semites. These jokes can be seen in some sense as reflecting the anti-Semitic ideology (or ideologies) which have been such a virulently destructive force in recent times. In Western Europe and North America anti-Semitism is now discredited and lacks respectability but it still grumbles beneath the surface and appears sometimes relatively innocuously in the unthinking remarks of powerless little people and sometimes menacingly in the rhetoric of politicians.[1] Meanwhile in Eastern Europe and especially the Soviet Union anti-Semitism flickers and flourishes often with official support.[2] There is also a third and often neglected category of jokes about Jews which I shall call Hebredonian jokes. These are jokes which employ a ritualised rather than a hostile ethnic stereotype of the Jews, or indeed the Scots or the Dutch, as being 'canny' (i.e. shrewd and thrifty). These jokes are readily transferred between a large number of ethnic groups with this reputation. Jokes about Jews that can be readily interchanged with Scots or Dutch jokes of this type, I have termed 'Hebredonian' (a hybrid word from Hebrew and Caledonian). The affinity of such jokes with Scottish/Dutch ones indicates both that they are not specifically Jewish and that they are relatively unlikely to be rooted in the hostile prejudices of others. These jokes may be favorable, neutral or critical but they are not linked to an organised ideology[3] like anti-Semitism, or even to a mobilisable pattern of prejudice such as those that have led to the persecution of the Armenians, the overseas Chinese or the East African Asians.[4]

Jokes involving Jews cannot always be easily or conclusively sorted into these three categories and in any case jokes can change their social meaning very dramatically depending on the context in which they are told. (Who tells the jokes, how and to whom? What are the joke-teller's motives and intentions?). However, it is possible to make reasonable judgements about the *probability* of a joke belonging to one (or none) of the three categories on the basis of style and content alone. There are two key tests that can be applied which I shall term *switchability* and *congruence*. Some ethnic jokes (for example a great number of simple put-down jokes) are almost completely free-floating and can be attached to virtually any group or groups. A writer or teller of jokes who wishes to *switch* such a joke from one group to another can do so without any great exercise of skill or effort and with minimal rewriting. Other jokes are so rooted in the cultural traditions, social position and even ways of thinking of a particular ethnic group that they cannot be switched around in this way or at least not without the kind of major surgery that either kills the joke in the process or else creates a new joke which has only a distant connection with the original. Many Jewish jokes fall into this category — they are unique and cannot be switched to any other group. Jewish jokes about religion, morality or traditional learning usually do not and perhaps cannot have analogies in other ethnic groups.[5] These jokes are not for export. There is also, however, a significant stock of Jewish jokes particularly those deriving their humor from a distinctively Jewish use of indirect and elliptical but relentlessly consistent reasoning that perhaps *could* be adapted to fit the circumstances of another group but in practice rarely are. Jokes such as the following display a logical sleight of hand and a feat of language compression that cannot readily be fitted into other people's idioms.

For twenty years the same customer visited a certain Jewish restaurant and, without fail, always ordered the same dish — borscht! In all that time he never once complained about the food or service — the model customer.

One evening, when the waiter had served the customary plate, the customer called him back to the table.

"Waiter, taste this borscht!"

"Why, what's the matter with it?"

"Just taste it!"

"Listen, it's too cold, it doesn't taste right, whatever, I'll take it back and bring you another serving."

"Taste the borscht!"

"Why should I taste? You don't want it you don't want it. So I'll bring you a change. Why should I argue with a good customer?"

The customer, his face dark with fury, stood up. "For the last time, TASTE THE BORSCHT!"

Intimidated, the waiter sat down. "All right, if you insist." He looked around. "Where's the spoon?"

"Ah-HAH!" exploded the customer.[6]

Mrs. Kotchin and Mrs. Mishkin sat rocking on the porch of the Villa Lipshitz, a Catskill resort, when a young man approached.

'Gottenyu!' exclaimed Mrs. Kotchin. 'Look at that boy! Did you ever see such a big nose? Such shifty eyes? Such a crooked mouth?'

In a freezing voice, Mrs. Mishkin replied, 'It so happens, you are talking about my son!'

'Well,' said Mrs. Kotchin, 'on him, it's becoming!'[7]

Both these jokes could be even more succinctly worded but only within the existing tradition. To try to transfer them to another group would somehow entail loosening the mainspring of the joke so that it would not be as funny as the original. Such jokes are indisputably Jewish, because to switch them would spoil them. However, there are some instances where genuinely Jewish jokes are shared with one or more other groups simply because there is an overlap of social experience or cultural tradition between them. In order to be *truly* Jewish a joke does not need to be unique to the Jews. There are many jokes which fit *equally* harmoniously into the traditions of perhaps two or three peoples but which cannot be readily switched outside this limited range. Here for instance are two Welsh jokes that have Jewish counterparts, yet which do not thrive if transplanted elsewhere.

A Russian spy was dropped by parachute in the Welsh hills with instructions to contact a Mr. Jones who lived in the small village of Llanfair and give him the code message, "The tulips are blooming today." Arriving at the village he asked a small boy where Mr. Jones lived and was directed to a cottage at the end of the village.

He knocked on the door and the owner emerged. 'Are you Mr. Jones?' 'I am,' 'The tulips are blooming today.' Mr. Jones stared at him in amazement and then smiled. 'Ah, you must have come to the wrong house. It's Jones-the-spy you want.'[8]

This joke is very Welsh but an equally authentic Jewish version of it about Horowitz the spy occurs in Leo Rosten's *The Joys of Yiddish*.[9] In theory it could be tinkered with to fit any group but it only really works well for peoples who (a) have lived in communities where everyone seems to know everyone else's business and no one has any successful secrets and (b) who distinguish between people with the same surname by giving them a nickname referring to their occupation. Ocky Milkman is first cousin to Tevyeh the Dairyman.[10]

> *A Welshman was shipwrecked at sea and marooned on a desert island. When a passing vessel picked him up five years later, the crew were amazed to find his little island covered in fine buildings that he had built himself. With pride the Welsh Robinson Crusoe took the captain round the island and pointed out to him his house, workshop, electricity generator and two chapels.*
>
> *'But what do you need the second chapel for?' asked the captain.*
>
> *'Oh' he replied, 'That's the one I don't go to.'*[11]

This joke too appears in Jewish guise in Henry Spalding's *Encyclopaedia of Jewish Humor*[12] and is just as much a Jewish joke as a Welsh one. It would not, however, sound at all plausible if it were told about, say, the Swedes or the Italians or the Irish. The joke depends on the fact that both Welsh nonconformist Protestantism and modern western Judaism are argumentatively democratic religions in which the congregation is not overawed by an ordained hierarchy (like say the priests and bishops of Roman Catholicism) with special sacred powers. Religious communities of this kind are likely to disagree among themselves and to produce divisions between 'the one I attend and the one I don't go to.'

Before going any further with the analysis of what constitutes Jewish, Hebredonian and anti-Semitic jokes and where the differences between them lie, it is useful first to ask what it is that all these types of jokes have in common. In this way it will be easier to see exactly where the relevant differences and contrasts lie without other aspects of the content of the joke getting in the way.

One consistent theme that is to be found in all three categories of jokes is the notion that the Jews are clever. It is not in the attribution of cleverness to the Jews but in its nature and evaluation that the differences occur. The attribution of cleverness to the Jews is of course part of a much broader and more general pattern of cultural assumptions shared by Jews, Gentiles and anti-Semites alike. As Raphael Patai has put it:

> *Superior Jewish intelligence is part of the Jewish self-stereotype. No person knowing Yiddish (and until one or two generations ago most Ashkenazi Jews knew Yiddish) can be unaware of the two expressions: Yiddisher Kop (lit. Jewish head) meaning cleverness and its opposite, Goyisher Kop (Gentile head) denoting stupidity. Cleverness or intelligence take an honored place among the qualities Jews like to attribute to themselves. The same rumor*

is mooted by Gentiles as well. Those of them who are free of the taint of anti-Semitism simply refer to it as a fact, without any emotional overtones, unless it be a twinge of envy or a note of grudging admiration. The anti-Semite will find it possible to speak of Jewish intelligence only in terms of negative connotations such as shrewdness, sharpness, craftiness, cunning, slyness and the like. He will see in these traits examples of the many Jewish features which are blameworthy and thus justify his Judeophobia. Characteristically, however, even the fiercest enemies of the Jews, including the Nazis, have never alleged that the Jews were stupid or obtuse. All people who know Jews, whatever their reaction to them otherwise, subscribe to the rumor of their intelligence.[13]

The Jewish pride in and preoccupation with cleverness takes many humorous forms that are much less common in other people's jokes. Four of the more important of these may be cited.

1. Jokes that state directly or indirectly a pride in intelligence or in intellectual or occupational success. Sometimes as in the jokes about Jewish parents being excessively ambitious for their children or too openly proud of their achievements, there is also an element of self-mockery but it is mockery of the 'faults of our virtues.'[14]

> *A man was approached in the street in Moscow and asked 'Are you Jewish?'*
> *'No,' he replied, 'I simply look intelligent.'*[15]

> *What is the shortest Jewish joke in Russia? A Jewish street sweeper.*[16]

> *A proud Jewish mother was propelling a push-chair with two small boys in it along a crowded street in London when she met an old friend of the family.*
> *'Goodness how your children are growing up,' the friend exclaimed. 'How old are they now?'*
> *'Well,' said the mother, 'the doctor is three and the lawyer is nearly two.'*[17]

> *What is an accountant?*
> *A Jewish boy who stutters and can't stand the sight of blood.*[18]

> *A Jewish family were taking a holiday on a ship in the Mediterranean when the eldest son of the family fell overboard.*

His distraught mother ran up to the bridge shouting: 'Captain, Captain, my son the doctor is drowning.'[19]

2. Jokes in which Jews outwit a prejudiced outsider or anti-Semite in a particularly clever way. All ethnic groups tell 'put-down' jokes in which one of their members outwits a prejudiced member of a rival group but Jewish jokes (a) reflect the fact that Jews have faced much greater danger from hostile outsiders than almost any other ethnic group; what was at stake was not mere national prestige, pride or even independence, but sheer survival, and (b) show the prejudiced outsider being outmanoeuvred in a much more subtle, clever, and indirect way than is the case in jokes relating to other ethnic rivalries and conflicts.

> *During the Nazi reign of terror in Germany Horowitz was dragged from his tailor shop in Berlin by two burly Gestapo men. After roughing him up one of the Germans said, 'Who was responsible for our defeat in World War One?'*
> *'The Jews and the pretzel makers,' replied the little tailor.*
> *One of the Nazis scratched his head and asked, 'Why the pretzel makers?'*
> *'Why the Jews?'*[20]

> *A Jew was walking on a street in Berlin when he accidentally brushed against a black-shirted stormtrooper.*
> *'Swine!' roared the Nazi.*
> *'Plotnick,' said the Jew, bowing.*[21]

> *A teacher in a German private school was berating her only Jewish pupil.*
> *'You are just like the rest of your race — selfish, greedy, and inconsiderate of others. Here your father pays tuition for only one student, but are you satisfied, Jew? No, you have to learn enough for three.'*[22]

> *An official brought the chief rabbi of a town before the Court of the Inquisition and told him 'we will leave the fate of your people to God. I'm putting two slips of paper in this box. On one is written 'Guilty,' on the other is written 'Innocent.' Draw.'*
> *Now this Inquisitor was known to seek the slaughter of all the Jews and he had written 'Guilty' on both pieces of paper.*
> *The rabbi put his hand inside the box withdrew a slip of paper and swallowed it.*

80

'What are you doing?' cried the Inquisitor, 'How will the Court know —'

'That's simple,' said the rabbi. 'Examine the slip that's in the box. If it reads 'Innocent' then the paper I swallowed obviously must have read 'Guilty.' But if the paper in the box reads 'Guilty' then the one I swallowed must have read 'Innocent'.'[23]

3. Jewish jokes reveal a capacity for manipulating concepts and logic and for subtle indirectness that is unique. These jokes are not a statement about Jewish cleverness but a display of that quality in action. It is impossible for unbiased outsiders to read or hear such jokes without thinking to themselves — 'that was clever! Why couldn't we think of that?'[23]

Rabinowitz was staying at a plush Miami Beach Hotel. He picked up the phone one morning and asked for room service.

'May I take your order,' said a voice at the other end of the line.

'Yeah,' snapped Rabinowitz. 'I want three overdone fried eggs that are hard like a rock. Some burnt toast that you could hardly swallow and a cup of black coffee that tastes like mud.'

'I'm sorry, sir,' said room service. 'We don't serve a breakfast like that.'

'Oh no? You did yesterday!'[24]

Item from the reading of a Jewish will by the lawyer to the relatives:

'And to my cousin Louie whom I said I would remember in my will — Hello Louie!'[25]

A great king grown old and eccentric called before him the chief rabbi of his realm. 'Before I die there's something I want you to do, Rabbi. Teach my pet monkey how to talk!'

'What?'

'That's a command: Teach my monkey how to talk within one year or your head will be chopped off!'

'But your Majesty, to carry out a request like that I need more than a year — I need at least ten.

'I'll allow you five and not a day more.'

The rabbi returned to his flock and told them what had happened. And they all cried out in sympathy. 'But what will you do, Rov?'

'Well,' said the rov, *'in five years many things can happen. For instance the king could die. Or I could die. Or — the monkey*

*could die. And besides, in five years, who knows — maybe I can
teach that monkey to talk.'[26]*

4. The Ashkenazi Jews from Eastern Europe who have had such an impact on the humor of the English-speaking world have introduced into English words of Yiddish origin such as schlemiel, schlimazl, nebbish, chutzpah, naches, schnorrer, that have no equivalent in pre-Yinglish English.[27] Many of these words that have been or are being absorbed into English deal with subtle differences between types and aspects of cleverness and stupidity, of success and failure, and they are often used in a humorous context. The fact that such words exist and catch on indicates (like the alleged plethora of words for various types of snow and ice among the Eskimos) a preoccupation with themes of cleverness–success/stupidity–failure

Table 1

Country in which jokes are told	Allegedly Stupid Groups	Allegedly Canny Groups
England	Irish	Scots
Wales	Irish	Cardis
Scotland	Irish	Aberdonians
Ireland	Kerrymen	Scots
United States	Poles	New England Yankees
Canada	Newfies/Ukrainians	Scots/Nova Scotians
Mexico	Yucatecos	Regiomontanos
France	Belgians	Scots/Auvergnats
Low Countries	Belgians	Dutch
Germany	Ostfrieslanders	Swabians
Sweden	Norwegians	Scots
Finland	Karelians	Laihians
Greece	Pontians	Scots
Bulgaria	Šopi	Gabrovonians
India	Sardarjis (Sikhs)	Gujaratis
South Africa	Van Der Merwe (Boers)	Scots
Australia	Irish	Scots
New Zealand	Irish, Maori	Scots

(For most of these countries one can also add the Jews to the list of canny groups — like the Scots they provide international jokes about canniness — hence my term Hebredonian.)

which characterises both Jewish jokes and culture and the outlook of the modern English-speaking world.

The Ashkenazi Jewish immigrants provided the Anglophone countries with words they could use but had previously failed to invent and jokes were a key vehicle for conveying an understanding of these terms to the recipients, rather in the way that the Scots word 'canny' has caught on.[28]

The most common ethnic jokes of the modern world are about alleged canny (i.e. shrewd, calculating, thrifty) and stupid groups.[29] Every country has its own 'stupid' and 'canny' groups about whom it tells jokes.

Table I above illustrates the widespread modern preoccupation with the contrast cleverness–success/stupidity–failure. This theme which is so subtly handled in Jewish jokes is elsewhere dealt with by pinning these opposed qualities on pairs of ethnic outsiders in a very routine way. Hence the Hebredonian jokes which the Jews share with the Scots and others. The following Scots jokes for instance are also told about Jews:

> *A Scotsman got on a bus in London, put his suitcase under the stairs and said 'The Houses of Parliament please!'*
> *The conductor said, 'Five pence and two pence for the suitcase.'*
> *The Scot said, 'I'm not paying for the suitcase.'*
> *The conductor said, 'If you don't pay up I'm going to throw the suitcase off the bus.'*
> *The Scotsman still refused to pay. So the conductor picked up the case and threw it off the bus — straight into the River Thames.*
> *The Scot was livid. He yelled and screamed: 'You're not satisfied with trying to rob me you English swindler, but you're also trying to drown my wee boy as well.'[30]*

> *There was great excitement on Deeside. A boy had fallen in the river and had been rescued just in time by a passer-by. When things had calmed down a bit the hero was approached by the boy's father and questioned:*
> *'Are you the man that saved my laddie?'*
> *'Yes!'*
> *'Whaur's his bonnet?'[31]*

> *An Aberdonian asked by a London friend the secret of his success in London and elsewhere replied that it was just brain due*

*to a fish diet and agreed to send a regular consignment of
Aberdeen fish to his friend. Some time later they met and the
London man being asked how he liked the fish said that they
were good, but he had discovered that he could get similar fish in
London at less cost. 'Ah!' said the Scot, 'I'll stop sending more. It
seems that what you have has proved effective at last.'*[32]

Hebredonian 'canny' jokes (a) cannot easily be related to any significant or systematic pattern of hostility on the part of the joke-tellers towards the subjects of these jokes and (b) are often inter-changeable between the various allegedly 'canny' groups without any loss of humor in the process. Hebredonian jokes involving Jews are neither specifically Jewish jokes nor in general anti-Semitic. Jokes that can also be told in much the same form about, say, the Scots, the Netherlanders or the Cardis, who are not the victims of anti-Caledonian, anti-Dutch or anti-Cardi hostility[33] are probably not anti-Semitic. They reflect general pressures in modern society to laugh at canny peoples and not the kind of anti-Semitic (or anti-Armenian) prejudices discussed later. Many Hebredonian jokes about Jews are so similar to those told about the Scots that Seth Kravitz on the basis of his fieldwork investigating the jokes told by Londoners concluded that Scottish jokes were a "modified sub-set of Jewish jokes"![34] It would be more accurate to say that there is a degree of overlap between Scottish and Jewish jokes and it is the overlapping area that I have termed Hebredonian. Indeed one way of distinguishing Hebredonian jokes about Jews from anti-Semitic jokes would be to ask the question 'Can this joke easily be told about a Scotsman?' If it can and would, then it is not likely to be anti-Semitic.

However, if instead of stressing the similarity of jokes about Scots and jokes about Jews we look at some of the contrasts between them then it becomes apparent that many of the elements present in the jokes about Jews that are not found in jokes about the Scots are congruent with the core beliefs of anti-Semites. These elements are largely absent from jokes about indigenous 'canny' groups like the Scots, the Dutch or the Cardis that have not been the victims of persecution but are often present in jokes about persecuted entrepreneurial and trading guest peoples such as the Armenians, the Chinese of South East Asia or the Asians of East Africa.[35]

One of the contrasts that has been noted between British jokes about canny Jews and those about canny Scotsmen is that the former are relatively more likely to be set in a business context and the latter in a domestic one.[36] This ties in with two broader general differences between jokes about Scots and jokes about Jews told in Europe and America generally, viz (i) In Scots' jokes the victims of the canny Scotsman's shrewdness are very often himself or his own immediate family or associates, whereas in jokes about Jews the victims of Jewish cleverness are often outsiders and sometimes society in general. (ii) the canny Scotsman is shrewd in avoiding expenditure and obligations but is relatively rarely depicted as swindling people, whereas jokes about Jewish swindling and business malpractice are common. The contrast is summed up in the joke about the shortest books in the world which includes 'Jewish business ethics' and 'La dolce vita in Scotland'.[37] To these two key differences between jokes about Scots (or Dutchmen, Regiomontanos, Cardis, and the indigenous canny generally) and jokes about Jews (and other 'guest' peoples such as Armenians, overseas Chinese, etc.) may be added a third: many jokes about the latter groups but not the former depict them as using their cleverness in ways disloyal to the host-nation. It is also significant that jokes about clever guest peoples often depict them as lacking in the more heroic or brutal virtues.

This exceedingly negative comic portrayal of Jewish cleverness is so congruent with the basic belief of anti-Semites that the Jews are diabolically cunning swindlers and enemies of society that such jokes may reasonably be termed anti-Semitic.[38] It is not the existence of a negative comic image of Jews as such that leads me to call a particular group of jokes anti-Semitic for there can be other reasons for the existence of hostile or offensive jokes, e.g. a conflict within the Jewish community itself.[39] Rather it is the close correlation between the *particular* negative image of the Jews in the jokes and what we know on the basis of *quite different data* to be the views and prejudices of anti-Semites that is crucial.[40] One form of joke that is commonly told about Jews and rarely about Scots and which epitomises the nature of the hostility and fears of the anti-Semite regarding the sinister ends which he thinks are being pursued by cunning Jews is that in which Jews commit arson to defraud an insurance company. It is almost a prototype of anti-Semitic jokes in general.[41]

> *I noticed some bottles on a shelf in Robinski's shop.*
> *'Vot vas dose?' I said.*
>   *'They is fire extingvishers,' he replied.*
>   *'Grashus!' I said, 'vy do you keep fire extingvishers?'*
>   *'Because,' he said, 'I get 20 per shent off ze premium of insurance.'*
>   *'And vot vas in ze bottles?' I asked.*
>   *'I do not know vot vas in zem,' he said, 'but it is kerosene now!'*[42]

> *Talking about insurance, Robinski he said 'Here is a strange letter I got from ze insurance company about a shop of mine in ze Brompton Road —*

Sir, — we understand you effected a policy of insurance over premises occupied by you in Brompton Road yesterday forenoon. We are informed that the premises took fire at half-past four the same afternoon when considerable damage was done. Kindly explain the delay.

It is very funny Robinski, he said, and I do not know vot to write in reply.[43]

A Jew crossing the Brooklyn Bridge met a friend who said: 'Abe, I'll bet you ten dollars that I can tell you exactly what you're thinking about.' 'Vell!' agreed Abe, producing a greasy bill, 'I'll have to take dat bet. Put up your money.'

The friend produced two fives. 'Abe,' he said, 'You are thinking of going over to Brooklyn, buying a small stock of goods, renting a small store, taking out all the fire insurance that you can possibly get and then burning out. Do I win my bet?'

'Vell,' replied Abe, 'You don't exactly vin, but the idea is worth de money. Take id.'[44]

A month after he had taken out his fire-insurance policy, Mottel's store burned to the ground and with it his entire inventory of last season's merchandise. Surprisingly, none of the new merchandise had been damaged. By a strange and fortuitous coincidence he had removed all new shipments to another location. Naturally he notified his agent at once. The agent, in turn, was ordered by his office manager to bring an insurance adjuster with him and, together, they sifted through the charred ruins for a full eight hours. At the end of the day, they returned to their office where the manager understandably nervous awaited them.

'Did you find out what caused the fire?' he asked.

'Yes, friction,' said the adjuster tersely.

'You mean something rubbed up against something else?'

'Yeah,' the adjuster affirmed. 'The fire was caused by rubbing a $25,000 insurance policy against a $10,000 dry goods store.'[45]

Hearing that Isaac had had a fire on his premises, I hailed him with: 'How did you get on with the Insurance Company, Isaac?'

'Hush,' he replied, 'it is not till next week.'[46]

There had been a conflagration at Isaac's tailoring establishment and the usual enquiry was taking place.

> *'And what do you think was the cause of the fire?' asked the*
> *Insurance Inspector. 'I think it was the gas light' replied Isaac.*
>
> *The Inspector looked dubious; so Isaac's friend Cohen broke*
> *in with: 'You vos wrong, Isaac mine frient. I think it vos the*
> *electric light.' But the Inspector wrote down in his report: 'Cause*
> *of fire — Israelite.'*[47]

> *Bronstein's Law: "Three fires = one bankruptcy. Three*
> *bankruptcies = a new house."*[48]

> *Blumenthal asked Schwartz, a clothing store proprietor, 'How's*
> *business?'*
>
> *'Not so good,' said Schwartz, 'It looks like a sure-fire*
> *proposition.'*[49]

These jokes are significant both as a piece of literal anti-Semitic folklore — 'the Jews are swindlers' — and at a symbolic level. An attempt to defraud an insurance company by deliberately setting a building on fire (rather than, say, faking a burglary or an accidental loss) threatens not just the profits of the insurer but also in an urban area people in that building or neighbouring buildings who may get burned in the fire. Anti-Semitic jokes about Jews committing arson are a very specific metaphor of the general anti-Semitic belief in secret Jewish conspiracies that destroy people, economies and societies so that the Jews may prosper.

It is significant that the only joke about Scots and fire-insurance that I can recall is far more innocuous:

> *A Scottish farmer put in an insurance claim after one of his*
> *barns burned down. The insurance agent who came round to*
> *settle the claim took the opportunity to try and sell him some*
> *more insurance. Why don't you take out insurance against theft*
> *he asked him, or even against floods.*
>
> *'Floods?' queried the canny Scot. 'Floods?' How do you start a*
> *flood?'*[50]

It is innocuous partly because of its *rural* setting. An isolated barn burning down does not constitute a threat to other people's lives or property. The insurance company loses (and so do its other customers) from such an illegal and anti-social act, but it does not pose a direct sinister threat to the rest of society.

The image of the Scot as crofter, farmer, manual worker is also a benign one and is in contrast to the anti-Semitic view of the Jew as a smart but unheroic urban trader[51] lacking in physical hardiness and courage.[52] This comes across consistently in jokes that *compare* a canny Jew and a canny Scot. George Orwell wrote about British music-hall jokes:

> *Occasionally a story is told (e.g. the Jew and the Scotsman who went into a pub together and both died of thirst) which puts both races on an equality. But in general the Jew is credited merely with cunning and avarice while the Scotsman is credited with physical hardihood as well. This is seen, for example, in the story of the Jew and the Scotsman who go together to a meeting which has been advertised as free. Unexpectedly there is a collection and to avoid this the Jew faints and the Scotsman carries him out. Here the Scotsman performs the athletic feat of carrying the other. It would seem vaguely wrong if it were the other way about.*[53]

Orwell's point seems to be substantiated by the following examples also:

> *An Aberdonian and a Jew had an argument and decided to settle it in the ring. The Jew thought to pull a fast one so he bet the Aberdonian to win. But the Aberdonian thinking along the same lines bet the Jew. In the ring the Aberdonian threw a punch, the Jew lay down, the referee started to count. At the count of nine the Aberdonian went over to where the Jew was lying and kicked him. The Aberdonian lost on a disqualification.*[54]

> *The usual trio consisting of an Englishman, a Scotsman and a Jew (the Irishman was ill) had a nine course meal at an expensive restaurant and the waiter presented them with a bill for £42.*
> *'I'll pay that,' offered the Scotsman.*
> *Prominent headlines in the following day's paper said:*
> *'JEWISH VENTRILOQUIST FOUND DEAD IN ALLEY.'*[55]

The use of force by the Scots is contrasted here with the sneaky behavior of the Jews. The Scotsman's tough brutality is almost a virtue and certainly a reminder of the Scots' reputation as dependable patriotic fighters who uphold the nation and the state. By contrast, the cleverness of Jews and other trading 'guest' peoples is often seen by their prejudiced hosts as directed against their nation, state or people and this view too emerges in jokes.

> *Definition of a patriotic South African — a Jewish doctor who can't sell his house.*[56]

Two Jews who had not seen each other for several years met by chance in the street in Warsaw and began to exchange news about their families.

'Tell me,' said one, 'What is your eldest boy Moishe doing these days, he always was a bright lad.'

'Yes indeed,' replied the father, 'He's made a brilliant careeer for himself in Prague. He's been really successful there and everyone says he's helping to build socialism.'

'And what about your second boy Chaim?'

'Well he's working in Moscow now and he's done very well too. He's getting a very good salary and doing really skilled work. And of course he's helping to build socialism there.'

'Now didn't you have a third son Isaac? What has become of him?'

'Oh he's done better than any of them. He emigrated to Israel and he's gone straight to the top of his profession.'

'And is he helping to build socialism too?'

'Oh no, he wouldn't do a thing like that, not to his own country.'[57]

Who has got the "largest collection of flags" in South-East Asia?

The Chinese — "one for each government that might come into control of the state."[58]

The head of the Bulgarian secret service desperately needed to obtain some vital documents that were in the possession of the British intelligence service. He sent his two best agents to London to try and get them back, but they failed to return. Finally he called in an Armenian agent from Plovdiv called Kirkov.

'Do you think you can get those papers back for me?' he asked him.

'Of course,' replied the Armenian, 'My friend Garabet works for British intelligence in London and I'll get him to procure the documents for you.'

'But how do you know he will do you such an enormous favor?'

'Why not? He owes me several such favors.'[59]

Conclusions

On the basis of the arguments and evidence presented above it is possible to suggest ways of systematically distinguishing between Jewish, Hebredonian and anti-Semitic jokes. The use of the two tests of congruence and switchability is summed up in Table 2 to which a comment is added on the view of Jews embodied in the jokes.

Table 2

	Jewish jokes	Hebredonian Jokes	Anti-Semitic Jokes
Congruence test	Congruent with the Jewish cultural tradition, social experience and use of language	Congruent with the widespread pattern of 'canny' ethnic jokes told in many countries	Congruent with anti-Semitic prejudice, ideology and propaganda
Switch-ability test	Very limited degree of switchability but jokes can sometimes be transferred to one or two other groups	Can be switched to any group with a reputation for being canny	Can be switched to other 'guest' trading minorities subject to discrimination and persecution but *not* to indigenous 'canny' groups
Attitude towards Jews implied in jokes	Generally favour-able but with a very large range from highly positive to moderately negative	Generally neutral but can be moderately positive or moderately negative	Highly negative but probably not negative enough for the most bigoted anti-Semites

NOTES

1. The remarks of some politicians in the course of the 1984 American primaries are an unpleasant reminder that anti-Semitism still flourishes in some quarters even in the western democracies.

2. See for example Bernard D. Weinryb, *Anti-semitism in Soviet Russia* and Zev Katz, *After the Six-Day war* in Lionel Kochan (ed.) *The Jews in Soviet Russia since 1917* Institute of Jewish Affairs/Oxford University Press. London 1970 pp. 228–339. Also the introduction by Leonard Schapiro, pp. 1–13.

3. There is no such thing as anti-Caledonianism. In the eighteenth century in Britain there was some anti-Scottish feeling, partly because of the influx of educated and entrepreneurial Scots into England but the Scots have rarely been seen as threatening aliens in any of the countries where they have settled. In most of the English-speaking world they are seen as a talented indigenous group, 'sagacious and determined as well as canny'. See W. Turrentine Jackson, *The Enterprising Scot*, Edinburgh University Press, Edinburgh 1968.

    There may well be numerous scattered individuals who do not like the enterprising Scot but this has no *social* significance. Similarly people joke about the commercially minded Dutch referring to them as the Pepper-sacks (in Germany) or the Tulip-munchers (in New Zealand) and there are numerous jokes about canny Dutchmen in Belgium. However, there is no anti-Batavianism corresponding to anti-Semitism. Jokes about the Scots or the Dutch represent a recognition of acumen that is not accompanied by any great fear or hostility. This is also a view that has been taken of the Jews by non-Jews who are not anti-Semitic and who may indeed praise the Jews for their 'Smilesian virtues'. See Colin Holmes *Anti-Semitism in British Society. 1876–1939.* Edward Arnold 1979 p. 19.

4. For a comparative discussion see Christie Davies, Asians of East Africa *Quest* Number 77, July–August 1972, pp. 33–39. See also Arnold J. Toynbee, *Armenian Atrocities, the murder of a nation,* Hodder and Stoughton, London 1915.

5. To take just one instance there are many Jewish jokes about dietary taboos that are probably incomprehensible to most gentiles. The latter can appreciate jokes about avoiding pork or possibly even keeping meat and milk products apart but jokes about permitted versus forbidden types of fish and sea-creatures or the use of separate cutlery for meat and dairy products probably have no meaning for them. It *might* be possible to alter the content of such jokes to fit, say, the beliefs and practices of the Parsees who have detailed notions of purity and pollution absent from the thinking of most Europeans but I would not like to try (see George William Carter, *Zoroastrianism and Judaism,* AMS, New York, 1918 and Maneckji Nusservanji Dhalla, *Zoroastrian Theology,* AMS, New York 1914).

6. Henry D. Spalding, *Encyclopaedia of Jewish Humor*, Jonathan David, New York 1973 p. 255.

7. Leo Rosten, *The Joys of Yiddish*, W.H. Allen, London 1970, p. 433.

8. I have deliberately quoted the non-Jewish versions to underline my point about switchability — the reader should be able to construct the Jewish version from the

non-Jewish one. Christie Davies, *Welsh Jokes*, John Jones, Cardiff, 1979, p. 11. See also Christie Davies 'In search of the real Welsh joke', *Western Mail*, Cardiff, 4th July, 1979.

9. Rosten, p. 453.

10. Ocky Milkman, like Dai Bread, is a character in Dylan Thomas's radio play 'Under Milk Wood." Oliver Cromwell whose original family name was the common Welsh Williams is called Williams-the-Conqueror.

11. Davies, *Welsh Jokes*, 1979, p. 25.

12. Spalding, 1973, p. 102.

13. Raphael Patai, *The Jewish Mind*, Charles Scribner's sons, New York, 1977, p. 287.

14. This joke was told to me in Los Angeles in 1979 by an American Professor of English who is a Russian Jewish emigrant.

15. This joke was told by the Russian Jewish humorous writer Emil Draitser (he formerly wrote for Krokodil using his patronymic i.e. Emil Abramovitch as a pseudonym but now lives in the United States) in the course of a paper he gave at the University of Reading, (England) on Soviet humor, in 1980.

16. I stress this point because many scholars have suggested that such jokes involve a degree of self-dislike, self-abasement or even self-hatred based on willingness to accept a stereotype imposed by the dominant social group. Andrea Greenburg for instance implies that it is factors of this kind that lead Jews to invent and tell jokes based on Jewish striving for financial success and social status. See Andrea Greenburg, 'Forms and functions of the ethnic joke', *Keystone Folklore Quarterly* winter 1972 vol. XVII, No. 4., p. 147. What Greenburg fails to take fully into account is that striving for money and status is a key aspect of most people's behaviour in western societies and particularly the United States. To seek and achieve success by legitimate means is considered laudable. Jewish jokes that mock Jewish ambition are not an index of self-hatred and indeed may be an indirect way of stating pride in success in societies where individual success is valued. These jokes are so distant from the anti-Semitic caricature of Jews as pushy or the anti-Semitic fear that 'the Jews monopolise the professions' that to see them as a manifestation of self-hatred is absurd. Greenburg (p. 145) accuses Alan Dundes of being simplistic in stressing the positive side of these jokes (see Alan Dundes: 'A study of ethnic slurs; the Jew and the Polack in the United States', *Journal of American Folklore* vol. 84, April–June 1971, No. 332 pp. 186–203) but ironically Dundes's article is subtle and insightful and it is Greenburg who is simplistic.

17. I heard this joke from an English Jewish lawyer in London in the 1960s. There is an American version in Leo Rosten, *The Joys of Yiddish* W.H. Allen, London 1970, p. 203.

18. This joke is currently being told in Britain. There is an American version about a 'C.P.A.' in Larry Wilde *The Last Official Jewish Joke Book*, Bantam New York, 1980, p. 167.

19. I heard this joke from an English Jewish student in Cambridge in 1964. For an American version see Rosten p. 445.

20. Larry Wilde, *The Last Official Jewish Joke Book*, Bantam New York, 1980, p. 2. There is another well-known version with "bicycle riders" in place of 'pretzel makers'.

21. Larry Wilde 1980 p. 115.

22. Spalding 1973 p. 195.
23. Rosten p. 110.
24. Wilde 1980 p. 2.
25. Told me by a British Jewish student of Economics in Cambridge in the 1960s.
26. Rosten pp. 314–315 and also see pp. 101–102, 112–113, 118, 165–166, 170, 188, 231, 257–258, 371–372, 397, 433, etc.
27. The fact that non-Jews often have some idea of the meaning of these terms and use them, albeit in ways that might make a Yiddish scholar shudder, is an indication of their force and usefulness.
28. It is significant that 'canny' is a Scots word. Hence Lewis Carroll's logical joke based on the subtle lack of fit between the two 'opposites' canny and uncanny:

    All Dragons are uncanny

    All Scotchmen are canny

    Therefore all Dragons are not Scotchmen.

    All Scotchmen are not Dragons.

    Curiously enough the people of the red dragon are just as canny as the Scots.
29. I have dealt with this point at greater length in Christie Davies 'Ethnic jokes, moral values and social boundaries', *British Journal of Sociology*, Volume XXXIII No. 3, September 1982 p. 383–403. See also Christie Davies, *Jokes are about peoples* Indiana University Press (forthcoming).
30. Ken Irwin (ed) Laugh with the Comedians, Wolfe/Independent Television Books, London 1972 p. 140. See also Lewis and Faye Copeland *'10,000 Jokes, Toasts and Stories'* Garden City Books, Garden City, New York, 1940 p. 718 and Hervé Nègre, *Dictionaire des histoires drôles* Fayard Paris 1973 p. 365–396. The Jewish version is in Spalding (1973) p. 49. For a Trinidad version about an (East) Indian see Louis Carballo, *Laughter from Trinidad,* Rilloprint, San Fernando, 1977.
31. Allan Junior *'Canny Tales Fae Aberdeen,* Valentine, Dundee, 1927, p. 17. There is a Jewish version in Ike' nsmile Lettslaff *'Jokes, jokes, jokes',* London 1937, p. 48–49.
32. Max Gilbert Frost, *Merry Stories Omnibus book,* T. Werner Laurie, London, 1933, p. 307 joke 1991. There are many Jewish versions e.g. that in A.C.H. Newman, *The select-a-joke book,* Elliot Right Way Books, Kingswood, U.K. 1979, p. 75–76.
33. Sometimes a neutral or amiable joke about the Scots gets so drastically rewarded so as to become a new and hostile joke about Jews and slides over into the anti-Semitic category usually by adding one of the anti-Semitic canards discussed later. However, many jokes remain essentially the same in tenet and tone (i.e. when told) whether they refer to Jews or Scots.
34. Seth Kravitz, London jokes and ethnic stereotypes, *Western Folklore* volume XXXVI No. 4, October 1977, p. 287–289. The examples of overlapping between Jewish and Scottish jokes that he cites are my 'Hebredonian jokes'. However, there are aspects of Scots cannyness that cannot be transposed into Jewish jokes e.g. jokes about the dour, ascetic nature of Scots cannyness or the conflict between thirst, thrift and Calvinism when it comes to alcohol.
35. 'Guest' peoples is the term given to peoples who (a) are immigrants or the descendants of immigrants whose ancestors came from a different place and (b) have a social existence which sets them apart from the local population. This may be from choice or as a result of discrimination. If they are successful in commerce they may suffer

prejudice and persecution. Indigenous canny groups (a) live in their ancestral homeland as say Scots in Scotland or the Dutch in Holland, or migrate internally within a nation as say Scots going to England, or migrate to countries where they or their co-nationals are the dominant ethnic group as say Scots going to Canada, New Zealand or even the United States, and (b) are characterised by weak social boundaries between themselves and the local or dominant people. The terms 'guest' and 'indigenous' people are intended to be purely descriptive. There is an evaluative ring about them but it is difficult to find words for which this is not the case that express this contrast adequately.

36. See Kravitz p. 288.

37. This is a very common joke involving a string of stereotypes. Other such books include 'Italian war heroes', 'Irish Intellectuals', etc.

38. In the sense that if there were no anti-Semitism I doubt the jokes would exist. The tellers of such jokes and the editors of anthologies including them are by no means necessarily sympathetic to anti-Semitism. Most of the jokes cited below were told to me by Jews and two of the editors of anthologies including such jokes interviewed by me were also Jewish. None of these individuals were in any sense anti-Semitic or characterised by any degree of so-called Jewish self-hatred. I share the scepticism expressed by Dan Ben-Amos in 'The myth of Jewish humor' *Western Folklore* vol. XXXII No. 2. p. 112–131 concerning the view that self-hatred is a characteristic of Jewish humor. Rather I would suggest on the basis of hearing such jokes in context that those Jews and philo-Semites who enjoy anti-Semitic jokes do so as one means of handling the harsh fact that anti-Semitism exists. Such jokes *in this context* are funny for the same reason that sick or black humor is. People often joke about what they fear most. Editors of contemporary anthologies of jokes whether they are Jewish or not recognise, however, the double-edged nature of jokes about, say, Jews setting fire to buildings to get the insurance money and often a joke on this theme with a wide oral circulation appears in print in a very curiously doctored form. For a statement of the view that anti-Semitic jokes are anti-Semitic, period, see Sig Altman *The comic image of the Jew,* Fairleigh Dickinson U.P. Rutherford, U.S.A., pp. 14–19.

39. See Ben Amos (above note 38). The most significant instance of highly derogatory jokes involving Jews that cannot be related to anti-Semitism are the so-called J.A.P. (Jewish American Princess) jokes which depict Jewish women as whining and sexless, cold towards their husband, possessive towards their sons and manipulative towards both. I have discussed these jokes with examples in Christie Davies 'Commentary on Anton C. Zijderveld's trend report on the sociology of humor and laughter' *Current Sociology* Vol. 32 Number 1, Spring 1984, pp. 152–153 and rejected any link with anti-Semitism. They emanate from within the Jewish Community in America and do not fit at all easily into the stereotypes held by anti-Semites.

40. The assumption about the nature of anti-Semitism which I have used as the framework of my analysis of anti-Semitic jokes is based on (a) Studies of anti-Semitism such as Holmes (1979) and James H. Robb *'Working-Class Anti-Semite'.* Tavistock. London, 1954. (b) The writings of influential anti-Semites such as Alfred Rosenberg, *Selected writings,* Jonathan Cape, London, 1970; Adolf Hitler, *Mein Kampf,* A.B.C. Publishing. New Delhi India 1968 and in a different translation Hutchinson London 1969. Karl Marx, *A World without Jews,* Philosophical Library,

New York, 1957. (c) Commentaries on the above by Robert Pois (editor of Rosenberg); D.C. Watt (introduction to Hutchinson edition of Hitler); Dagobert D. Runes (introduction to Marx); and Nathaniel Weyl, *Karl Marx; Racist* Arlington House, New Rochelle, New York, 1979. Very briefly the key beliefs of anti-Semites seem to be that the Jews are (a) cunning heartless swindlers (b) dangerous and malevolent conspirators (c) lacking in national loyalty to the country of which they are citizens, cowardly and capable of treason. My own work on the pattern of prejudice against Asians living in East Africa (see above) indicates that a similar set of beliefs is held about them. I have tape-recorded interviews with anti-Asian Africans who expressed not merely the same kinds of sentiments as anti-Semites in Europe but used the same kind of imagery. (see also Toynbee pp. 19–20, 26, 34).

41. In Robb's study of anti-Semites one of the extreme anti-Semites he interviewed (p. 109) "Says they (the Jews) are black marketeers and firebugs (Calls fire engine bells 'Jew's wedding bells')". Another of those interviewed (p. 107) Robb describes as "Nervous about the possibility of the house burning down and takes elaborate precautions to prevent this."

42. W.H. MacDonald *'Yarns ancient and modern'*, William Hodge, Edinburgh 1943 pp. 61–62 and in identical form in James Ferguson *The table in a roar,* Methuen, London 1933 p. 168. There is an extremely skilled attempt to turn this into a philo-Semitic joke in Larry Wilde (1980) p. 116 but despite the skill employed the switch does not work.

43. MacDonald p. 62 and Ferguson p. 168.

44. William Patten, *Among the Humorists and After-Dinner Speakers,* P.F. Collier, New York 1909, p. 173.

45. Henry D. Spalding, *A treasure trove of American Jewish Humor,* Jonathan David, New York, 1976, p. 166.

46. Allan Junior, *The Aberdeen Jew,* Valentine Dundee, 1927, p. 21. (see also p. 34). Also found in George Robey, *After-Dinner Stories,* Grant Richards, London 1920, pp. 228–229 and Macdonald p. 62. This joke is still in oral circulation in Britain.

47. Junior (1927) p. 32. See also Ferguson p. 169.

48. Bronstein is the name I have given to the British Jewish banker who told me the joke when he was a student in the 1960s. He put his own name to the 'law' but I have given him a pseudonym to protect the guilty. The name Bronstein bears no relation to his own and is simply taken from a long dead politician.

49. Larry Wilde (1980), p. 161.

50. This Scots story is in oral circulation in Britain and I am reasonably sure I have seen it in print. There is a similar story in Kurt Ranke, *European Anecdotes and Jests,* Rosenkilde and Bagger, Copenhagen 1972, p. 119, joke 190 told about a German *farmer* urged to insure his *crops* against hail. In the commentary on p. 183, a Jewish version is quoted from Geiger's *Histoires Juives,* p. 11, No. 1, where Levy says, "I've just insured myself against both fire and hail". Levy's occupation is not given nor is it stated what it is that he has insured. It is very difficult to give a sympathetic humorous portrayal of urban arson because it is so dangerous. It is a measure of H.G. Wells' genius that he succeeds in doing so in his novel, *The History of Mr. Polly.* Mr. Polly, a well-nigh bankrupt small shopkeeper, burns his shop down for the insurance money, and sets an entire street of shops on fire and yet so skilfully does Wells structure the sequence of events that Mr. Polly emerges from the charred ruins as a hero to his

neighbours and has the entire sympathy of the reader. The scene where the burnt-out store keepers discuss the consequences of the fire later is one of the most amusing things Wells ever wrote.

51. A dichotomy that underlines much anti-Semitism is the dichotomy Us = honest, sturdy, long-settled working farmers the backbone of the nation, ever ready to defend our native soil as soldiers. Them = the Jews who are the opposite of us and, therefore, bad.

52. Kravitz cites this as a theme in jokes told by a British professional comedian which he (the comedian) found led to strong objections from Jewish audiences. Robb's anti-Semites often ascribed these qualities to Jews.

53. George Orwell, *The Collected Essays, Journalism and Letters of George Orwell*, Secker and Warburg, London, 1968, vol. II, p. 338.

54. From the file of Scottish jokes in the library of the House of Humour and Satire, Gabrovo, Bulgaria. It was originally entered in a Scottish-Gabrovonian competition for the best Aberdeen joke held in 1968 by a correspondent from Motherwell in Scotland.

55. Colin Crompton, *More Best Jewish Jokes,* Wolfe, London, p. 9.

56. I was told this joke by a South African industrial scientist in Botswana in 1983. I had heard it before in London.

57. A British university teacher who speaks Polish fluently heard this joke in Poland in 1980 and told it to me on his return. It is a joke that cuts many ways at once.

58. See Fred R. von der Melden, 'Pariah Communities and Violence,' in H. Jon Rosenbaum and P.C. Sederburg (eds), *Vigilante Politics,* University of Pennsylvania Press, 1976, p. 218.

59. I was told this joke in Bulgaria in 1981 by an English speaking Bulgarian.

J. Kauffman

GALLOWS HUMOR AND JEWISH HUMOR: A READING OF "THE DANCE OF GENGHIS COHN" BY ROMAIN GARY

JUDITH KAUFFMAN
Bar-Ilan University, Israel

GALLOWS HUMOR AND JEWISH HUMOR
A reading of "The Dance of Genghis Cohn", by Romain Gary

What I shall try to do here is to point out the specific Jewish characteristics in Romain Gary's humor. I have chosen this writer because it is quite unusual to find both a reflection on Jewish humor and its application in the same text. *The Dance of Genghis Cohn* presents a vast illustration of what Jewish humor is, as conveyed by the hero, Genghis Cohn, a Jew and a humorist as well.

The novel tells the story of Cohn, a well-known *khokhem* of the old Yiddish burlesque in Warsaw. He has, for the past twenty years, been the *dybbuk* of his murderer, *Hauptjudenfresser* Schatz. The ex-SS officer, at present police commissioner in the little town of Licht ("Light"), has to solve a range of mysterious murders: all the victims are men who died with happy smiles on their faces. Lily, Baron von Pritwitz's wife, is suspect number one. She may be a dangerous nymphomaniac, looking for a superman. Florian, her husband's game keeper, kills every man who has not succeeded in giving her that total fulfillment for which she is longing.

Lily may be Germany, helped by Florian, the demoniac and impassive German death, and Schatz, the German conscience possessed by six million Jewish *dybbuks*. Lily could just as well be Humanity in search of the Absolute: when violence is the highest value, the quest leads to pornography . . . To these interpretations suggested by Gary, the reader will add his own.

In order to avoid excessive generalisation, I have decided to base my presentation on a short excerpt from the book:[1]

> *We both laugh. An ideal partner.*
> *"I know another one", says Florian, feeling encouraged. "During a prorom, Cohn's wife is being raped by the Cossacks in front of her husband. First it's the soldiers who have her, then their officer comes in and helps himself too. So Cohn says to him: 'Can't you ask permission first, you, an officer and a gentleman?'"*
> *I roar with laughter. "That's terrific! I love our folklore."*
> *"I know another one —"*
> *I interrupt him politely. I really don't intend to spend my time listening to our history. I know it by heart already.*
> *"Did you say Cohn? Which Cohn was that?"*

B/1

C

B/2

C

A/2

B/3

"Well, you know, it's always the same one."

"It wasn't Cohn from Smigla Street, was it?"

"No, it was Cohen from Nazareth."

I laugh. "Mazel tov! Congratulations. Your memory!"

"Zu gesundt."

'Oh, so you speak Yiddish?"

"Fluently."

"Berlitz?"

"No, Treblinka."

We both laugh.

"I've always wondered what Jewish humor is, exactly," he says. "What do you think it is?"

"It's a way of yelling."

"What use is it?"

"The power of cries is so great that it will shatter the rigors decreed against man."

"Kafka," he says. "I know, I know about it. Do you really believe in it?"

I wink at him and we both laugh.

"That Cossack story you told me . . . You said Cohn? It wasn't Leiba Cohn, of Kichenev, by any chance? He was my uncle, and it must have been him, because he told me the same story. It was his wife whom the Cossacks raped in front of him. She had a child after that adventure and my uncle, who was very vindictive, revenged himself cruelly on the Russian goyim. He treated the child as his own son, and brought him up as a Jew."

Florian is absolutely sickened. "Really, what a swine! Fancy treating a child like that!"

"Yes, we are a merciless race. Indeed, we crucified Our Lord Jesus Christ, peace be to His ashes."

"Excuse me, excuse me! You always try to claim everything for yourselves! Nothing for other people... Such greed! Pope John XXIII declared that you weren't guilty."

"Not guilty? So, for two thousand years, it has all been for nothing?"

"All for nothing, for nothing. You only think about doing a little business!"[2]

I found four groups of elements in the text which will form the basis of my paper. There are two Jewish jokes, A/1 and A/2; three groups of puns, B/1, B/2, and B/3, two exclamations in Yiddish, C, and one definition of Jewish humor, D. The plan of this paper will be as follows:

100

1. Yiddish, its presence and function,
2. Puns,
3. A definition of Jewish humor, illustrated by the two stories.

1. Yiddish, its Presence and Function

This novel is full of Yiddish expressions. It is undoubtedly Gary's most exotic book for the French reader who is far from being as well acquainted with this language as the American public. For this reason, the presence of Yiddish is all the more effective.

We find cooking vocabulary such as *cholent* and *gefilte fish, tsymes, kneydl,*[3] as well as *kosher*[4] with the more general meaning of acceptable. We have usual words with such strong Jewish connotations that they cannot be properly translated, like *tsuris, Yiddishe hutzpeh, shtik, khokhme, Yiddishe khokhem* or even *mensh.*[5] We also have insults: *mishugeh, ganif*, and exclamations like *mazel tov, rakhmones, gevalt.*[6] Each time the evil has to be waved off, we have people *tfou tfouing* around[7] ... There are some echo-combinations: *values-shmalues, voices-shmoices, happy-shmappy.*[8]

Born in Eastern Europe, but becoming transnational because of its speakers' migrations, the Yiddish language survives mostly by means of isolated expressions. The single Yiddish word found imbedded in another language discourse, is acquiring the function of a recognition mark for a dispersed collectivity. It is a linguistic *yellow Jewish star* creating a situation of connivance between the members of the same diaspora, and excluding all the noninitiated at the same time.

Still, unlike what happens with other languages, the acquisition of which is ever possible and is ever an enrichment, Yiddish is, for the non-Jew, a trap and an alienating activity. Why is that so? When seen from the outside, Yiddish is no more than the spoken language, the jargon of a minority. It is a language you learn at home through everyday life. One should not forget that being a Jew is a way of dying as well as a way of living. You do not learn Yiddish at the Berlitz school, but at Treblinka,[9] and when you speak it, it does not mean you have acquired some new kind of knowledge; it means that by speaking Yiddish, by using this basically familiar language, you are part of the intimacy[10] of the Jewish people, and you take part in this essential complicity, Jewish Destiny. Humor develops to its best in this climate of connivance and familiarity.[11]

Besides, Yiddish itself has a humoristic value, for it is, as pointed out by Genghis Cohn himself, no less than the caricature of Goethe's language,[12] especially in Jewish names such as Jasza Gesundheit, Tsatsa Sardinenfish, Zigelbaum, Schwanz, Gedanke and Gutgemacht ...

Up to this point, I have spoken of *direct* manifestations of Yiddish; there is also a form of *allusive* presence in the English or French adaptation or parody of Yiddish clichés. These are of three sorts, all used as refrains in a repetitive technique. The first structure is based on the model "It's anti-Semitism, that's what it is!"[13] The second one, "A thing like that, I wouldn't wish it on my best friend," as in, for instance, "Resurrection, I wouldn't wish that on my best friend . . ."; "A business like that, I wouldn't wish it on my best friend."[15] The third kind of repetition includes proverbs or quotations presented by the structure: "As we say in Yiddish . . ." ' "As we say in Yiddish, it's no more love, it's pure hate." Or "As we say in Yiddish, mea culpa."[16] — and "As a Yiddish poet wrote . . ."

These cases of mechanical repetitions account for elementary mechanisms of humor. But the fact that they are linked to Yiddish gives them a special dimension of complicity and intimacy.

Let me go back to the last example: "As a Yiddish poet wrote . . ." Here is the complete quotation. Genghis Cohn tells how he was sitting under an oak, listening, "as a Yiddish poet wrote, to the 'sobbing of the violins of autumn', autumn 1943 to be precise."[17] The French reader has immediately identified the last century French poet, Paul Verlaine. The "Yiddishization" of respectable, well-known and established values of western civilization leads to the immediate devaluation of these values. What remains of Verlaine's poetry, of the so light and sweetly French "les sanglots longs des violons de l'automne" in the middle of autumn 1943 and the Nazi Apocalypse? This cultural "annexation," as one more manifestation of international Jewish complicity, is nothing less than the specific *Yiddishe hutzpeh* of the Jewish humorist. Now that the public has been prepared, the artist can begin his show, step forward on the stage and play with words and ideas.

2. Play of Words and Ideas

Generally speaking, the play of words proceeds from the substitution of one word for another. It is a "quid pro quo," one word hiding another, in the way the basic plot of the novel could be described as "one man hiding another." When *Hauptjudenfresser* Schatz opens his mouth, you never know if he, or maybe his Dybbuk Cohn, will speak.

The humoristic substitutions are of three sorts:
— one word appears instead of another, because of partial semantic analogy,
— synonyms,
— one word, is substituted for another, because of partial phonetic analogy,
— homonyms,
— the same word can be understood in two different ways — polysemy.

Arthur Koestler has coined the word "bisociation"[18] to define the association of two mutually incompatible associative contexts, or, in other

words, the association of contexts both unexpected and perfectly logical —
that is, of a logic not usually applied to the situation first announced, as in
the following examples:

a. *Cases of synonymy:* There is the grim bisociation Berlitz/Treblinka as
schools of Yiddish, and there is the similarity of victim status of both the Jew
of Smigla Street and the Man of Nazareth. "Which Cohn was that? Well, you
know, it's always the same one." The play of words comes like a history
course: Jesus is the Jewish scapegoat "par excellence". He is "the Mensh"[19] as
Genghis puts it in Yiddish.

b. *Cases of polysemy:* Having lived through two thousands years of
meaningless persecutions and strong feelings of culpability, Cohn exclaims:
"It has all been for nothing?" Traditionally, the Jew is full of cupidity, thus
money has to be a genuine obsession for him: "All for nothing, for nothing.
You only think about doing a little business," is Florian's answer. Innocent
words are, by means of history, charged with new irremediable connotations.
That is exactly what happened with the *soap.* Since Auschwitz, Schatz has
never touched a bar of soap. "You never know who's in it!"[20] he explains.
And Genghis comments: "How should I know! It was mass production, they
made soap wholesale, nobody marked Jasza Gesundheit or Tsatsa
Sardinenfish on it." Grammatical confusion — *who's* in instead of *what's* in
— develops into a confusion between species, this one quite similar to the
SS's habit of calling a man dog and a dog man. Nazis have proved that words
cannot be trusted anymore. If you eliminate the difference between proper
and figurative meaning of words, you get this *khokhme* from a German
executioner: "This is a de luxe cake of soap, because it is made with the
chosen people."[21] Words can kill sometimes. And there is a contamination of
perversion from language to ideas and behavior. It is not irrelevant to notice
that soap may also be a good means for a definition of *culture.* This occurs
when Genghis establishes a comparison between the Simbas of Congo, who
were savages, and the Germans. "The Germans had Schiller, Goethe,
Hölderlin, and the Simbas of the Congo had nothing. The difference between
the Germans, heirs to an immense culture, and the savage Simbas, is that the
Simbas ate their victims, whereas the Germans turned theirs into soap. This
need for cleanliness, that is culture."[22]

c. *Cases of homonymy:* This is the pun's field of predilection, the first being
found in the title, in which we have a bisociation of Genghis Khan the
Barbarian to Cohn the Jew, traditional symbol of weakness. The synthetic
formula expresses both revolt and its own impossibility; in other words, the
basic situation of the Jew in front of his persecutors. How could this one who

103

is going to be shot, transform his passivity into aggressiveness?

When he lies naked in the common grave, facing both his executioners and posterity, Genghis Cohn has one single weapon left, obscenity, the obscene gesture: "to show his ass"[23] — or *tokhes* —, and the obscene word *"kush mir in ...."*

The insulting exclamation is a kind of variation for the cry, and brings us back to Genghis's definition of Jewish humor: "It's a way of yelling." Still, what follows in the text must be read also. Kafka is mentioned but not taken seriously with his "powers of cries (... that will shatter) the rigors decreed against man." The cry is immediately followed by its own negation. Genghis winks at Florian and they both laugh. Jewish humor is exactly that *simultaneous* expression of contraries, cry and laugh at the same time, or speaking like Genghis, who gives another definition, this time with a pun, Jewish humor is "une sorte d'agression à main désarmée" — "a kind of unarmed aggression."[24]

3. A Kind of Unarmed Aggression: Jewish Humor and Jewish Stories

Let me go back to the first Jewish story. There is something of a blasphemy in this joke which implies that we forget, or at least minimize, a scandalous premise: the collective rape. The indecent submission of the husband, which is a kind of self-mutilation, may be interpreted as a form of masochism. But it means that we understand nothing of what Jewish humor is. Suffering gives the Jew no pleasure whatsoever.[25] He simulates adhesion to his executioner's point of view, by the use of *gallows-humor*.[26] With this kind of black humor, you pretend being deceived by appearances, in order to deny the horror of what things really are — and you deny it "by words alone."[27]

When you know that rebellion is useless, you pretend to give up. In this way you deprive your persecutor of the pleasure of mocking at you and of continuing to torture you. Apparent self-disparagement and self-aggression are actually forms of self-defence. The opponent will not escape from it without damage. Criticizing the officer for not behaving as a gentleman, is, by understatement, a way of scoffing at the European way of life and at European morals; it is a way of hunting down false values.

Take Buchenwald as evoked by two members of the German "elite": "Did you see the pictures of all these bodies one on top of another at Buchenwald? What pornography! It was so lacking in decency! People shouldn't be allowed to take pictures of things like that, and even less to allow them to be published. All those naked bodies, they shouldn't have been allowed to exhibit them. It was an invasion of privacy, my dear. [...] These indecent

104

pictures have caused more damage than the actual action. The executions were certainly a crime against the Jews, but publishing these photographs is no less than a crime against humanity."[28]

In 1967, when the novel was published, talking freely about sex was still considered a provocation. In order to prevent the survivors of Auschwitz from marching blindly towards the hydrogen bomb, in order to shake their conscience, Gary thought that they should be given a picture of humanity caught in the system of violence, as a nymphomaniac victim of an innocent dream.[29] That is what a figurative interpretation of the novel proposes to us. So, the last meeting of Lily with Genghis, which was kindly "sponsored" by Hitler, is described by Florian, as "six millions ago, not including the soap . . ."[30]

In the same way, we should try to understand what Treblinka really was. Genghis comes to our help: "Anyway, everyone knows that the Jews weren't assassinated. They died voluntarily . . . I recently discovered some reassuring evidence about that in the book of a certain Jean-François Steiner Treblinka: 'We stood obligingly in line, in front of the gas chambers, we never resisted extermination. There were but a few rebels, here and there, particularly in the Warsaw Ghetto, but as a whole, there was an eager, obedient will to disappear . . .' Collective suicide, that's what it was . . . You see, Jews wanted to die, while making some profit on the side. How? I'll tell you how. We didn't commit suicide with our own hands, as the insurance company wouldn't pay up, and our survivors couldn't have recovered any damages. So . . . [. . .] Somewhere there must be an author willing to unveil our diabolical maneuver, and describe how we transformed the Nazis into a blind and obedient tool in our hands."[31]

By using the well-known caricature of the Jew as a greedy Judas, endowed with supernatural powers, and by unfolding the reasoning up to its final conclusion, the writer leads us towards the distortion that is integral to the absurdity of black humor.[32]

This is where we have arrived with the first Jewish joke. Let us go to the next part — that is, the second joke. Cohn is taking his revenge. How? The child born after the rape is Jewish. For Florian, the non-Jew, the outsider, it is a dreadful punishment to cast the destiny of the Jews upon an innocent baby.

But let us step into Cohn's shoes: it is an extraordinary message of hope and love the Jewish father gives his bastard whom he adopts as a legitimate child. The revenge of the Jew as an action implies a nonspoken reply to his executioner which could be as follows: "You didn't care for *me* as a Jew. Now I deny *your* existence as a Goy. I'm your equal. Moreover, I leave you far behind me, for unlike you, I don't destroy. I build, even though I have to cohabit with horror, in order to realize that creation."

It is certainly not by chance that one of the recurrent images of the novel is precisely a certain snapshot of an old Hasidic Jew being dragged by his beard by a German, and his fellow soldiers laughing at him, while he, the old Jew, is *laughing too.*[33]

The Jew's laughter is turned towards posterity; that is his way of challenging his executioners. When Gary evokes this scene for the last time he points out that: "The smile is immortal and the shame is such that we must be approaching *eternity.* "[34] This laughter is also a challenge to Him who did not show up, He who chose to be silent in Auschwitz, through absence or impotence,[35] "unless," as Genghis would say, "you consider this world to be a creation, an insult which would not even spring to the mind of an atheist."[36]

This laughter bursting out, at the moment man almost touches what may be *nothingness* or *infinite,* this laughter of *unarmed aggression* is more than the blasphemous laughter of black humor. It is this superior form of Jewish humor we have, when *Comic* and *Cosmic,* usually opposite notions, come together in an ultimate bisociation called "humour blanc" — white humor, by the French novelist, Michel Tournier.[37] Our novel illustrating this "humour blanc" ends with the vision of Genghis Cohn, the *Wandering Comic Jew* marching along his Via Dolorosa: "He is bent double under the weight, but He can still perform, as long as there is an *audience,* and He obstinately follows His beloved, dragging His heavy cross on His back."[38]

Here I cannot help myself evoking Romain Gary the man, who often spoke of himself as "a sort of Genghis Cohn." Between 1973 and 1980, while writing as Romain Gary, he published four novels under the name of Emile Ajar. He never recognized that he was Emile Ajar, and when it became necessary for Ajar to show up, one of Gary's relatives, Paul Pavlowitch, played the part. Only six months after Gary committed suicide the whole truth was revealed in a little posthumous book. I wonder if this Gary-Ajar relationship was not a good *dybbuk* story too, and as a conclusion, I shall leave the last words to Gary, those last words of his testament, which are in a very "genghiscohnish" way of speaking:[39]

Je me suis bien amusé, au revoir et merci.
I had a lot of fun, good bye and thank you very much.

NOTES

1. The novel was "translated from the French by Romain Gary with the assistance of Camilla Sykes." A comparative reading of the two books shows quite a number of alterations. The English text is shorter (40 chapters for 44 in the French) and sometimes simplified — what remains allusive in the French novel is explained in the translation. I preferred working with the original novel, quoting the English where possible, translating by myself where necesary.

2. *The Dance of Genghis Cohn,* New American Library, New York, 1968, Part two: "In the Forest of Geist", chapter 23: "Death has a flat", pp. 141–142.

    La Danse de Gengis Cohn, Paris, Gallimard, 1967, Deuxième partie: "Dans la forêt de Geist", chapitre XXVII, "La Mort en panne", pp. 166–167.

3. *G.C.,* p. 9, p. 53.

4. "There's something going on here that isn't very *kosher.*" *G.C.,* p. 73.

5. *tsuris, G.C.,* pp. 20, 243; *Yiddishe hutzpeh,* p. 211; *shtik,* p. 198; *khokhmé,* p. 85; *Yiddishe Khokhem,* p. 215; *mensh,* pp. 215, 236, 242.

6. *mishugeh, G.C.,* p. 211; *ganif,* p. 240; *mazel tov,* p. 140; *rakhmones, gvalt,* p. 213.

7. *G.C.,* pp. 65, 98, 209, and especially 241: "The Jews are the only ones who have ever turned into soap, this is History, man! The greatest *shtik* of all our repertoire . . ." "*Tfou, tfou, tfou.* A *shtik* like that..."

8. *G.C.,* p. 64 and 235; 89; 243.

9. See the play of words in the excerpt.

10. Theodor Reik, *Jewish Wit,* Gamut Press, New York, 1962, "The Intimacy in Jewish Wit", p. 188.

11. Reik, *op. cit.,* p. 190.

12. The English text has jumped on the sentence: "Il faut bien connaître l'allemand pour comprendre avec quel art de la drôlerie le jargon yiddish caricaturait la langue de Goethe." French text, p. 176.

13. Here is a conversation between Schatz and Cohn: "The public is saturated. They had enough of the Jewish *shtik.* Things're happening, you know. They want the Negro *shtik* and the Vietnam *shtik.* You can't keep six millions Jews on the best-seller list for ever . . ." — "what kind of talk is this? Anti-Semitism. That's what it is!" *G.C.,* p. 235.

14. *G.C.,* p. 124.

15. *G.C.,* p. 213: "We are all brothers!" "*Gevalt!* Enough of your atrocities!" He opens his arms: "Cohn, come along with us! It won't cost you anything, it's always the others who pay! You'll be doing good business!" — "A business like that, I wouldn't wish it on . . ."

16. *G.C.,* pp. 144 and 56.

17. *G.C.,* p. 108. This verse was the message to be broadcast by the B.B.C. to announce to the French Resistance the arrival of the Allied troops. It was first to take place in autumn 1943!

18. Arthur Koestler, *The Act of Creation, a study of the conscious and the unconscious in science and art,* Dell, New York, 1964, "The Logic of Laughter", p. 35.

19. *G.C.,* p. 217.

20. *G.C.,* p. 84.

21. *G.C.,* p. 85.

22. *G.C.,* p. 59. Cohn's friend, Sioma Kapelusznik, on the edge of the grave, gives his own description of culture, in a Witz also: "Culture is when mothers who are holding their babies in their arms are excused from digging their own graves before being shot."

23. *G.C.,* p. 59.

24. *G.C.,* p. 174.

25. Theodor Reik, studying "The Aspect of Self-Degradation" criticizes Martin Grotjahn's masochistic theory: "Self-degradation and self-humiliation are perhaps a measure of defence protecting (the Jew) against greater danger, a kind of sacrifice in order to survive (. . .) That implied conviction and hope is one of the many things the Jews have in common with the teaching of that Rabbi from Nazareth later called the Savior." (*op. cit.,* p. 222). Reik's conclusion is what he calls the "pseudo-masochistic character" of Jewish humor.

26. See Michel Borwicz, *Ecrits des condamnés à mort sous l'Occupation,* Paris, Gallimard, Idées, 1973, pp. 265–272, and William Novak, Moshe Waldoks, *The Big Book of Jewish Humor,* Harper and Row, New York, 1981, p. 74: "Gary's work is in the tradition of Galgenhumor (gallows humor), which has been a part of the Jewish response to anti-Semitism for centuries."

27. Title of the book on "the Holocaust in Literature" by Sidra Ezrahi, University of Chicago Press, 1980.

28. This entire passage has been omitted in the English text. It takes place in the French novel, in chapter XVII, "On nous l'avait caché", pp. 104–105.

29. See Romain Gary, *Pour Sganarelle. Recherche d'un personnage et d'un roman,* Paris, Gallimard, 1965, p. 431: "Je vais traiter de la bombe à hydrogène par la biais de la pornographie sexuelle, parce que cette époque très éclairée continue à faire de la pornographie une notion exclusivement confinée dans le domaine de la sexualité."

30. *G.C.,* p. 135.

31. *G.C.,* p. 83.

32. One can find the same distortion in the trap brotherhood sets to the Jews: There is a way of suppressing the Jew morally and spiritually "by fraternizing (him), and thus forcing (him) to shoulder the collective responsibility of the species, which would have, among other grisly consequences, that of making (him) responsible for (their) own extermination." *G.C.,* p. 209.

33. *G.C.,* pp. 37, 171, 197, 198.

34. *G.C.,* p. 240.

35. *G.C.,* p. 118.

36. *G.C.,* p. 125.

37. Michel Tournier, *Le vent Paraclet,* Paris, Gallimard, Folio, 1977, p. 201. See also Charlotte Wardi, "Le génocide des Juifs dans la fiction romanesque française: 1945–1970. Une expression originale: "La Danse de Gengis Cohn" de Gary", Paris, *Digraphe* 25, printemps 81.

38. *G.C.,* p. 244.

39. Romain Gary, *Vie et mort d'Emile Ajar,* Paris, Gallimard, 1981, p. 43.

E. Fuchs

HUMOR AND SEXISM: THE CASE OF THE JEWISH JOKE

ESTHER FUCHS
Texas University, U.S.A.

HUMOR AND SEXISM
The Case of the Jewish Joke

In current humor scholarship the term "sexual joke" usually designates what is known as the "dirty" or "obscene" joke, the joke that pokes fun at human sexuality. Studies from Freud (1960) to Legman (1975) fail to distinguish between jokes ridiculing members of a particular sex — notably the female sex — which I will henceforth designate as sexist jokes, and jokes referring to human genitalia and sexual behavior. Drawing on feminist theory and criticism I would like to suggest in this paper that sexual humor is not inspired by male *sexual* aggressiveness, as is commonly believed, but rather by *political* aggressiveness, namely by the ideology of masculist sexism.[1] In the first part of the paper I focus on the sexism of the innocent joke, in the second part I deal with the dirty joke, particularly with its major scholarly treatments. My case study in the first part of the paper is the Jewish joke. The examination of the sexist Jewish joke will enable me to draw analogies between the sexist and racist joke, specifically between misogynist and anti-Semitic humor on the one hand, and Jewish and feminist responses to such jokes on the other.

It is commonly believed that the jokes I will consider later are inspired by censor evasion. Yet, as we shall soon see, the jokes which are commonly anthologized as "family *tsores*" or "marital *mishmash*" attack the bride, the wife, the mother-in-law and the mother, while the assailants are the groom, the husband and the male joke teller. It is the preponderance of women as the butts of marriage and family jokes that requires a reexamination of the assumption that all these jokes are inspired by a revolutionary anti-conventional and anti-institutional vision.[2] Since it is impossible to survey within the confines of the present study all the categories of the sexist Jewish joke, I will focus in what follows on three of the most popular and pervasive ones: the Jewish-European bride joke, the Jewish wife joke and the Jewish-American mother joke.

> *Bornstein the Shadchan introduced his client Yonkel to the prospective bride. Yonkel was disappointed. "What are you doing," he said to Bornstein, "making a fool out of me? Look at her! She is ugly and she's old. She squints. Look at those false teeth." "Why are you whispering?" said the matchmaker. "She is deaf too"* (Wilde, p. 46).

111

The motif of the mismatch is perfect material for a joke because of the numerous possibilities it offers for the creation of incongruities. The prospective groom who resorts to the *shadchan* is obviously interested in a bride who will match his expectations. Usually, these expectations are in line with standard western masculist preferences, namely that the bride be physically attractive. Since the implicit androcentric expectations rarely pertain to the bride's mental, creative, or intellectual capabilities, the *shadchan* joke is not likely to frustrate the listener's expectations by presenting a stupid or illiterate bride. The disappointing features we are most likely to encounter in such jokes are related to the bride's physique and physiognomy. The variations in the bride's deficiencies are numerous, ranging from limping to venereal disease. In response to the client's inevitable complaint, the *shadchan* either tries to minimize what is obviously an unforgivable defect or, as in the joke here, inadvertently makes his client privy to yet another defect in the prospective bride.* It is clear for example, that the above joke pokes fun at the naïve and trusting prospective groom for choosing an inept matchmaker. *Shadchan* jokes often ridicule the *shadchan* himself whose profession is to find appropriate matches, but who invariably finds the wrong one. Nevertheless, the bride is the only one who is derided for incorrigible defaults, usually related to her physical appearance. Since the bride is implicitly defined as a prized object, what most *shadchan* jokes consist of is the frustration of this expectation.

Very few *shadchan* jokes poke fun at an ugly or impotent groom. Both the expectation and the frustration are defined from a masculist point of view. The following joke further exemplifies this tendency:

> *The would-be bridegroom complained that the bride had one leg shorter than the other and limped. The Shadchan contradicted him: You're wrong. Suppose you marry a woman with healthy, straight limbs! What do you gain from it? You never have a day's security that she won't fall down, break a leg and afterwards be lame all her life. And think of all the suffering then, the agitation and the doctor's bill! But if you take this one, that can't happen to you. Here you have a fait accompli* (Freud, pp. 62–63).

A gender reversal may detract from the effectiveness of the joke, among other reasons, because jokes thrive on conventional thinking, and according to nineteenth century Jewish European social convention it is inappropriate and therefore unlikely that a woman should use a broker to find a man to her liking. Underlying the social convention which permits only grooms to take the initiative for finding a marriage partner is the premise that the bride is an

---

*   I am not arguing that all *Shadchan* jokes disparage *only* the bride.

object to be chosen by a groom, and not vice versa. The sexist definition of groom as subject and bride as object which underlies the above joke is what makes the set up familiar and therefore convincing. In Jewish jokes, a bride is not likely to complain about her groom's appearance or defective masculinity, because in the dominant androcentric culture what matters in a marital transaction is the *woman*'s physical appeal. This does not mean that the bride is the only victim in the joke, but as we shall soon see she is victimized more virulently than the male parties involved. For, while the *shadchan* may be ridiculed for his illogical rhetoric, the joke implies that his apparently illogical thinking hides a shrewd sense for business. After all, what matters for him is not the groom's satisfaction, but the fee he receives for the transaction. What the *shadchan* discloses despite himself, however, is that the whole deal is not worth much; even a healthy and good-looking bride is, in the final analysis, a source of trouble. The butt of the joke may very well be the groom, not for his choice of an incompetent broker, but for his desire to marry a woman, for marrying a woman is a no win situation whichever way man may look at it.

It would be inaccurate to confer ideological respectability on this kind of joke by ascribing to it a revolutionary insight into the drab nature of social institutions, as Freud does in *Jokes and their Relation to the Unconscious* (1906: 30). The fact is that the *shadchan* joke does not question but reinforce conventional thinking. We laugh not only because the joke contains an element of surprise, but because it presents us with familiar scenarios, scenarios which are familiar not because they reflect authentic personal experience, but because they draw on shared cultural stereotypes. The ugly bride is funny because in a patriarchal culture brides are expected to be beautiful, because women are perceived and defined primarily as sex objects.

Thus, although the *shadchan* and the groom are ridiculed too, each in his own way, theirs are corrigible flaws. The *shadchan* is in all probability aware of the flawed logic of his argument, and the groom has hope, for if he has any sense at all he will relinquish the idea of marrying a woman altogether. The bride, however, is the only truly incorrigible victim. The invalid bride is the only one who is radically caricatured, her physique distorted in a grotesque fashion. The joke that reduces a woman to the sum total of her limbs reflects a sexist sense of humor, just as a joke reducing a male Jew to the size of his penis and the shape of his nose reflects an anti-Semitic sense of humor.

In the following joke, it is the *male* Jew who is caricatured in an irremediable fashion:

> *"What happens when a Jew with an erection walks into a wall?*
> *He breaks his nose"* (Knott, p. 20).

Unlike the innocent Jewish *shadchan* joke, this anti-Semitic joke is a dirty joke, as it caricatures not only physiognomical parts but genital organs too. Yet by caricaturing the physique of their butts, both jokes imply that their butts are incorrigible. Both jokes use physical distortions as a means of attacking their victims. The *shadchan* joke caricatures the Jewish woman by reversing the stereotype of the beautiful bride, the anti-Semitic joke caricatures the male Jew by manipulating the conventional stereotypes of the male Jew's long nose and small penis. This analogy enables us to notice the similarities between racist and sexist jokes. It also points up the areas where the Jewish joke is most likely to strike: it will strike at physical defects in a female Jew but rarely will it make reference to physical defects in a male Jew, particularly where the Jewish nose or the Jewish sex organ is concerned. By contrast, the anti-Semitic joke, both the innocent and dirty variety, normally attacks the *male* Jew.

While European *shadchan* jokes thrive on caricaturing the bride, contemporary jokes tend to caricature the wife. In wife jokes the wife is mostly ridiculed for her disappointing character traits. Foremost among them are her frigidity, stupidity, and greed. In most jokes the husband emerges victorious. The following joke confers victory on the husband by allowing him to deliver the defeating and definitive punch-line:

> *For their twentieth wedding anniversary, Shimsky bought his wife a family plot at the Hillside Memorial Park. As their twenty-first anniversary approached, Mrs. Shimsky asked, "What are you going to give this year for our anniversary?" "Nothing," he replied. "You still didn't use what I gave you last year"* (Wilde, p. 51).

The incongruity between the wife's expectations for a gift on her marriage anniversary and the husband's response which intimates that he is disappointed at her failure to drop dead is only one set of incongruities this joke manipulates. Another one is the incongruity between the conventional act of bestowing a gift, and the real hostility implied in the husband's hope for his wife's death. The joke bestows victory on the husband not only by giving him the punchline, but also by intimating that he is justified in his wish to rid himself of his spouse. For one thing, his wife is stupid. She did not catch the hint from Shimsky's first anniversary gift, accepting it as a real gift rather than as an offensive hint. Not only is the wife stupid, she is also greedy, selfish, and a nag. Who could blame Mr. Shimsky for buying her a burial plot?

Like the *shadchan* joke, this joke too cannot simply be categorized as an antimarriage joke. What is ridiculed is not the institution of marriage *per se* but the woman involved. Under attack is the stereotypical Jewish middle class wife, whose idleness, greediness, and selfishness justify her husband's

114

wish to see her dead and buried. Along the lines of the anti-Semitic joke, "a good Jew is a dead Jew," the implication of the sexist joke can be summarized as "a good wife is a dead wife". Jewish JAP (Jewish American Princess) and wife jokes often use stereotypes which anti-Semitic jokes traditionally attribute to Jewish men. Foremost among these stereotypes is the victim's unbridled greed. In the anti-Semitic joke it is the male Jew who is often ridiculed for his all consuming passion for money. For example "What's the definition of a queer Jew? Someone who likes girls more than money" (Knott, p. 20). Here it is the Jewish male who is being ridiculed for his lust for money, which normally overrides, it is implied, his sexual lust. In Jewish jokes, however, it is more often the Jewish wife or the JAP who is ridiculed for her lust for money as in the following example: "My wife divorced me for religious reasons. She worshipped money and I didn't have any" (Novak and Waldoks, p. 257).

This is not to say that Jewish jokes do not ridicule Jewish males. The opposite is in fact the case. The Jewish joke has become famous for its disparagement of Jews in general, including male Jews — a tendency criticized as masochism or eulogized as healthy self-criticism. But in my view what distinguishes the Jewish self-disparaging joke from the anti-Semitic joke is the former's tendency to avoid the anti-Semitic stereotypes of long noses, small penises and insatiable greed. Jewish jokes will take a bold self-critical attitude in matters pertaining to Jewish religion, Jewish history, specific Jewish professions, Jewish paranoia, xenophobia and even anti-Semitism (Reik, 1962), but it is rare to find authentic Jewish jokes jibing at Jewish stereotypes as defined by anti-Semitic humor. On the other hand, we are likely to find in Jewish jokes a transference of anti-Semitic stereotypes to female Jews, notably to wives.

But JAPS and wives are not the only female models ridiculed in current Jewish jokes. Superseding them in popularity in Jeewish-American humor is the omnipresent *Yiddishe Mamma*. If in previous generations, notably in the Jewish European context, it was the mother-in-law who was ridiculed for her Gershom parochialism and pettiness, currently it is the Jewish mother herself. Legman points out that Jewish humor outdoes any other ethnic humor in what he calls "the defiling of the mother" (1975: 392). Drawing on the Freudian theory of censor-evasion, Legman explains that the phenomenon is related to the formal respect Jews have traditionally been enjoined to show their mothers, something analogous to the institution of the Virgin Mary in Catholicism. I would like to suggest that the surge in antimother jokes might also be related to the increasing influence and popular appeal Freudian psychology has enjoyed especially since the end of World War II in the United States. Freudian theories concerning the mother's allegedly irreversible impact on her child's development continue to enjoy wide popularity. The

115

following joke exemplifies the dreaded influence of Jewish mothers on their vulnerable defenseless sons:

> *One summer day, Mrs. Saperstein took her little boy Alan to Jones Beach. As soon as she settled under a beach umbrella she cried out to her son: "Alan, Alan, come here! Don't run into the water. You'll get drowned! Alan, don't play with the sand. You'll get it in your eyes! Alan, Alan don't stand in the sun. You'll get sunstroke! Oy Vey! Such a nervous child"* (Novak and Waldoks, p. 30).

The overprotective mother, it is implied, is the source of her child's neurosis. By projecting her phobias onto her son, she manages not only to restrict his freedom and enjoyment of life, but also to inculcate into him her own fears of nature and good times. Once this maternal duty is successfully accomplished, she manages to develop in her son an awareness of his own inadequacy as the nervous child that she herself turned him into. It would be inaccurate to define such jokes as parental jokes because they rarely address a father-daughter or a father-son relationship. The critic in these jokes is the child — frequently, the son — and the butt of the joke is the mother. What Jewish jokes about mothers point up is that the mother's overprotectiveness not only derives from her own insecurities but it also ends up victimizing her child.

The following joke is based on an exaggeration *ad absurdum* of the popular stereotype of the ever nourishing over nourishing mother:

> *A Jewish gangster was dining at a kosher restaurant on New York's lower East Side when members of the mob came in and pumped him full of lead. He crawled out of the restaurant and stumbled up Rivingson Street to the tenement of his childhood. With hands clutching his bleeding stomach, he crawled up three flights of stairs and banged on the door of his mother's flat. He began sobbing "Mama! Mama!" His mother opened the door and discovered her only son lying in a puddle of blood. Again he wailed, "Mama! Oh, Mama!" The old woman looked down at him and said: "Bubeleh, come in and eat — you'll talk later!"* (Wilde, p. 42).

The joke offers an exaggerated variation on the character of the *Yiddishe Mamma,* who is exclusively and eternally preoccupied with her son's appetite while ignoring his other more vital needs. To be sure, the joke jibes not only at the mother, but at the son as well, at the stereotype of the Jewish Mamma's good boy, who abandons at the moment of truth all external trappings of tough virility, only to crawl back whining to his mother. On

116

another level, however, the joke intimates that a Jewish man will never be able to be a "real" gangster; namely a tough independent and genuinely virile man, just because of his fatal dependence on his mother's nurturance. The reference to food, at the beginning of the set up ("A Jewish gangster was dining at a kosher restaurant"), and at the punchline ("Bubeleh, come in and eat"), may imply that it is the obsessive concern of the mother with her son's appetite that has brought about his death. Unlike other jokes of the same genre, the mother is not shown to gorge her son to death, but indirectly the joke implies that were it not for the upbringing of the *Yiddishe Mamma,* her son may have been more cautious and effective as a gangster, and that rather than dining nonchalantly at a kosher restaurant or crawling back to his mother's home, he could have acted in a manner more congruent with our expectations of a real gangster. What is more obviously funny however, is the mother's inability to notice the pool of blood around her son's body and her continued preoccupation with food. Using Bergson's theory of laughter, we may conclude that what makes the mother ridiculous is her mechanical response to the needs of her dying son. The drastic circumstances which require an appropriate adaptation of behavior and attitude do not make a dent in the mother's nurturant behavior. The implication is that behind the mother's nurturance is neither love nor understanding, but mechanical reflexes and biological instincts.

I would like to suggest that the *Yiddishe Mamma* jokes reveal not only an impulse to defile the mother as a gesture of rebellion against a hallowed institution, as Legman suggests (1975: 392), and not only a backlash at the all devouring omnipresent Freudian Mother. The *Yiddishe Mamma* constitutes yet another aspect of the female butt in the Jewish sexist joke. Whether she appears as bride or mother-in-law, as wife or single JAP, as prostitute or as mother, it is *she* who is the butt of the joke and it is relentlessly and ubiquitously an androcentric joke which finds her ridiculous.

I would like to stress that the jokes I have used to exemplify the sexist bias in the Jewish jokes are not classifiable as "dirty" jokes. In comparison to the jokes quoted in Gershon Legman's two volume study of the dirty joke, the jokes I have drawn on are not only innocent, but humanitarian and benevolent. Yet it seems to me that it is precisely this benign sexism of the Jewish joke that can shed light on the more virulently sexist bias of what I defined earlier as the dirty joke, which pokes fun at human sexuality. Acknowledging the sexism underlying both Jewish and non-Jewish, innocent as well as dirty jokes, I intend to reframe the phenomenon of the so called sexual joke in a way that will make its motivation more understandable, though admittedly, to some listeners at least, not as funny.

In the following brief survey of humor scholarship on the so called dirty joke we notice a kind of evasiveness; an admission and a disclaimer, a

117

hemming and hawing about the motivations and possible functions of the dirty joke. According to Freud, the motivation of the teller of the dirty joke is sexual: "Smut is like an exposure of the sexually different person to whom it is directed. By the utterance of the obscene words, it compels the person who is assailed to imagine the part of the body or the procedure in question and shows her that the assailant is himself imagining it. It cannot be doubted that the desire to see what is sexual exposed is the original motive of smut" (p. 98). Although Freud uses in his description of the allegedly seductive denudation of the female listener terms such as "assail" and "assailant" which would better fit a political or martial context rather than a sexual one, he still insists that the obscene joke constitutes an autonomous category distinct from what he calls the "aggressive joke" and the "cynical joke" (p. 115). The purpose of the dirty joke is, according to Freud, a seductive procedure which is supposed to turn the female listener on. Freud's interpretation of the sexist joke as sexy precludes the possibility that the real motive behind the dirty joke told by a man to a woman in a private setting is political rather than sexual. In my opinion, the dirty joke is identical to the aggressive joke whose intent is to degrade and assault the fictional victim of the joke as well as the listener. The proclivity of the dirty joke to disparage female anatomy and to reduce woman to the sum total of her genitalia is a power-related process, intended among other things to imply that the teller of the joke is superior to the fictional butt of the joke, *and* to the female listener. The joke teller implies that the woman listener must submit to his will and his desire, for after all she is nothing more than a vagina or a prostitute (Legman, 1975). The fact that dirty jokes are normally told in Western white society by men in all male groups supports this theory even further, for it is clear that in an all male group there is no attempt to seduce a female listener. Rather, the antifemale dirty jokes help solidify male bonding by attacking and demeaning the female Other.[3] When a female listener is included in the group, the purpose is not so much to seduce her as to subject her to a test. If she reacts with hostility, she fails because she demonstrates a lack of a sense of humor; if she finds the dirty joke funny she implies that she disowns her links with her female sex group and that she is worthy of the men's trust. Either way, she is doomed, and either way she must renounce her female identity as a source of pride.

In his monumental study of the dirty joke, Gershon Legman notes: "One fact strikingly evident in any collection of modern sexual folklore, whether jokes, limericks, ballads, printed 'novelties', or what not, is that this material has all been created by men, and that there is no place in it for women except as the butt. It is not just that so preponderant an amount of the material is grossly anti-woman in tendency and intent, but also that the situations presented almost completely lack any protagonist position in which a woman can identify herself — *as a woman* — with any human gratification or pride. (1968:217; italicized in the original).[4] What is astonishing is that despite his recognition of the misogynist nature of so many dirty jokes, Legman endorses Freud's interpretation of the dirty joke as a verbal seduction: "It cannot of course be overlooked that the telling of sexual jokes *to* women by men is certainly and inevitably a preliminary sexual relation, and represents a definite sexual aproach, just as listening to (or telling) such jokes by women implies a readiness for or acceptance of such an approach" (1968:218; italicized in the original). Despite the unquestionable evidence of sexist hostility in most dirty jokes, Legman does not relinquish the notion that this hostility is an expression of sexual appetite.[5] Nevertheless, he admits that he is annoyed and "turned off" by dirty jokes told by women: "More than once, however, I have had hostile and reclamatory bitches of the classic penis-envy type tell me such stories [dirty jokes]... with the obvious intention of turning off or parrying my expected sexual approach" (Legman 1975:35). While women who tell men dirty jokes are according to Legman "bitches of the classic penis-envy type," men who tell women dirty jokes are normal men of the healthy virile type. Although he interprets a woman's dirty joke as a "turn off" signal he maintains that a man's dirty joke is a seductive "turn on," intended to titillate the female listener. Legman appears to be particularly annoyed by women who refuse to play the traditional female role and who instead of blushing, or applauding the wit of the male performer, demonstrate that they are neither shocked nor tickled. He is particularly revolted by women who rebuff the sexist dirty joke by telling dirty jokes themselves. This rebuttal on the part of the subjugated sex constitutes according to Legman an expression of penis-envy and self-hatred. "By telling dirty jokes," he argues, woman "is effectively denying her own sex as a woman" (Legman, 1975:35).

Although it may not be the best response, it seems to me that women telling dirty jokes protest against the submissive role assigned to them by a patriarchal society. These women are doing something analogous to what Jews have done with anti-Semitic jokes. By using the same weapon, the weapon intended to humiliate them, women telling sexist dirty jokes, and Jews telling anti-Semitic jokes, do not deny their identities or manifest envy of their opponents, but, in a way, disarm their traditional oppressors. Martin Grotjahn compares the anti-Jewish joke to a mock suicide aimed at undermining the original hostility of the anti-Semitic joke. It is as if the "witty Jewish man carefully and cautiously takes a sharp dagger out of his enemy's hands, sharpens it so that it can split a hair in mid-air, polishes it so that it shines brightly, stabs himself with it, then returns it gallantly to the anti-Semite with the silent reproach: Now see whether you can do it half so well" (1957:22–23). The result according to Grotjahn is "not defeat or

119

surrender but victory and greatness" (p. 22) *Pace* Legman, it seems to me that women's dirty jokes constitute an act of self-defense although there are, admittedly, other effective strategies.

Leonard Feinberg appears to abandon to some extent Freud's theory of seduction, opting instead for the latter's theory of aggression as the underlying motivation of the dirty joke. Nevertheless, he ignores the anti-female aggression in so many of the examples he deals with, and argues that the aggression of sexual jokes is directed against the societal restrictions against sexual activity (1978:118). In addition, he argues that sexual humor is aggressive, not because of the power relations between the sexes but because "sex is physically aggressive" (p. 90). Consequently, Feinberg implies that sexual humor in all its guises is a healthy and normal expression of human drives. What Feinberg overlooks is the culturally constructed, androcentric underpinnings of the definition of sex as an aggressive phenomenon. This omission contributes to the general evasion by most critics of the political dimension of sexual humor, or more specifically of sexist dirty jokes.

Christopher Wilson is somewhat less bound by the male centered, white middle class view of his predecessors. He notes that while white women and black men and women tend to share dirty jokes in mixed as well as in single-sex groups, white males tend to tell most of their dirty jokes to each other. According to Wilson, this "suggests one function of such joking: it may express and foster the particular values of the male groups within which it [the dirty joke] is voiced" (1979:188). Still, like his predecessors, Wilson fails to account for the differences between white men and women in terms of their respective social expressions of sexual humor.

It is clear that the definitive study on sexual humor has not yet been written. My intention here was to offer a feminist perspective on sexual humor, a perspective which takes into account the male dominated structure of Western society. My distinction between sexist and sexual jokes was meant to point out the thin boundaries between the so called innocent antifemale joke and dirty antifemale joke. The fact that in both "innocent" and "dirty" jokes, it is the woman rather than man who is ridiculed should help us reframe our investigations into the nature of sexual humor, by calling attention to the political element inspiring so much of traditional and contemporary sexual humor. The androcentric and misogynist streak in "innocent" and "dirty" jokes should alter critics to the fact that although dirty jokes appear to address human sexuality, they are in fact motivated by a patriarchal will to power, by an androcentric urge to subordinate and control the female Other. Finally, by drawing on the Jewish joke, I hoped to call attention to the significant analogies between sexist humor and racist humor. In both cases the butt of the joke is the Other, the pariah, the social and cultural outsider. In sexist humor the Other is woman; in anti-Semitic

120

humor the Other is the Jew. This, however, does not mean that Jewish jokes are less sexist than other ethnic jokes, although they may perhaps be less dirty. At this point I am incapable of offering conclusive statements about the extent or nature of sexism in the Jewish joke in comparison to other ethnic jokes. Too little has been done in this area and I am in no position to draw final conclusions. What I hope to have done is to raise questions about the sexist joke, the Jewish joke, and the possible relationships between them.

NOTES

1. For a definition and discussion of these concepts and their manifestations in Western culture and society see Simone de Beauvoir (1952), Kate Millet (1969) and Janssen-Jewrriet (1978).

2. Freud argues that what he defines as "cynical" jokes are popular because they attack social institutions: "Among the jokes that cynical jokes are in the habit of attacking none is more strictly guarded against by moral regulations but at the same time more inviting to attack than the institution of marriage, at which accordingly, the majority of cynical jokes are aimed" (1906:110). Freud exemplifies this category of jokes by citing the following joke: "A wife is like an umbrella — sooner or later one takes a cab" (p. 110). The "one" in the joke is a man and a husband. A man must give up his umbrella and resort to a cab when under heavy rain, just like a husband cannot count on his wife to provide him with his sexual needs so that sooner or later the husband will be compelled to take a cab and resort to a prostitute who will take care of his needs. The explicit analogy between a wife and an umbrella hides an implicit equation between a wife and a prostitute. In the final analysis both of them are meant — from a man's point of view — to provide sexual services. The joke implies that the wife may in fact be a poor substitute for a prostitute, as she may be able to respond to her husband's superficial sexual needs only. To use the joke's simile, she may protect him from a little bit of rain (allusion to torrential ejaculation?) but she cannot satisfy him in times of real need. The reduction of a wife to a sexual instrument intended to relieve her husband's sexual needs, and the implied analogy between a wife and a prostitute reveals a sexist point of view because at bottom it is neither the wife nor the prostitute that are being derided but woman as an instrument whose sole function is sexually to satisfy man. "Sexist" seems to me a more appropriate definition of this kind of joke than "cynical."

3. The communication of the dirty antifemale joke to a woman listener implies that she was selected because the listener believes her to be different from her female counterparts, and therefore worthy of being told of the repulsive features and degrading functions of female sexuality. In this sense the technique and function of the dirty sexist joke are strikingly similar to those of nonjocular pornographic literature. As Andrea Dworkin (1944), and Susan Griffin (1981) have shown, the pornographic female image is a male-defined female, the female as man wants her to be: submissive, lacking a will and a mind of her own, a sex object whose sole function is to please her master-inventor. By reducing her to her genitals, pornography strips woman of her human dignity and turns her into a sexual automaton, giving vent to man's antifemale

fantasies. Like the endless pornographic variations on the motif of the seductive rape, and not unlike the Freudian ideology of female masochism, many sexual jokes imply that woman wishes to be degraded and raped. The implied message of the teller of the joke, or the aggressor, is that the female victim only pretends to be a victim and that in actuality she has only waited for her male partner to assault and degrade her. As Susan Brownmiller (1976) demonstrates in her study on rape, this ideology has more in common with intersexual power relations than with sexual desire.

4. It should be stressed that although women figure as the most frequent victims in dirty jokes, men too appear as butts of dirty jokes; especially those concerning sexual potency, and the size of the penis. Legman argues that these jokes are not invented by women, but rather by men as projections on the female speaker of male anxieties (1968:319–334). Legman's argument has yet to be ascertained. No systematic effort has yet been undertaken to identify the originators of dirty jokes (Feinberg, p. 101). It would be more accurate at this point to accept Legman's assertions on this matter as hypotheses.

5. Legman is less resolute in regard to the seductive impact of dirty jokes on women in the second volume of *The Rationale of the Dirty Joke*, where he admits that he does not know if dirty jokes indeed arouse female listeners (1975:35).

References

Beauvoir, Simone de, 1952. *The Second Sex,* tr. and ed. H.M. Parshley (New York: Vintage).

Bergson, Henri, 1977. *Laughter,* tr. Tred Rothwell, (Philadelphia: Richard West, 1977).

Brownmiller, Susan, 1976. *Against Our Will,* (New York: Bantam Books).

Carter, Angela, 1978. *The Sadeian Woman and the Ideology of Pornography* (New York: Pantheon).

Dworkin, Andrea, 1974. *Woman Hating,* (New York: Dutton).

Feinberg, Leonard, 1978. *The Secret of Humor,* (Amsterdam: Rodopi).

Freud, Sigmund, 1960. *Jokes and their Relations to the Unconscious,* tr. and ed. James Strachey (New York: Norton).

Grotjahn, Martin, 1957. *Beyond Laughter,* (New York: McGraw-Hill).

Janssen-Jurreit, Marie Louise, 1982. *Sexism: The Male Monopoly on History and Thought,* tr. Verne Moberg, (New York: Farrar Strauss and Giroux).

Knott, Blanche, 1981. *Truly Tasteless Jokes,* (New York: Ballantine).

Legman, Gershon, 1968. *Rationale of the Dirty Joke: An Analysis of Sexual Humor,* vol. I (New York: Grove).

Legman, Gershon, 1975. *Rationale of the Dirty Joke,* vol. II (New York: Grove.

Millet, Kate, 1970. *Sexual Politics,* (New York: Ballantine).

Novak, William and Moshe Waldoks, 1981. *The Big Book of Jewish Humor,* 1981. (New York: Harper and Row).

Reik, Theodor, 1962. *Jewish Wit,* (New York: Gamut).

Wilde, Larry, 1980. *The Last Official Jewish Joke Book,* (New York: Bantam).

Wilson, Christopher P., 1979. *Jokes: Form, Content, Use and Function* (London: Academic Press).

L.E. Mintz

THE RABBI VERSUS THE PRIEST AND OTHER JEWISH STORIES

LAWRENCE E. MINTZ
University of Maryland, USA

THE RABBI VERSUS THE PRIEST AND OTHER JEWISH STORIES

There has been a great deal of discussion concerning the motives and functions of ethnic humor, including accounts which are widely disparate, even paradoxical. It is useful to consider the entire range of possible reasons for this kind of joking, outlining the contexts in which the jokes are told and heard, as well as analyzing the texts themselves. Who tells these jokes to whom; why? No single, simple explanation is sufficient. This essay examines jokes which feature Jewish-Christian confrontation, most of which are frequently cited in literature devoted to Jewish humor, with a specific reference to their appearance in the folklore of Jewish youths in a mixed Jewish-Gentile environment in the Bronx, New York during the 1950s. The joke-telling is analyzed within a continuum description of the motives and functions of ethnic humor.[1]

The continuum description sets up four categories for ethnic joking, *critical humor,* or jokes told about a group by members of another group; these jokes are for the most part highly critical, relying upon negative ethnic stereotypes; *self-deprecating humor,* or humor told by members of the group itself, apparently self-critical, accepting of the negative stereotypes; *realistic humor,* or jokes which are less critical than they are exploring of the amusing aspects of ethnic interaction in a pluralistic society; *ironic humor,* or jokes which turn the weaknesses into strengths, the criticism into ironic self-congratulation, the vulnerability into victory for the traditional victim of the joking. For each category, a number of possible motives and functions are described theoretically and illustrated by jokes commonly told in the target environment.[2]

Critical humor in Jewish jokes focused on two stereotypes, the Jew as financially dishonest and obsessed with money, and the Jew as weak and cowardly. The Catholics told these jokes to each other, perhaps to enhance their group identity and morale, to assert their superiority and even to express their group identity and morale, or to express their hostilities in a licenced, acceptable manner. "Why do Jews have big noses? Because air is free." "Moishe had a candy store/the business was so bad/he asked his wife what should he do/this is what she said/take a little kerosene/spread it on the floor/take a match, give a scratch/no more candy store." "The priest offers a nickel for the little boy who correctly answers the question: who was

125

the greatest man who ever lived? The black kid chooses Jackie Robinson . . .
The priest acknowledges Robinson's status as a credit to his race, but denies
the reward. The Irish kid chooses St. Patrick, causing the priest a moment of
dilemma (he was an Irish priest), but again, the answer is wrong. The Jewish
youth correctly answers Jesus, collects his prize, and when he is questioned
as to why he supported the Christian creed, he answers that 'business is
business.'" Jewish kids are described as being issued violin cases and glasses
to discourage them from fighting, and in one joke, a Jewish mother asks her
kids what they are doing in a closed bedroom. When they answer that they
are fucking, she replies, "that's ok, just don't fight." Jewish kids heard these
jokes from close Christian friends, perhaps in the spirit of what Lawrence
LaFave calls the "irony of ironies."[3] The jokes are told to signify the
transcending of prejudice or hostility. "If I weren't obviously and unquestionably without prejudice I couldn't tell you this joke." For the hearer, laughing
at the joke provided an opportunity to be a "good sport," a person who was
not too sensitive or too ethnocentric.

The texts of the so-called *self-deprecating humor*[4] were very similar to
those of the critical humor; indeed many of the same jokes were told by
Jewish kids to their co-religionists. In many cases the alleged stereotypical
behavior of mercenary concern and cowardice is accepted with near-pride,
making the joking in this category sometimes almost indistinguishable from
the ironic humor to be discussed below, but it is nonetheless useful to
separate making peace with a negative image from turning it into a positive
one. "The Minister sings 'Rock of Ages' and his congregation contributes
$1,000. The priest sings 'Ave Maria' and his parish coughs up $2,000. The
rabbi sings 'There's a Gold Mine in the Sky' and two hundred Jews join the
Air Force." "The Israeli soldier captures an Arab tank every day to win a
weekend pass, but when he is forced to reveal his method it turns out that he
is trading an Israeli tank for each one of the enemy's." Traditional jokes
about Jewish "schnorrers" are reflective of the victory of the weak and
vulnerable, but the stereotype of the clever, but dishonest, money-obsessed
Jew is dominant.

More recent jokes maligning the so-called Jewish American princess and
Jewish mothers are similarly self-deprecating, even if they do represent a
male criticism of a separate (female) group. Their picture of Jews as sexually
repressed, more concerned with material possessions and status, appearance
than sex or affection, reveals a willingness to joke about a less than
admirable self-image. Perhaps as Dan Ben Amos's thesis suggests, these
jokes do separate assimilated Jews from "greenhorns," or serve as corrective
criticism of error within the group rather than of the group, but it is not
unreasonable to theorize that such self-criticism may also make self-doubt
less threatening, less hard to face, and may make it easier to live with the

126

realization that these stereotypes are attributed to Jews as a part of the popular culture.

The category of *realistic humor* designates jokes which deal with the realities facing a minority group living within a larger, dominant culture without much criticism attending the observations. It might be argued that there is implied criticism in most of the jokes, for instance, of the apostates and deviates from the traditions of the group, but, for the most part, these jokes acknowledge inevitabilities with humor rather than animosity or fear. A whole series of jokes deal with apostasy, one group humorously describing the effect of conversion or intermarriage on the parents of the apostate, and another group dealing with conversion as insincere and/or incomplete.

> *A daughter phones her mother to report that she is marrying a gentile. The mother seems surprisingly unalarmed, even when the daughter adds that her husband-to-be is unemployed and that they will have to live in the family home. The mother offers her own bed, in fact. When the daughter wonders where the mother will sleep she is told, 'don't worry about me. The minute you hang up I'm going to kill myself anyway.'*

> *A son calls his mother and informs her that he is marrying a gentile girl. The mother accepts this evenly, but he further informs her that the girl is a schvartze. The mother is unflappable: 'you can have her Tuesdays and Thursdays, by me she'll clean Mondays and Wednesdays.'*

Or in another variant, he prepares the mother for a shock, she is unshaken when he sequentially tells her he is getting married, not to a gentile girl, not to a black woman, but to a *boy!* Her only response is, "a nice Jewish boy?"

> *A haughty Jewish woman converts and studiously avoids all references to her former status, but when she slips into an icy swimming pool at her new exclusive country club she exclaims, 'oy gevalt! . . . whatever that means.'*

> *Three converts discuss their motives for becoming Christian. When one insists that he is motivated by genuine religious feeling the other two reply, 'what do you take us for, a couple of goyim?'*

> *A man converts to Christianity for a monetary reward. When his wife and children ask for the money, he moans, 'the minute an honest Christian earns a little money, the Jews take it away.'*

> *A new Christian impresses the priest with his knowledge of the Christian holidays until he gets to Easter, which he describes as*

127

celebrating Jesus's emergence from the cave, the spotting of his shadow, and his return for six more weeks of winter!

Such jokes surely ridicule the converts, but they are less functional as ethnic criticism than they are expressive of the reality of assimilation and a desire to cope with it as more amusing and silly than threatening.

Another *realistic* joke may be cited as an example of an acknowledgment of the humor in the inevitable Jewish-Christian acculturation experiences.

A Jewish juvenile delinquent (that we had them was a source of ethnic pride, in the neighborhood . . . perhaps itself indicative of acculturation) *gets thrown out of a succession of public, private and Jewish schools for violent, antisocial behavior. His father, in desperation, sends him to a Catholic boarding school* (famous for discipline in our folklore). *His first two report cards are all 'A's with a special commendation for good behavior. His amazed father makes a special trip to visit the boy, who greets him neatly dressed and groomed, calling him 'sir.' When the father asks him what they have done to him to make him behave he replies, 'nothing yet, sir, but when I saw the man they had nailed to the wall here, I knew I had better not mess around.'*

Such jokes recognize the uneasiness generated by the familiar Christian icons as well as the reputation of the Catholic schools, but there is no real criticism in any direction. Rather the joke acknowledges Jewish-Christian contact in a humorous spirit. Realistic humor allows for a consideration of the multiethnic environment and its threats, its problems, mediated by the license of the comic mood.

The fourth category of Jewish jokes told in this cultural milieu is perhaps the most significant both quantitatively and in terms of social and cultural meaning. *Ironic humor* provides a comic victory for the traditional victims of ethnic joking, turning their weaknesses into strengths, their vulnerability into triumph, their faults into virtues. In this mode, weakness, cowardice, and even mercenary obsession are presented as cleverness, as tools for survival, as means of transcending the attacks and insults provoked by the status of a marginal, minority, frequently deprecated group. Many of these jokes feature a gentle, but pointed confrontation between a rabbi and a priest or between rabbis, priests, and ministers. Waldoks and Novak acknowledge the prominence of these jokes in modern American Jewish humor:

Jokes about ministers, priests, and rabbis (or, in lay terms, a Protestant, a Catholic and a Jew) reflect the recent American tendency toward ecumenism and the public ascendency of Judaism to the trinity of official religions. These have come to replace earlier jokes about conversion and assimilation. (1979, p. 95)

Ed Cray properly places these tales in the folk tradition of the trickster (1964), and we can add the conventions of the wise fools and the "little man" as well.[5] Above all, these jokes allow for the celebration of the triumph of the Jew through the employment of wit over the stronger or at least self-confidently "superior" gentile:

Priest to rabbi during interfaith banquet: 'When are you going to give up your antiquated customs and eat some of this delicious ham?' Rabbi: 'At your wedding, Father.'

Priest to rabbi: 'Tell me, rabbi, did you ever cheat and try eating ham?' Rabbi: 'Well, to tell you the truth, I did break down once, just out of curiosity.' Rabbi to priest: 'Since I've confessed my experiment to you, let me ask, have you ever had a woman?' Priest: 'Yes, though I hate to admit it, earlier in my career I just had to find out what it was like.' Rabbi: 'A lot better than ham, no?'

Priest and rabbi hear confession together: priest treats two women who confess adultery on three occasions by demanding ten 'Hail Marys' ten 'Our Fathers' and ten dollars for the collection plate. When the priest has to go to the bathroom, the rabbi takes over. A woman comes in and confesses committing adultery twice; he invites her to take advantage of the special, three for ten dollars.

The priest 'baptizes' his new Cadillac with a bucket of water so the rabbi cuts two inches off the taillight.

The three chaplains (representing the three faiths) *are playing cards after lights out. The general catches them, but the two Christian clerics deny the transgression; the rabbi asks 'with whom shall I play?'*

The rabbi enrages the priest and the minister by insisting that he is Jesus and he can prove it. He takes them to a house of ill repute where the madam exclaims, 'Jesus Christ are you here again?'

The priest and rabbi survive a plane crash. The priest looks over and sees the rabbi apparently crossing himself and exults 'in your time of true testing you turn to the one true faith.' The rabbi replies, 'what true faith, I'm just checking my spectacles, testicles, wallet and cigarettes.'

Some of these jokes are "better" than others, i.e. they are constructed more cleverly, they reveal more wit, but their reception was at least in part affected by our sense of the ambivalent relationship between Jews and Catholics in our place and time. We were friendly and for the most part not overtly hostile, but we were definitely separate communities with a sense of opposition, of conflict, of competition. These jokes fit in *precisely* with that cultural climate (which is not to say that they cannot at all be appreciated in other contexts). They reflect rivalry and muted confrontation, a strong identity and ethnic pride, a constant awareness of the primacy of ethnicity, neighborhood, and community, and a realization that Jewish-Catholic interaction, however ambiguous we found it to be or ambivalent we might feel about it, was inevitable and ultimately survivable.

The continuum of the motives and functions of ethnic joking acknowledges that no single theory explains the phenomenon. The meaning of the joke telling is tied to the teller and the audience as well as being in the text, and the effect of the humor can be subtle and complex. In this sense the ethnic joking experience corresponds to the serious relationship of Jews and Gentiles in an urban, mixed religious, mixed ethnic environment, providing a safe, traditionally-licensed opportunity for exploration and expression of sensitive social and cultural needs.

NOTES

1. The texts of two papers in which the continuum description was designed are not available in published form, but abstracts of both presentations have been published. Lawrence E. Mintz, "A Continuum Description of the Motives and Functions of Jewish Humor," Modern Language Association Conference, December 1976, in *American Humor: an Interdisciplinary Newsletter*, IV:1 (Spring, 1977) and "A Continuum Description of the Motives and Functions of Race, Sex, and Ethnicity in Humor," Second International Conference on Humor, August 1979, in Harvey Mindess and Joy Turek, eds. *Proceeding of the Second International Conference on Humor*. Los Angeles, 1980.

2. The time and place referred to for the context of the joking is the late 1950s in the Bronx, NY. The writer lived in an almost exclusively Jewish community closely bordered by an Italian Catholic and Irish Catholic neighborhood. Contacts between Jews and Christians were mostly related to school and sports activities and were for the most part friendly, but the social groups were quite distinct. The jokes discussed in this paper were told to and by the Jewish youths in the area and dealt with Jews and their relations with Gentiles. Another dimension would be provided by an examination of jokes aimed at the Gentiles, but these were not available for consideration.

3. Lawrence LaFave, "An Irony of Irony: The Left-Handed Insult in Intragroup Humor," in Antony Chapman and Hugh Foot, eds. *Its a Funny Thing, Humor*. NY:

Pergamon Press, 1977. pp. 283–285. See also the other essays in the section on ethnic humor and the discussion of the presentations by this writer.

4. Perhaps the most spirited discussion in the literature devoted to ethnic humor is over the question of the motives and functions of self-deprecating humor. For two very different positions, see Martin Grotjahn's characterization of such humor as reflecting self-hatred, "Jewish Jokes and their Relation to Masochism," in Werner M. Mendel, ed. *A Celebration of Laughter*. LA: Mara Books, 1970, pp. 135–144, and Dan Ben Amos's account of this kind of joking as a form of internal criticism and ironic transcending of familiar criticism, "The Myth of Jewish Humor," *Western Folklore* 32:2 (1973), 112–131.

5. Ed Cray, "The Rabbi Trickster," *J. of American Folklore,* 77 (1964), 331–345.

References

Adler, Bill. *Jewish Wit and Wisdom*. NY: 1969.

Ausubel, Nathan. A Treasury of Jewish Humor. NY: 1951.

Ben-Amos, Dan. "The Myth of Jewish Humor," *Western Folklore* 32:2 (1973), 112–131.

Boskin, Joseph. *Humor and Social Change in Twentieth Century America*. Boston: 1979.

Cray, Ed. "The Rabbi Trickster," *Journal of American Folklore*, 77 (1964), 331–345.

Dorinson, Joseph. "Jewish Humor: Mechanism for Defense, Weapon for Cultural Affirmation," *Journal of Psychohistory,* 814 (Spring, 1981), 447–464.

————. untitled ms. of Jewish humor c. 5/80.

————. "The Gold Dust Twins of Marginal Humor: Blacks and Jews," Popular Culture Association, April, 1984.

LaFave, Lawrence. "An Irony of Irony: the Left-Handed Insult in Intragroup Humour," in Antony Chapman and Hugh Foot, eds. *Its a Funny Thing, Humour.* NY: 1977.

Mindess, Harvey. *The Chosen People?* LA: 1972.

Mintz, Lawrence E. abstract, "A Continuum Description of the Motives and Functions of Jewish Humor," *American Humor: An Interdisciplinary Newsletter,* Spring, 1977.

————. abstract, "A Continuum Description of the Motives and Functions of Race, Sex, and Ethnicity in Humor," proceedings of the Second International Conference on Humor, Harvey Mindess and Joy Turek, eds. LA: 1980.

Novak, William and Moshe Waldoks, eds. *The Big Book of Jewish Humor*. NY: 1981.

Reik, Theodor. *Jewish Wit*. NY: 1962.

Spaulding, Henry D. *Encyclopedia of Jewish Humor*. NY: 1969.

Whitfield, Stephen J. "Laughter in the Dark: Notes on American Jewish Humor," Midstream, XXIV:2 (Feb. 1978), 48–58.

Y. Friedlander

HALACHIC ISSUES AS SATIRICAL ELEMENTS IN NINETEENTH CENTURY HEBREW LITERATURE

YEHUDA FRIEDLANDER

Bar Ilan University, Israel

HALACHIC ISSUES AS SATIRICAL ELEMENTS IN NINETEENTH CENTURY HEBREW LITERATURE

He who scofs at the words of the Sages will be
condemned to boiling excrements."
(The Babylonian Talmud, 'Erubin' 21b)*

The Halacha is interpreted in four ways in the Haskalah literature and in Judaic writings: (a) through clarification of the Halacha itself according to the thirteen principles by which the Torah is interpreted and according to early and later Rabbinic authorities; (b) through clarification according to history — the evolution of the Halacha and its development against a historical, social, cultural and perhaps even economic background; (c) through actualization — the search for links with reality and the detachment of the Halacha from its context; (d) by way of aesthetics, analysis of the aesthetic qualities of Halachic issues and the examination of their role in the fabric of fictional literary works.

Modern Hebrew satire from the end of the eighteenth century, being a literature whose purpose was to change the face of Jewish experience in the Jewish communities of Europe, required all the above-mentioned four ways of interpretation, at times by intermingling them and at others each on its own; at times openly and at others by implication.

It is not my intention in this article to deal with linguistic references in the Halacha literature which have been interpolated into satiric works, but rather with extracts from the Halacha that have been introduced intentionally with definite satirical aims. An examination of a number of satirical texts has revealed that the Halachic issues exist both in the surface structure and the deep structure of satirical works.[1] There are Halachic issues that constitute a sort of primary matter (Urstoff), others constitute a means for creating characters and atmosphere, and yet others constitute a motif or an obvious object for satirical criticism.

* All extracts from the Babylonian Talmud are from: "The Babylonian Talmud, translated under the editorship of Rabbi Dr. I. Epstein, London, The Soncino Press, 1938.

There are three elements common to the variety of Halachic issues found in the satiric text: (a) the issues deal with concrete matters and specific events in Jewish life, but are given representative characteristics in the satirical text with the intention of presenting the world of Halacha in its entirety; (b) the "representative" sample is designed to undermine the basic authority of the Sages in the past and the present and to propose new attitudes and approaches to the world of Halacha in all its aspects; (c) the Halachic issues quoted are designed to arouse the reader's scorn, and to enable the satirist to create a mantle of "credibility" which exists in satirical illusion.

These three elements are only general outlines, while the unique character of each individual work is determined by the creative ability of the satirist in the way in which he introduces the Halachic issue into the text, and creates the internal links between the components of the work.

In order to illustrate the place and role of Halachic issues within the framework of modern Hebrew satire, I shall present here some examples of satirical texts written at the end of the eighteenth and during the nineteenth centuries. An analysis through intertextual reading will reveal to us a complex and stimulating aspect of the internal structure of the best of modern Hebrew satire.

A. The Halacha as Primary Matter (Urstoff)

Y.L. Peretz's story "A Ruined Sabbath", first published in *Kalendar* edited by Appelberg in 1892[2], appears to me to be a satirical story. We have here a description of an episode whose main (neurotic) concerns are the warm, naive relations between Zerah, a young husband and Miriam his wife, who live with his surly mother-in-law, the widow Seril, a woman meticulous with her daughter about all matters relating to marital relationships as set down by the Halacha, and who keeps a strict eye on the younger woman. The mother is particularly concerned that her daughter should be certain that she is clean during the days close to her menstruation period:

> *"My dear Mother," Miriam wanted to know. "Why shouldn't Zerah be concerned about these things? Why does he laugh when I toss him the keys, instead of handing them?"*
> *"Men are pranksters by nature," the Mother would reply. "They make sport of everything. What will they lose by sinning? They merely pick up a book, go through a chapter of Mishnayyot, and sixty pages of sins are wiped off their record!"*[3].

Towards the end of the story there is a description of how Zerah returning from the synagogue after the Friday evening service wakes his wife with a kiss:

"Damnable sinner!" the Mother screamed, raging up from her chair.
Miriam fell into a faint. She was brought to quickly — but the Sabbath was ruined"[4] *Translated by Israel I. Taslitt.*

Peretz was not quoting Halachic issues, but introduced into the story Halachic rulings relating to the menstruation period which served him as primary matter for his satirical design. In tractate "Shabbath 13a–13b" we find the ruling "Even any form of intimacy is forbidden" and it continues,

Tanna debe Eliyahu: It once happened that a certain scholar who had studied much Bible and Mishnah and had served scholars much, yet died in middle age. His wife took his tefillin and carried them about in synagogues and schoolhouses and complained to them, "It is written in the Torah, for that is thy life, and the length of thy days: my husband, who read [Bible], learned [Mishnah] [13b] and served scholars much, why did he die in middle age?" and no man could answer her. On one occasion I was a guest in her house, and she related the whole story to me. Said I to her: "My daughter! how was he to thee in the days of menstruation?" "God forbid!" she rejoined: "he did not touch me[5] *even with his little finger." "And how was he to thee in the days of white garments?" "He ate with me, drank with me and slept with me in bodily contact, and it did not occur to him to do other." Said I to her, "Blessed be the Omnipresent for slaying him."*

The Code of Maimonides, Book Five, the Book of Holiness, (Yad Hehazaka) Forbidden Intercourse, Chapter XI, 18, states: "A Man is forbidden to come in close contact with his wife during these seven days of cleanness, even if both she and he are fully clothed. He should not approach her, not touch her even with his little finger, nor eat with her out of the same dish." (Translated from the Hebrew by Louis I. Rabinowitz and Philip Grossman. Yale Judaica Series, editor Leon Nemoy, Volume XVI, New Haven and London, Yale University Press, 1965).

The "Maggid Mishneh" points out (Halacha 19): "There are those who say that it is forbidden to transfer anything from his hand to hers lest he touch her."[6]

There is no doubt that Peretz created the characters in the story "A Ruined Sabbath" on the basis of the Halacha that relates to the menstruation period in general, and especially against the background of the story quoted in the "Shabbath" tractate. The reader's affection is drawn towards the young couple, of course, while the widow Seril is portrayed as a particularly cruel character, representing "Halachic" Judaism in the manner Peretz the satirist wished to present it. It is possible that Peretz was influenced by M.L. Lilienblum ("Hataot Neurim") in his portrayal of neurotic people who are motivated by religious coercion·where strict observance of the Halacha is concerned, and he serves as an intermediary link between Lilienblum and M.Z. Fireberg ("Le'an?"). The direction of the satirical story "A Ruined Sabbath" is in keeping with the general, basic purpose of the satirist in Hebrew literature of the nineteenth century — the creation of the confrontation between natural human emotions and the severe demands of the Halacha, with the Halacha considered as "inhuman". Thus from the thematic point of view there is no innovation in the story "A Ruined Sabbath", and Peretz's contribution with this story is mainly in the portrayal of a situation and the description of characters.

A comparison of the works of Peretz and Lilienblum could cast additional light on the ways in which they exploited Halachic issues in the texts of satirical works.

I will illustrate my contention with two extracts from "Hataot Neurim" by Lilienblum (1876):

> (a) My stupid uncle used to say that on the night of the New Year and the night of the Day of Atonement he was unable to sleep: on the night of the New Year — lest he have a bad dream; on the night of the Day of Atonement — lest he experience a pollution. As it is stated in Yoma 88a: "One who experiences a night pollution on the Day of Atonement, let him be anxious throughout the year (lest he might die)"[7]

> (b) After the "Kol Nidre" prayer I said the confessional prayer, I read the first four chapters of Psalms, as was my wont, as they are an incantation against impure occurrence — and I lay down to sleep. In the middle of my sleep I woke up with a start, and my heart almost stopped beating . . . I discovered . . . that I must be anxious throughout the year!!
> Do not laugh dear reader, so that you might not put a person to shame."[8]

Unlike Peretz, Lilienblum quotes the Halachic source for the hero's nightmare. Let us look at the original:

> Out Rabbis taught: One who experiences a pollution on the Day of Atonement should go down and immerse himself and in the evening he should rub himself off properly. [. . .]
> A tenna recited before R. Nahman, To one who experiences a

*pollution on the Day of Atonement, all sins will be forgiven.
[...]
In the School of R. Ishmael it was taught: One who experienced a
night pollution on the Day of Atonement, let him be anxious
throughout the year, and if he survives the year, he is assured of
being a child of the world to come.
R. Nahman b. Isaac said: You may know it [from the fact that]
all the world is hungry, and he is satisfied. When R. Dimi came,
he said: He will live long, thrive and beget many children (Yoma,
88a. Vol. 7, pp. 440–441).*

Rashi's commentary on this passage states:

*"One who experiences pollution on the Day of Atonement"; and
not intentionally, all sins will be forgiven — this is a good sign
that he will be blessed with seed — and will have a long life.
"Let him be anxious throughout the year"; Lest his fasting not be
accepted and that he be sworn to whatever oath it may be wished
that he be sworn to, like a slave who fills the cup of his master
and spills the whole jug over his face.
"He will live long"; He who experienced a pollution on the Day
of Atonement — will thrive and beget many children — children
and grandchildren for this is the sign that he will be blessed with
seed — and will have a long life.*

Let us return to Lilienblum's description: "My stupid uncle used to say:"
This is a two-faced portrayal of the uncle. At first reading it would appear
that his stupidity derives from his naive belief in the words of the School of
R. Ishmael, but from an intertextual reading it appears that the uncle's
stupidity derives from the fact that he was not careful in his selection of the
more serene passages relating to this Halachic issue, and that he had not
studied it to its conclusion. But the uncle plays only a minor role in the story,
for his description serves as a sort of background to the behaviour of the
protagonist Tslopahad Bar Hushim Hatoheh, who in actual fact is as stupid
as his uncle. The ironic attitude towards the uncle is, of course, full of self
pity. The autobiographical story "Hataot Neurim" is not satirical in the
generally accepted manner of the genre, but there are certain satirical
elements in the various scenes of the story.

Both in "A Ruined Sabbath" by Peretz and in "Hataot Neurim" by
Lilienblum, the Halacha serves as primary matter (Urstoff) for the creation
of the characters. It is not the Halacha itself that is the subject of the satirical
story (in the examples quoted above), but rather the hero, who is attracted to
certain Halachic issues by virtue of his neurotic personality.

A certain similarity in the use of Halachic issues in the presentation of the story is to be found in "Le'an?" by Fireberg (1899), even though this is not a satirical story. There is a certain similarity to be found between the behaviour of the hero of "Le'an?" and that of the hero of "Hataot Neurim". Nahman, the extremely neurotic character in "Le'an?" is suffering from mental torment: "But — this thought added to his suffering — why was such a terrible world created? G-d is good, and if you have not been meticulous in washing the hands, you will be reincarnated as a frog . . . he created himself a weak and humble man and expects him to have god-like strength . . . no, no, I am not a sinner, G-d is good. Good, good . . . Oh, get thee before me evil!"[9]

Let us, therefore, turn to the sources. In tractate "Shabbath 62b" it says:

> **R. Abbahu said — others say, In a Baraitha it was taught: three things bring man to poverty, viz., urinating in front of one's bed naked, treating the washing of the hands with disrespect, and being cursed by one's wife in his presence.**

And in the tractate "Sotah 4b" we find:

> **R. Zerika said in the name of R. Eleazer: Whoever makes light of washing the hands [before and after a meal] will be uprooted from the world.**

Reincarnation as a punishment is not mentioned in the Talmud, but rather in the Kabbala. The punishment of reincarnation is a sort of measure for measure. He who is not careful to carry out the washing of the hands in running water without a break . . .[10]. What Peretz and Lilienblum did with the Halacha, Fireberg did with a combination of Halacha, Aggada and Kabbala. The similarity between them is the use of the sources as primary matter as background to the story.

B. The Halacha as a Motif

One of the main characteristics of Hebrew literature at the end of the eighteenth century is the use of well-known Halachic issues as a motif in the controversy between the Berlin Maskilim and Orthodox Jewry. The main desire of the Maskilim was to present the Halacha as a legitimate authority for their demands for reform in Jewish religious practice. One of the most outstanding examples of this was the desire to introduce prayer in German into the synagogue. In the satirical work by Aharon Wolfsohn of Halle "Siha Be'eretz Hehayim" which appeared in periodical episodes in "Hameasef" during the years 1794–1797[11], preceding the temple controversy in 1819, there is a caustic satirical dialogue, the main gist of which is the justification of prayer in pure German. Moses Mendelssohn insolently places before his rival the Polish rabbi his claim:

> *"Guard your vineyard! You have not guarded your vineyard. For you have not studied full well the teachings of our brother Moses ben Maimon in his work 'Yad Hehazaka'. He has stated there: 'A man may read the Shema in any language, and a person reading in any language must be most careful not to be mistaken in that language.'"*[12]

The Polish rabbi who appears in the above-mentioned play as So-and-So replies:

> *"(angrily) who are you, that you dare to say such things to me: You have not studied well the 'Yad Hehazaka'? How dare you boast your superior knowledge about this work over which I have toiled throughout my entire life? What do you know about it that I do not know? I have known the writings of our brother, but I have also been aware that Rabbi Abraham the son of David questioned this statement and stated: 'it is not conceivable that the languages can be interpreted, and who will examine the meaning he has given it?'"*[13]

Wolfsohn in his editorial annotations presents quotations from the Rambam's "Regulations concerning the reading of the Shema," Chapter 2, 10, and from the author's "Kessef Mishne"[14] Let us look at this in greater detail.

> *In tractate Sotah 32a Mishna it is stated: "The following may be recited in any language: the section concerning the woman suspected of adultery, the confession made at the presentation of the tithe, the 'Shema', the 'prayer', the grace after meals, the oath concerning testimony and the oath concerning a deposit."*
> *The Gemara on this 32b states: "The Shema. Whence have we it that this [may be recited in any language]? As it is written, Hear, O Israel — in any language you understand."*

The Ramban on the basis of tractate "Sotah" pronounces on the regulations concerning the reading of the Shema, Chap 2, 10: "A man may read the Shema in any language that may be understood. And he who reads in any language must be careful of any mistake in that language; be precise in that language as you are precise in the holy language." Despite the objection of the Rabbi Abraham, son of David the majority of the rabbinical scholars stated that it is permitted to pray in any language.[15]

Wolfsohn, followed by Eliezer Liberman, Meir Israel Breslau and others, argued against the Orthodox rabbis (Hatam Sofer, Rabbi Akiva Eiger, the judges of the high rabbinical court in Hamburg and others)[16] that their objection to allowing prayers to be said in German was contrary to Halacha.[17]

This Halachic issue, and others like it, constitute a motif in the scholastic satire of the end of the eighteenth century and later; Wolfsohn and his school present themselves in their satirical works as defenders of the Halacha whenever it was seen to be supportive of their struggle.

C. The Halacha as a Subject of Satire

Modern Hebrew satire is in the main expressly anti-Halachic, and the "Haskala" writers were wont to choose well-known Halachic passages couched in what seemed to them to be "strange" language, and present them as individual examples which prove the rule — and they were not short of suitable examples. Let us examine some of them. Shaul Levin-Berlin in his satirical work "Ktav Yosher" (1794) describes the "Kosher" Jew as one who does not urinate in public places on the Sabbath.[18] This is based on the Mishna in tractate Erubin 98b:

> *A man may not stand in a private domain and make water in a public domain or in a public domain and make water in a private domain, and the same applies to spitting.*

As far as the surface structure is concerned this piquant example of urinating on the Sabbath is the subject of a satirical work, but as far as the deeper structure is concerned, it is the Halacha taken out of its context that constitutes the subject for satirical criticism because the Maskilim wished to annul this Halacha completely, as it did not seem to them commensurate with modern Jewish life. The choice of this example helped them in presenting this Halachic issue as ridiculous.

Itzhak Erter followed the same pattern in his well-known satirical work "Tashlich" (1840). The devil castigates the narrator: "The learned of your land have sinned greatly, in writing books full of foolishness; your rabbis have sinned in continuing through their writings to place restrictions on the soul to the extent that the burden can no longer be endured".[19] The narrator gradually succumbs to the words of Samael the devil, and is forced to turn to the reader and say: "I have come today to present some of the complaints I have heard against my Jewish brethren, which are marginal to this work, in order that they might search among the books mentioned here to see if this is true, are such things to be found within them? are they written there?"[20] In a marginal note Erter brings a quotation from the book "Mei Niddah" written by R. Shlomo Kluger, one of the great Rabbinical scholars in Galicia of the nineteenth century, published in Zolkawa in 1834:

142

For we see in truth that the matter under discussion that virginity which appears or not is not a matter of nature, but rather a decree of the Creator and the Torah, and if this is so, it is difficult to understand why for a female proselyte who has been proselytized it is not stated thus, for according to the Torah, a proselyte who has been proselytized is a baby that has been born, and if it is so why did her virginity not reappear as that of a Jewish girl before she is three years and one day old?[21]

Erter's intention was to describe the basic absurdity, in his opinion, of discussing the virginity of a three-year old girl, and the analogy of a female proselyte who has been raped after childhood. The quotation is surprising on its first reading, and the reader tends to accept Erter's militant, critical arguments. However, anyone well-versed in this Halachic issue immediately perceives the "adaptation" of the text to the requirements of the satirical aim of placing the Halacha in an absurd light. We can, therefore, see the Halachic picture in a wider context. The Mishna, tractate "Niddah" 44b opens thus: "A girl of the age of three years and one day may be bethrothed by intercourse." The Gemara brings a Baraitha:

Our Rabbis taught: A girl of the age of three years may be bethrothed by intercourse; so R. Meir. But the Sages say: Only one who is three years and one day old.

The Gemara tries to understand the cause of the controversy between R. Meir and the Sages and asks:

What is the practical difference between them? — The School of R. Jannai replied: The practical difference between them is the day preceding the first day of the fourth year. R. Johanan, however, replied: the practical difference between them is the rule that thirty days of a year are counted as the full year.

Rashi and the Tosaphists explain the principles of the controversy according to the opinion of the school of R. Jannai as well as of R. Johanan. The question under discussion is that of what is the legal definition of the term "year" in the Halacha? Does the last day of the year end the computation, or does one wait until the first day of the following year, or does the Halacha consider the first month of a year as a year from the legal point of view? The Tosafists, referring to the term "Thirty Days" explain:

The controversy is in fact over the question whether one day of the year is counted as a year — in the opinion of Rabbi Meir, two years and one day suffice, he does not dispute the Beraitha that follows and in his opinion one day in the third year is not considered as the third year.

In the book "Mei Niddah" (96, 72) it is written:

This should be explained further, for we see in truth that the matter under discussion, that virginity which reappears or not, is not a matter of nature, that is to say that in so and so many years it does not reappear and in less than that reappears; for if the matter were one of nature, what is the reference here to thirty days in a year being considered as a year or one day in the year? Let us examine what is the factual truth, whether it is natural for virginity to reappear or not, and how does the matter of computation of a year or a day relate to this?

R. Shlomo Kluger discusses later in his work whether the legal principle can also be applied to a female proselyte, and whether there is any significance to the fact that the third year is a leap year in the Hebrew calendar.[22] An examination of the text in its entirety will immediately reveal that this is a discussion of a certain *legal* reality which has implications for the Halacha relating to "Nidda" and not to practical reality. Anyone conversant with this issue in the Halacha and the Tosafists will understand the difference between the "law of virginity" and the physiological reality. Erter, who well knew the nature of this distinction, intended to blur it, and thus describes the words of the author of "Mei Niddah" in their full absurdity. But here this specific Halachic issue has been selected as an example of the world of the Halacha as the subject of satirical criticism.

This approach by Erter, used in the satire "Tashlich," is not especially common in his works, and apears a number of times only. However, he was excelled by his friend Yehoshua Heshel Shor in his writings. Shor's satirical works, both his prose writings and essays, are full of Halachic issues which come under satirical criticism.[23] I will present one example which can provide an additional perspective to the examples I have quoted from other satirical works.

In the satire "Taryag" (1853), a discussion is reported between the narrator and the Talmudic Sage and expositor of the Scriptures, R. Simlai (third century C.E.) who visits him on the eve of the New Year. The narrator complains to him about the Talmud and Gaonic and Rabbinic writings written after the death of R. Simlai. The latter expresses surprise and says: "I did not know a book other than this Scroll of the Law (the Torah) and the Prophets and Writings, and it was not permitted to write other than these, for the sayings of the Kabala were passed on by word of mouth, as they were wont to change according to the needs of time and place, and if anything was committed to writing they were restricted to secret scrolls, [for if they were tiny they would be lost][24] but were not written down in book form to be preserved forever. Thus, if this is so, what are these many large and broad, long and thick books?!"[25] The narrator wishes to incite R. Simlai against the Halachic rulings quoted in the Babylonian Talmud: "I read to him: Abbayeh and Raba both stated: anything that has any medical attribute has no part of superstition."[26] R. Simlai replies in amazement: "There is an explicit Mishna which states that the Sages forbid the going out even on week days with the nail of the crucifixion for medical purposes for fear of superstition."[27] Shor attributes the source of Abbayeh and Raba's commentary to the tractate "Shabbath 87", but this is incorrect as the quotation is from "Shabbath 67a".

It should be noted that Shor has the narrator quote Abbayeh and Raba (4th century C.E.) who even condone the use of magic for medical purposes, while R. Simlai is much more strict in matters relating to superstition and prefers to rely on the Mishnaic ruling. The satirical stratagem is obvious, for Shor wishes to attack the Babylonian Talmud, full of magic, and even prefers the strict R. Simlai to it. Shor is prepared to accept the severe rulings of the Halacha when it suits his general purpose. Anyone familiar with the works of Shor is aware of the fact that he is not prepared to forego any opportunity to attack the Babylonian Talmud, and prefers to rely on the Jerusalem Talmud in those cases where the latter is in keeping with his satirical purpose.[28] In the deep structure of the conversation between the narrator and R. Simlai, we find an attempt totally to undermine the Babylonian Talmud because in the main it was this work that set the basis for Orthodox Jewish life which became the main target for the barbs of modern Hebrew satire. For this reason Shor, unlike his predecessors in satire, wrote a scathing attack on the Babylonian Talmud in the first issue of "Hehalutz" (1852). In his controversial article "An examination of the Mishna and Gemara"[29] which opens with the motto: "He hath made me dwell in dark places refers to the Babylonian Talmud."[30] Shor dares doubt the validity and credibility of many Halachic rulings: "And who knows how many Halachic pronouncements, laws, regulations and decrees have been added by pupils which are to no avail".[31]

The quotation from Shor's satire "Taryag" raises the point of view that the earlier generations take precedence on the strength of being first. R. Simlai belongs to the generation of Rabbi Johanan who said: "The fingernails of the first ones are preferable to the bellies of the later ones,"[32] and this approach could be expedient to the "protestant" aims of Shor. However, Shor is prepared to rely on the later ones when they are to his advantage. He concludes the above-mentioned article on the Mishna and Gemara with the call: "And from those of this generation versed in Torah I would request that they sacrifice before us similar articles to those *(op. cit.)* and that they reveal and show the truth, for the word of G-d does not speak from out of their mouths, and we are not always responsible for their pronouncements, their decrees and regulations, and we are not inferior to them to change, to annul and to formulate new regulations suitable and proper for our place and time, according to which 'perfection is not to be found among living creatures, even among the most select of them, until the last ones will not be permitted to share with them' (Hameiri in his introduction to Avot).[33] Moreover, Shor is not the only one to behave in this way.[34]

It is interesting, by the way, to point out that in his satire "Taryag" Shor's attack on the Halachic rulings condoning magic for medical purposes, to which the rationalistic Shor did not agree, was a continuation of the line taken by Y.L. Mizes in his satirical work "Kinat Ha'emet" (1828), but Mizes put the blame on Hassidism, and quoted against them sources from the works of the medieval sages Rabbi Sadya Gaon, R. Yehuda Halevy, R. Avraham Ibn-Ezra, Maimonides among others. Shor went even further than his predecessor and placed the blame on the Babylonian Talmud and its influence on all Orthodox Jewry, including those who objected to Hassidism.

In summary: The Halachic issues that have been discussed in this article are only a very small selection. But even on the basis of these few examples it can be stated that one cannot carry out an in depth study of modern Hebrew satire without a consistent and detailed examination of the Halachic issues found in it, issues which have determined its character and defined its aesthetic quality.

NOTES

1. See Noam Chomsky, *Language and Mind,* Harcourt Brace Johanovich, New York, 1972, p. 46-21.
2. See *Kol Kitveh Y. L. Peretz,* Dvir, Tel Aviv, 1961, Vol. IV, Book I, pp. 28–36.
3. *Ibid.,* p. 32.
4. *Ibid.,* p. 36.
5. The word *bi* (me) appears in the original in square brackets.
6. See *Ibid.,* Halacha 19, and "Maggid Mishneh". *ibid.* See also chapter 21 and "Nosseh Keilim," *ibid.*
7. See *Moshe Leib Lilienblum, Ketavim Autobiographiim,* edited with an introduction by Shlomo Breiman, "Dorot" series, Bialik Institute, Jerusalem, 1970, p. 115.
8. See *ibid.,* p. 117.
9. See *Kitvei Mordechai Ze'ev Fireberg,* compiled by E. Steinman, fifth expanded edition, Knesset, Tel Aviv (n.d.), p. 53.
10. See Gershom Sholem, *Pirkei Yessod Behavanat Hakabalah Vesimleha,* Bialik Institute, Jerusalem, 1981, Chapter IX, pp. 308–357.
11. See Yehuda Friedlander, *Aharon Wolfsohn, Perakim Basatira Ha'Ivrit Beshalhei Hame'ah Hayud-het Begermania,* Papyrus, Tel Aviv, 1980, pp. 121–200.

12. *Ibid.*, p. 172. A photocopy of the manuscript of "Siha Be'eretz Hahayim" (ms. Warsaw 170) exists in the Institute for Photocopies of Hebrew Manuscripts at the National and University Library in Jeruaslem (registered 10105 x 'o).
The extract quoted here appears in the manuscript in a slightly different version.

13. *Op. cit.* In the manuscript the extract appears in a slightly different version.

14. *Ibid.*, p. 196. In the manuscript there is no annotation to the extract.

15. See Yehuda Friedlander, *Bemisterei Hasatira,* Bar-Ilan University Ramat Gan, 1984, pp. 132–136.

16. *Ibid.*, pp. 77–142.

17. In this connection it is worth quoting from the author of *Tiferet Yisrael* (R. Israel Lifshitz 1782–1860) in his commentary to the tractate Sotah, Chapter 7, Mishna 1:

> *"However, in our times there have recently arisen those desiring to make innovations and who wished to contradict this Mishna to pray in the synagogue in the Ashkenazi language [...] thus as the majority of the Sages, who are the scholars of the Torah, fear that in so doing the reverence of the holiness of repetition would decline [...] the Torah command negatively — that their demands should not be listened to [...] and even if it were a full precept in the Torah to pray in the Ashkenazi language, the sages of that generation have sufficient authority, abiding by their interpretations suited to the times, to remove a certain matter from the Torah by taking no action as in the case of one seeking a loophole."*

18. See Yehuda Friedlander, *Shaul Levin-Berlin, Perakim Basatira Ha'Ivrit,* (Note 11 above), pp. 93–94.

19. See Itzhak Erter, *Hatsofeh Leveit Yisrael,* Mahbarot Lesifrut, Tel Aviv, 1952, p. 69.

20. *Ibid.*, pp. 70, 72.

21. *Ibid.*, pp. 70–71.

22. "Mei Niddah", *ibid.*

23. See Yehuda Friedlander, *Ir'ur Ma'amda shel 'Emunat Hachamim' Be'aspaclaria shel Hasatira Halvrit Bamea Hatisha-Esrei,* The Sixth International Congress of Judaic Studies, Jerusalem 1977, Vol. III, pp. 369–376.

24. See *Babylonian Talmud,* Baba Batra, 14b.

25. See *Hehalutz,* Vol. II, Lewow, 1853, p. 4.

26. *Op. cit.*

27. *Op. cit.*

28. *Ibid.*, pp. 37, 43, and there are many further examples.

29. Yeshayahu Gafni in reference to research in this field, *Sekira al Hemehkar Hahistori shel Bavel Hatalmudit Badorot Ha'ahronim,* Bulletin of the World Union of Judaic Studies, 21 Autumn, 1983, p. 5.

30. See *Babylonian Talmud,* Sanhedrin, 24, a: "He hath made me to dwell in the dark places like those that have been long dead. This, said R. Jeremiah, refers to the Babylonian Talmud." See the issue there.

31. *Hehalutz,* 1852, p. 55.

32. *Babylonian Talmud,* Yoma 9, b.

33. *Hehalutz,* 1852, p. 56.

34. Yehuda Freidlander, *Bemisterei Hasatira* (Note No. 15 above) pp. 150–151.

A.E. Rivlin

TEVIE THE MILKMAN — INTERTWINING JEWISH DESTINY AND HUMOR

ASHER E. RIVLIN
Tel Aviv University, Israel

TEVIE THE MILKMAN —
INTERTWINING JEWISH DESTINY AND HUMOR

"Shalom Aleichem, you are the exalted classic portrait of our lives as the times and fate of the Jewish people in Eastern Europe change; You are the wonderful narrator of that life" (Dov Sedan, 1965).

"Apparently there is a no more enchanting mirror in which Israeli youth can observe the facets of the Diaspora, so foreign to them, than in Shalom Aleichem's jest" (Yeshurun Keshet, 1962).

The many scholars and interpreters of Shalom Aleichem perpetuated his historic stature with many such superlatives: the knight of humor, the wizard of language, the genius of the tale, the artist of the portrait, the magician of mimicry, the greatest Jewish dramatist; a man of sublime perception; or by pairing his name with highly esteemed peers — Shalom Aleichem and Mendele, Shalom Aleichem and Peretz; or again by analogue: Shalom Aleichem in Yiddish is like Bialik and Agnon in Hebrew.

The Knight of Jewish Humor

Within the varied works of Shalom Aleichem there are many different kinds of humor, expressed through a variety of methods: surprising idioms; linguistic verbosity; astonishing images; similes; mixed-up colloqualisms; sharp expressions; vulgarisms; popular blasphemies, nonsensical rhyming, etc.

On higher levels of expression one can discern the use of satire and irony; of the grotesque and the sarcastic, of wit and pretentiousness, of improvised quibbles and distorted interpretations; of linguistic entanglements and etymological legends. There is also figurative humor constructed on comic situations, on a comedy of errors, on slapstick and so on.

The Jewish humor of Shalom Aleichem has many faces as well, ranging from the good-hearted joke which is somewhat like the scholar jesting, to baneful, mordant wit, and even "black" humor. The local color stands out in the Jewish humor, which is unique in its mentality and in its socio-cultural extremities. For many this makes it a prototype of tragic humor, a somewhat destructive one, intended to cover for our weaknesses. The essence of Jewish humor explicates above all the use of self-criticism for self-defense and to support the struggle for survival.

151

Druyanov defined the basic characteristics of the Jewish joke as follows: "It is all wit, all war, all rebelliousness; it almost entirely lacks peace of mind and appeasement which are also a joke's components."

The humoristic techniques commonly found in Shalom Aleichem's works are:

1. Figurative expressions which combine terms and concepts from two different, unrelated fields.
2. Extreme figurative expressions whose language pattern is untranslatable into Hebrew and English.
3. Extreme figurative expressions whose uniqueness is in their sound.
4. Expressions with unique onomatopoeic, alliterative sounds. Puns and folkloristic rhyming are included in this type.
5. Expressions anchored in the shtetl and country folklore.
6. Similes as a natural humoristic means in Shalom Aleichem's use. He exploits the imagistic pattern to widen the gap between the parts of the simile. Such an exaggeration is at the same time both surprising and funny.
7. There are also mixed expressions using more than one of the above techniques.
8. Folkloristic curses, always juicy, are to be found in all languages and cultures. Their humoristic impetus is greater when they are intoned and rhythmic.
9. Paradoxes — at times uniquely intoned.
10. Colloquial language, freely spattered in complex sentences.
11. Foreign words which are twisted in their pronunciation.
12. Finally, "deaf-talk" — a common device of humor. This is also the basis for a comedy of errors of which Shalom Aleichem was very fond.

Shalom Aleichem exemplifies a real type of deaf-talk (when every conversationalist is certain that his partner is aware of what is being talked about) and an artificial type of deaf-talk (when one of the participants feigns innocence — as if not knowing what the topic of conversation is). Both types have a significant comic effect, but the second form also implies more than that — as will be shown later, but I will now discuss the special kind of Shalom Aleichem's humor in "Tevie the Milkman".

The Taste of Bitter Humor of Tevie the Milkman

In several aspects, in "Tevie the Milkman and his seven daughters", Shalom Aleichem reached the peak of his literary work. In it, there are all the comic factors and all his humoristic forms except pranks, verbal slapstick boisterousness per se, mockery or vulgarity and chutzpa.

The first part of the book contains a short prologue "I am not worthy", the exposition. It is followed by two chapters "The great prize" and "Attic", which form a sort of elaborate introduction to the second part of the book which is its essence.

The second part is composed of five monologues; each one is dedicated to one of Tevie's five daughters: Zeitel, Hodel, Chava, Shprintze and Byelke. Finally, there is an epilogue entitled "Go thee forth".

Every daughter's tale is a sad one of separation and of severance of ties from parents, home and heritage. Each one of the five girls is involved in a love affair or is wed by a matchmaker. Each of their five mates represents a certain ideological or social type; and each couple depicts a familial conflict on an ideological and cultural-national background at a critical period in the history of the Jewish people in Eastern Europe, at the turn of the twentieth century.

It might be said that the story of Tevie the Milkman from Anatevka borders on being an allegory and that the course of his life of troubles symbolizes that of many Jews like him. Tevie's misfortunes worsen at every stage: Golda, his wife dies of grief and Tevie, who is left with two daughters — a widow and a divorcée, and grandchildren too, is deprived of his house and native village.

Who could laugh at such a man or at such tragic circumstances? If Tevie survives these frequent blows it is because "The just shall live by his faith" (Habakkuk 2, 4). But with all the similarities his story is not the same as that of Job. We add to his faith his sense of humor; so paraphrasing the verse "and the righteous shall live by his faith and by his jest".

The Monologue as Narrative Art and as Means of Humor

In this work Tevie is the narrator, the witness and the judge, the interpreter and the characterizer — and above all— the most prominent figure. This multiplicity of roles serves as a basis for complexities and contradictions which produce humor. For example, let us observe self-characterization. For many hours a day, Tevie is alone (with his horse) and therefore forced to talk to himself and about himself in reaction to his experiences. This self-reference is one element of a self-defense mechanism he employs in order to survive, to exist and to continue bearing the yoke both of earning a living and of life itself. But concomitantly it is a humoristic technique, as a number of excerpts will show:

> *"If you only knew what troubles and pains this Tevie carries within him";*
> *"Tevie by nature trusts other folks; only the fool believes every one".*
> *"Tevie the good-for-nothing".*

153

"Tevie, Tevie you brute!"
"Be silent Tevie! Take your time!"
"But Tevie isn't a human!" (very frequent)
"But Tevie you're behaving like an old woman"

The choice of this form also seems to moderate the sorrow and shame, the sense of failure and disappointment of the narrating-hero; it is a way of speaking-out deep concerns.

In a humoristic style, at times on the verge of satire, Tevie recounts to Shalom Aleichem his complaints against the Lord-Almighty, the world and the Jewish gentry, and settles the account of debts and rights. Tevie rebels (according to Druyanov's definition of the joke) against those who are more powerful than him: god, government, gentiles, gentry, women, the younger generation . . . but he always comes out the loser. This literary device enables Tevie to send out a humanistic-Jewish message that emerges from his hardships in a-state-of sobriety, without blurring it with tears or excitement.

"As A Man Would Talk to his Neighbor"

Tevie the Milkman's attitude to God is a multiple one. The latent hero of the book is God. Tevie himself is a sort of anti-hero. Both are united in the name TUV-YA (YA being a shortened form of Yehova, the Lord) which sounds like fatal irony. The humanistic edge is in the way Tevie challenges godly justice by restating that he has no appeal against divine justice, because there is no cause or hope in appealing against the rule of the gracious merciful Lord.

The humor of Tevie's exclamations against God is at times a restrained satire, short of a final outright rebellion. The hope and faith, the imagination and the dream reinstate the necessary balance. In order to stay within the limits of humor, Tevie is never in need of black, macabre-like humor. The most common godly figure of speech in the book is "a compassionate and merciful God"; usually when the story displays mercilessness and no pardon.

The nucleus of humor is to be found in every unexpected diversion from the known linguistic norm, but in order to understand the duality of attitude and the source of humor precisely at such dramatic and tragic climaxes, it is necessary to analyze several instances of such talk, of pouring out one's heart, of laying bare one's plea. Tragic and comic, vigor and timidity, appeal alongside acceptance of judgment are all intermingled here. But there is no expression of self-pity. It seems that the situation of directly talking to God is well-known in sources of Jewish and general literature. Ordinarily it is a grave, serious situation, charged with religious tension and overloaded in a pathetic style, even when it is stylized as a reproach or in an accusing manner. In this work, moreover, the situation — distressing as it may be —

lacks pathos and is never dressed up in an artificial manner. The simplicity of every day colloquial language is a convenient bridge for creating a slightly humoristic atmosphere. The lack of heavy-handedness and linguistic pathos in Tevie's speech does not belittle the tragic feelings, but it does neutralize the fear and let out the mental tension. A defense mechanism is activated every time when he is on the verge of breaking down.

Tevie may laugh at himself and even deprecate himself, but it never reaches self-degradation, not even in self-defense at critical moments. Never does he appear as clownish or humiliated. Not even when he testifies to himself being "a man who doesn't care to be joked upon" because "they shall never know what's in his heart".

He has no extreme characteristics, but rather a mixture of giving-in from weakness and self-pride. Aware as he is of his traits he creates a convenient set for humor which is a mixture of laughter and tears: "One eye is laughing, the other weeping".

His image of a hard-luck person (shlimazel) amuses us, and the suffering he goes through shakes us, whilst Tevie's verbal reactions sharpen in us both reactions and we are activated in the manner that bitter wit moves us: one eye laughs, the other cries.

Tevie is not a fool, nor a "schlemiel"; he is not a miser nor a coward; neither a clown nor an entertainer; he is not an idler, and not handicapped in a way that might make it possible to laugh at his entanglements or deride his desolation. The reader laughs with him and for him, because Tevie does not pity himself and neither does he expect pity from the listener-reader.

When Tevie, as he frequently does, declares that he is a good-for-nothing, a luckless, unfortunate, a simpleton believer, a fool or a brute — he acknowledges his chronic ill-luck; and in doing so he pads the place where he falls or soothes his wounded psyche: "I've been a misfortunate all my life and as such I'll die".

When he interprets the proverb of Ecclesiastes: "All is vanity — everything will be alright" we laugh at the witty paradox. Perhaps there is no more a humorous interpretation reflecting most of his weltanschaaung and his self-image in the world than the following: "Man is formed of the dust and is to return to dust" meaning according to Tevie: "man is weaker than a fly and stronger than iron".

A basic quality of Tevie as a literary figure who creates humor is his quality of speech. Tevie is a fervent and empathic communicator. He says "whatever gets on his tongue". He professes to himself to hate reticents. He loves "conversationalists, with whom you could exchange words, verses, Midrash commentaries, world views, and miscellaneous ideas and opinions; that's how Tevie is". He discerns between the conversation of scholars and that of coachmen. He is fond of people who speak their mind and abhors "a man of secrets"; "where there is a secret — there is stealthiness". He testifies to himself as "Tevie isn't a prattler" but he certainly succeeds in converting gossip and chat into art.

Before I touch upon the uniqueness of the humor in this work of Shalom Aleichem, let me summarize the essence of Tevie the Milkman's character: Initially he has a favorable self-image in all aspects of self-disclosure — in personality and behavior. This is, naturally, part of the existence defense mechanism which he buttresses periodically. In fact he comes out of every confrontation defeated. He succumbs to the rich, the common folk, to the gentile, to women, and to the younger generation, to Epicureans too. This fixation of superiority in his self-esteem, while grounded in the reality of being a chronic loser, is the right and germinative set for comic sketches. It seems that the jokes are indeed the weapon of the weak. That "the hidden source of humor is not gaiety but grief" (Mark Twain). The apparent quiet talk, with a somewhat faint smile, at times a bit biting, covers over latent tension and pain.

Humoristic Facets in Tevie the Milkman's Language and Style

If we attempted to change Tevie's figure with that of another Jewish figure living under the same conditions, we would have to change his "knowledge" which impels his speech as well, and he who does not speak in that unique manner can not be Tevie. More than all qualities of that work, it is Tevie's *language* which grants it its folkloristic and literary stature among our people and its fame throughout the world. Tevie's language is also the rhythm and intonation of the story.

His fluency of speech is like the current of a river; flowing idly at times and gushing forth at others. It covers some ground with folk wisdom, and some other distance in clear lyrics. At one section it intensifies dramatically, at another it overflows its banks as in tragedy. All the patterns of sound and tempo are to be found in his loquacity.

His fluency and simple lively style are a buffer against mental weakness and a defense against slipping into sentimentality. It has been stressed that these tales do not contain mischievous pranks, nor grotesque situations, as can be found in abundance in other works of Shalom Aleichem. There is only a little buffoonery for its own sake, nevertheless we smile almost incessantly while reading. If it were not for the language, could we have laughed on hearing the sad tales of the suffering milkman? "How many calamities there are in these amusing monologues of Tevie" (Kariv). Tevie is conscious of his impulse to prattle, but he must speak out, unburden himself in order to maintain his mental balance and continue with his life-routine.

Tevie's language is not just a delightful treasure of words and proverbs. It

156

is not just a kaleidoscopic vortex of verse, Midrash commentaries and quips, twisted and straight; his language is not only "colorful, bursting bubbles" (Hrushovski) and not only a carrier of communication, a means of characterization and even not only a humor generating tool.

When Tevie distorts a verse, explains it crookedly — he enlivens it and throws light on it in a new and refreshing fashion. His surprising novelties express in themselves a creative act; and in this creative fabrication the secret of humor is concealed.

The Weapon of the Verses

Tevie is aware of the scarcity of his knowledge of the holy scriptures. He regrets it, and as every hard-working Jew, wishes for better times when he will be able to devote more time to studying the scriptures, the Torah. He is willing to divulge this weakness to Shalom Aleichem who listens to his tales with the intention of writing them down. But whatever knowledge he does possess he manages to use expediently in discourse, and what is more, as a weapon to match his friends, who are even more ignorant than himself on such matters. Tevie explains the distortion of verses and sayings: "there isn't anything straighter than a ladder, nor more crooked than a proverb".

Gradually he develops this weapon more elaborately and adjusts its calibre according to the perceptiveness and vulnerability of his foes; starting with his son-in-law, the teacher Parchick and finishing off with his boorish son-in-law Padhatzoor; not excluding the priest; Ephraim the match-maker, his daughters, his wife, Golda, his relative Menahem Mendel and not leaving out Leizer-Wolf, the butcher. The rule is that the more illiterate the foe, the greater the manipulation of the verse, the more acute the digression from the original text, the more twisted and false the outcome. Concommitantly, the more fun and amusement the well-read may derive.

Accordingly, the delight of the reader grows in similar proportion to Tevie's self-reference to his causistry of the Midrash-verse as a comic weapon. The reader enjoys sharing Tevie's secret and fixing up the foe, the fool and the folk.

It must not be forgotten that the weapon of the verse is first of all a defensive one. Its foil is drawn out in order to protect the foibles of the self-image; an image of a humble man whose advantage over the wealthy is in his knowledge. It is set in motion for self-defense against the crumbling of the spirit at a moment of crisis. "The joke is the weak's weapon": "Oh, how much I wanted to thrash him with several slick verses, with Midrash, so that he would remember me; this contractor". He thinks at a moment of rage: "Wait, wait my contractor, I'll thrust this verse into your ears till all you see is black" — — — and with this all his aggression is dissipated.

157

Why does a man like Tevie need to produce such a "lethal weapon"? Some limited knowledge, an original and creative thinking capacity, a rich and abundant imagination ("Tevie you're flooding the world with verses and commentaries"), to be an "inventor" at heart, to know "your enemy" and show the right amount of courage and optimism. The manipulations and elaborations that Tevie works out with verses and proverbs have been the object of many studies, but a comprehensive analysis of all forms and uses concerning their sources and the various techniques employed, has yet to be undertaken.

Shalom Aleichem did not invent Jewish humor with its different characteristics, not Jewish social satire nor the bitter wit or the self-jesting. The distortion of the verse and its meaning have their origins in the sources of our Sages (Chazal),in the Maqamas (rhymed prose) of the Middle Ages and in the satires of the Haskalah period extending till Mendele. But Shalom Aleichem developed this kind of humor into an independent art, a valid humoristic genre — and one of the foremost and sophisticated in the field of Jewish humor. Hence it is possible to mention only some of the types; not according to any distinct criterion of quality, value or purpose.

1) A weird and ridiculous interpretation to the expression extracted from traditional Jewish interpretive sources — the most common type of distortion performed for humoristic purpose.

2) An original interpretation of verse or saying from the prayer book. Different from the type mentioned above, this is not an attempt to interpret the origin, but to continue as if the additional commentary were just a logical outcome of the original one.

3) An integrated interpretation: the source being broken up into phrases which separately acquire various meanings.

4) A splinter of a verse correctly quoted (mostly from a prayer verse or from Biblical stories), its end being changed and applied to a different matter in a surprising way.

5) A part of a verse or proverb quoted precisely but interpreted for a different cause and conveying a digressive meaning.

6) A disruption of the original word or pronouncing it incorrectly in order to create a new and queer meaning.

7) Making up verses and sayings that are fictitious: this causistry is only employed against ignorants or gentiles that are presumably unable to detect its falsity. At times Tevie enlists the intonation of the Aramaic language to add a touch of validity to such a verse.

8) Reduction of expressions and original florid idioms in order to insert them into daily conversation. This type of common saying is used abundantly in Shalom Aleichem's writings in general. Such linguistic use in people's everyday conversations, while always intending to cause mirth, is analogous

to the insertion of verse and wise proverbs in the discourse of scholars.

Laughter mostly breaks out right at the beginning of a verse or at its interpretation, when knowingly or unwittingly it is not related to its correct source. The knowledgeable reader is amused when at the beginning of the interpretation Tevie uses the wrong term for the type of source discussed. Other falsifications occur when he attributes a fictitious saying to an authentic source, or when, for example, he attributes a commentary to Rashi which he never made, or when he relates an authentic proverb to a nonexistent source.

Rhythm and Intonation in the Service of Magnification of the Humor

Rhythm and intonation of a verse, idiom, proverb etc. may contribute significantly to a kind of humor whose basis is disruption, twist, and distortion.

Most of Tevie's quotations (the exact and the faulty) from the sources have a rhythmic pattern and most have a distinct tonal rhythm; there are multiple meanings to different words, synonymic parallelism, antithetical parallelism, or a complementary kind. It may be assumed that most of the sayings were selected by the speaker for their rhythmic tonal pattern. Its advantages are pleasant rhetoric, aesthetic charm, and the fact that they might be easily perceived and therefore easily distinguished for their distortion from the original form, a digression which is the cause of laughter. For these qualities of the pattern, proverbs and verses have become firmly embedded in folklore since time immemorial. Tevie depends on his listener's previous knowledge, and knows that the digression from the original is sure to be perceived. The verses serve Tevie as an efficient defense mechanism: counterbalancing the tears by arousing laughter. Prolixity is his strategy; the verse games, his tactics.

In the bok's first part the humor is slight, folkloristic, perhaps a bit vulgar. The product is strictly laughter derived from enjoyment. But in the second part of the book, the technique of insertion and interpretation undergoes a profound change, and reaches the artistic heights of bitter humor.

When he is pressed back by the gentile society surrounding him, he is in need of the verse weapon, to support, in his laughter, his Jewish identity, and to differentiate explicitly between Israel and other people. When he weakens in his struggle against all the forces opposed to him — the younger generation, the Epicureans, the rebels which pervade the traditional familial territory, he turns to verse-humor, and thus can accept his fate. When he is overloaded with complaints and reproaches against godly injustice, against the social inequity and against the hard-heartedness of the Jewish society he holds fast to the anticipated relaxation caused by verse-laughter. When he feels the undermining of his manly authority in the company of his wife and seven daughters, he blurs it by concentrating on verse and epigrams which uphold and uplift his paternal image and sense of domination. "You immediately come up with a verse for everything" exclaims his feminine company, and he evades them, and cunningly overcomes their protests by confusing them with his twists of the tongue.

Here is a fictitious dialogue reflecting the constant state-of-mind which the suffering Tevie is in and the way he deals with it:

> *A: While reading the tragic poem of Tevie the Milkman — one*
> *gets the feeling of wanting to cry.*
> *B: Then why do we laugh instead?*
> *A: Because Tevie himself amuses us.*
> *B: Why is he amusing?*
> *A: Because he himself wants to laugh.*
> *B: Why is that so?*
> *A: Because he must laugh.*
> *B: But why?*
> *A: So he won't cry.*
> *B: So why doesn't he simply cry?*
> *A: Because . . . "Tevie isn't a woman"*

Conclusion: "Tevie the Milkman" for the Young Generation

I have stated that this bitter humor that Shalom Aleichem created in this wonderful piece is one of the most sophisticated of its kind in Hebrew literature. Tevie's monologues are a sort of "entertaining quiz" for the reader. The reader must simultaneously perform several actions: uncover the reminders or hints relating to Jewish traditional sources, customs and folklore; to identify and locate the sources; to catch on to their connection with the text; to comprehend Tevie's "trick" and only then to reach laughter and enjoyment. In this complex process, the contemporary younger generation reader in Israel is already held back in the initial stage, due to his lack of knowledge of the sources.

Humor which is a product of cultural-ethnic folklore; which is constructed upon connotations and allusions belonging to a certain lingual sphere, which is based on figurative language and grammar forms typical of a particular society at a particular place and time — such humor has its unique code which might lose much of its brilliance even when its translation is excellent. The contemporary translators (Hrushovski, Aharony, Ben-Shalom) attempt to overcome this language barrier in order to attract back the younger generation to Shalom Aleichem in general and to "Tevie the Milkman" specifically. It is a generation for whom Yiddish is not the language, as is also the case for many of their parents; what is more, the place of the traditional literary sources in their education is on the wane.

REFERENCES

Aharony, A. *Shalom Aleichem: Tevie the Milkman.* Aleph publications & Siphriat Hapoalim, 1982.

Ben-Shalom, G. *Shalom Aleichem — Tevie the Milkman and his Daughters.* Tel Aviv, 1983.

Druyanov, A. *The Book of the Joke & the Jest,* Dvir Publications, 1963.

Gross-Zimmerman, M. "Freilecher Pathos" (Joyous Pathos), An Addendum to The Works of Shalom Aleichem. Yiwa Publications, Buenos Aires, 1969.

Halperin, S. "Concerning the term 'dramatic'", *Criticism & Interpretation,* No. 11–12, 1978, p. 259–268.

Hrushovski, B. *Shalom Aleichem — Tevie the Milkman & Monologues,* Siman Kriah Publications & The Kibbutz Meuhad, 1983, pp. 195–212.

Humor, miscellaneous encyclopaedias & literary dictionaries.

Jewish Humor, miscellaneous encyclopaedias & literary dictionaries.

Kariv, A. *Iyunim.* Dvir Publications, 1950, p. 36–41.

Keshet, Y. "Differentiations". *On Shalom Aleichem,* Dvir Publications, 1962, p. 7–33.

Miron, D. *Shalom Aleichem,* An Essay. Massada, T.A., 1970.

Penueli, S.I. *Sifrut Kipshuta.* Dvir Publications, 1963, p. 271–281.

Rivlin, A.E. *Unfolding A Story.* The Institute for Educational Means, 1984, p. 49–62.

Rozansky, S. "Old and new in Tevie the Milkman of Shalom Aleichem", an introduction to the works of Shalom Aleichem, Yiwa Publications, Buenos Aires, 1969.

Sadan, D. Avney Bohan. "The minister of humor" & "Between satire and humor", *Machbarot Lesiphrut,* T.A. 1951.

Shalom Aleichem, miscellaneous encyclopaedias & literary dictionaries.

Shmorack, H. "Tevie der milchiker — the history of the work" in *Hasifrut,* No. 26, 1978, p. 26–38.

Ziv, A. *Humor & Personality,* Pappirus, 1984, p. 55–72.

D. Alexander

POLITICAL SATIRE IN THE ISRAELI THEATRE: ANOTHER OUTLOOK ON ZIONISM

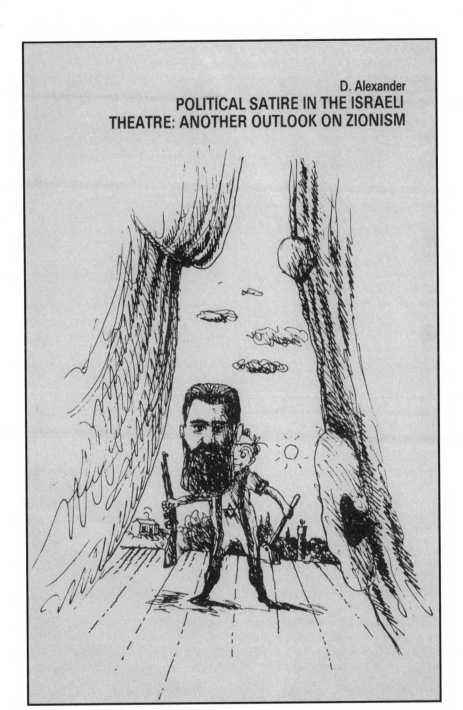

DAVID ALEXANDER
Tel Aiv University, Israel

POLITICAL SATIRE IN THE ISRAELI THEATRE
Another Outlook On Zionism

The early chapters in the history of Hebrew-speaking theatre in Israel introduced a very clear definition of the functions that local society attributed to theatre arts, namely, that theatrical activity was expected to be part of the pioneering process which strove to rebuild a new entity in an ancient land. Thus, stage-artists — amateur as well as would-be-professional — assumed the role of educators and of founding-fathers to a new brand of Jewish culture, and this objective preceded any other aim, either as considering the theatre a source of amusement, or as relating to it in the capacity of "art for art's sake."

During this period of the emergence of what was to become known as the "Yishuv" (The Jewish population in the land of Israel), stage productions — as indeed all other cultural activities — were evaluated according to the contribution they made towards ideological assets and national values. Quite a number of plays during the first thirty years of the present century were followed by intensive controversies which related not so much to artistic interpretations as to current social criteria. The basic question was one of what was fitting for the people as material for theatrical experience in view of the fact that entirely new walls were being created on traditional foundations. This yard stick was applied to the early productions that were presented by members of the "Lovers of the Hebrew Stage" (an amateur dramatic society founded in 1904), as well as to the repertoire of "The Tent" ("Ha'Ohel") a socialist-oriented studio (1925).

It is in this environment that one finds, towards the end of the twenties, the first satirical cabaret, "Ha-Kumkum" ("The Kettle"). The innovator and founder of what was supposed to be an Israeli version of the European "Kleine Buhne" was the Hungarian-born poet writer and essayist Avigdor Ha-Meiri. Ha-Meiri's first encounter with satiric activity in Palestine is another example of the idealistic nature of artistic expression referred to at the beginning of this paper. At the same time it reflects one of the major trends in the personality of a true satirist: a life-size "Chutzpa." Avigdor Ha-Meiri came to Palestine as an immigrant from Oddessa in the summer of 1921. Less than three months after his arrival he had already written and published a pamphlet, entitled: "Lev Hadash ("A New Heart"). This satiric newsletter (of which only 8 issues were published between 1921 and 1924)

165

had a very clear, prophetic-like charter inscribed on its front page:

Throw away all your sins, and create for yourselves a new heart.[1]

While watching his people arriving in the Promised Land, contaminated (as he put it) by deadly culture acquired along with the European flesh pots Ha-Meiri decided to assume the role of a modern robe-clad street-preacher, who was to conduct an ideological battle against all local sins and vices.[2] All this, it may be stressed once again, within a few months of his first landing at Jaffa port . . .

The same spirit prevailed in the Kumkum. On the opening-night, which was in Tel Aviv on the first of May 1927, the conferencier introduced the main topics with which the cabaret planned to deal. 160 perplexed witnesses were sitting around small tables sipping tea (one might view this as the local alternative to the classical night-club scene), listening to the master of ceremonies chanting Ha-Meiri's lines, elaborating on the fact that the whole system of the new Jewish settlement in Palestine was indeed going to be scalded by the Kettle's steam.[3]

The more poetic recollections relating to The Kumkum can be found in newspaper columns of those days:

It is the first time that they have shown us in the theatre a picture based on our thoughts and on the true reality of the Yishuv[4]

wrote one critic, and another of his colleagues added:

The Kumkum is the lighted mirror which reflects our national and humanistic entity.[5]

And yet, there was one more dimension worth mentioning related to Ha-Meiri's work with the satiric company (besides the fact that he was the sole writer of the witty material, the leader of the troupe and its manager). In his notebook he made rough entries under the heading: "On satiric theatre — lessons to the members of The Kumkum,[6] which are sketches stating his satiric credo:

The beauty and the ideal to which we strive are boring . . . lifeless formulae . . . in every charm there is a little of the distorted, and in every distortion one can always find some charm . . .
. . . so when we laugh at the distorted we do so out of the love we bear for it.
In every laughter there has to be love and joy. The things we do not care for, we never distort (we never make an object of laughter).[7]

I am not at all sure that all the respected gentlemen that The Kumkum satirically mocked would have agreed wholeheartedly with Ha-Meiri's declarations of "love and joy". After all, we have to realize that while waging war against various modes of Jewish life in Palesine, Ha-Meiri spared nothing and nobody: leaders of the Zionist Movement, institutions dealing with internal Jewish affairs, religious foundations, representatives of the British government in Palestine, a wide range of ideologies and beliefs, and a series of types presenting a diverse cross-section of the Jewish population gathering in Eretz Yisrael. All this was done, however, with empathy and care towards the objects under the satirist's dissecting knife. Satire, too, was expected to share the burdens of establishing a new society of pioneers. Satiric comments were not uttered in pessimistic hatred and out of despair, but rather were directed by an optimistic point of view which believed in healing vices.

A further confirmation of this conception is to be found in the apologetic-like comments made by members of "Ha-Matateh" ("The Broom") — the second satiric company in Palestine after The Kumkum — often on the verge of closing down their theatre. The Matateh, which was founded in 1928, was shut down after twenty-six years of constant activity — not only because of the withdrawal of the British mandate (foreign rule is always a much appreciated bitter enemy for satire), but first and foremost because "they had expected us to mock things that were being built right under our eyes, and we said: 'What?' We, who fought to get an independent state, should now get up and flog it?'"[8] This may be a somewhat unexpected declaration coming from an artist, a politically-involved actor, whose main target should have been the establishment and all institutions of government. It is not so surprising when one bears in mind that actors of the satiric stage, as well as other artists, did see themselves from the first wave of immigration to Palestine (1880) as fulfilling a Zionist mission; making their contribution on the front line of fighting towards the realization of a vision, stated a few years earlier.

One of the leading journalists in the Hebrew press, Uri Kaysari, devoted an editorial to the satiric theatre in those early years. One phrase in this article seems to me accurately to define the main motive and motivation of Hebrew satire:

The satiric theatre is the means to bring forth the deep tragedy of the beautiful dream about the redemption of Eretz-Yisrael, and the bitter realization of this dream.[9]

I wish to suggest, therefore, that satire in Israel — in prestate days as well as from 1948 onwards — has been, and still is, a reflection (in a distorted mirror) of the Zionist idea and vision. Whilst the approach changes from one period to another, styles and intonations, modes of design and points-of-view all undergo dynamic changes and shifts; nonetheless, the need for the

167

expression stems from the wish to present a first hand reaction and opinion to the constant process of rebuilding a Jewish homeland.

In direct continuation to the basic supposition that I make, I claim, further, that from the establishment of the State of Israel in 1948, we can observe two distinct trends in the evolution of local satire. This division created two dichotomously opposed approaches to the satirical treatment of the local, national and political scene.

If I refer once again to the theatre as a specific channel of satiric expression, this would be the place to note the fact that the two approaches also differ in their dramatic structure and stage form, as in the motifs expressed in them.

The one approach (first chronologically), seemed to continue the prestate times and to accompany the formation of a mixed society comprised of immigrants and refugees. It focused on social matters, on the raising of typical internal political problems ("wheeling-dealing") and exposés, as well as on condemnation of negative phenomena in the establishment. The big "hit" in the theatre of the early fifties was Efrayim Kishon's "His Name Precedes Him"; a comedy which describes new Israeli society as cultivating political "protectia" as a substitute for professional knowhow. The heroes of the plot are the bureaucratic establishment and an illegible signature on a letter of introduction.

The satiric tone governing this phase of satire bordered on the mildly ironic, and the humoristic barbs were unprovocative.

But above all, it was, to a great extent, satire written and produced by people who came to Israel as new immigrants from central European countries; artists who related to the tradition of the classical, witty and elegant cabaret — which was forced many times to find sophisticated solutions to express a political opinion in a restricting régime. Publishing satire in Israel was, therefore, both an advantage and a cause for frustration at the same time: freedom of political speech is always a virtue, and yet — as far as satire is concerned — the fact that it does not have to fight for its "survival" is one of the shortcomings of democracy.

"There is no law forbidding anybody to say all he wishes, and yet — there is no law forcing people to listen,"[10] complained Kishon, and Dosh (Kri'el Gardosh — a noted Israeli cartoonist and writer, who is also Hungarian-born) raised his eyebrows in a rhetorical question: "What is the big-deal about 'bold' satire in Israel? Attacking establishment is rather a quick way to earn your living."[11]

I dare say, then, that this dualism of admiration and frustration, along with the fact that they came over as "olim" (new immigrants) and were introduced right away into a "dream that has come true" created a kind of mild, forgiving approach to the ailments of Israeli society in the works of

Kishon, Yossef Lapid and Dosh. Following all this they have in fact become spokesmen for the nationalistic line based on a widely-held concept of a national consensus. Their satire seeks at one and the same time to represent the newly-conceived political entity of the Jewish people in Israel, and to *improve* its reality — not necessarily to *change* it.

To sum it up then, the first approach in new Israeli satire continued to strengthen the foundations of the Zionist vision and its dispositions, to follow it as it materialized, and to cherish its profile.

The second approach, which began to develop after the Six Day War (1967), attempted to sketch the state of our lives in drab colours and in an extreme style. This trend adopted an aggressive mode of artistic expression making use of grotesque, vulgar and violent means. The writers responsible for this brand of satirical comments were young, Israeli-born artists, who "recruited" satiric weapons (even for the anti-militarist satirist his art and its tools are indeed "heavy armor") in order to introduce a new interpretation of the Zionist crisis.

Without a foreign rule against which to direct poisonous arrows — but at the same time without a commitment to admire the actual fact of having become an independent state — a new generation of creators was born which relinquished humoristic occupation with domestic matters in favor of a direct and biting attack on values and basic ideological concepts.

The key word in defining the cause for this attack is "disappointment". Disappointment at the way things turned out; bitterness at the realization of the vision. The analysis of "A dream and an awakening" is the central theme in the satiric works of Amos Kainan, Hanoch Levin, B. Michael, Rami Rosen, Yehoshua Sobol and Yehonathan Gefen — to mention but a few of the leading representatives of this generation.

> *This play presents variations on the theme of murder. The*
> *murdered object is a dream, the murderers — are the dreamers . . .*
> *They murder their dream, and with it themselves. The main*
> *dream is our dream about the State of Israel . . .*[12]

— thus wrote Amos Kainan in the programme to one of his plays, "For I Still Believe in Thee", and Yehonathan Gefen intoned in one of his cabaret-lyrics:

> *This was almost it.*
> *We were right next to it.*
> *So what happened to this dream?*
> *What had caused it to melt away?*[13]

The period following the victorious Six Day War, signified by a wave of national intoxication, exaggerated pride and a series of newly-conceived myths was the turning point in local satiric expression. At first it was Hanoch Levin, who through two cabaret reviews,[14] made harsh proclamations about the war and its moral outcome. Needless to say that at the time these were very unpopular statements with the public. Very few theatre spectators were prepared to sit still at the Tel Aviv Kameri Theatre, while on stage Levin unfolded *his* concept of the last war. The liberation of the West Bank, including all holy places of worship, has become in his theatrical dialogue a mere family-feud over the right to "govern" the bathtub and the toilet.

This sacrilegious mini-drama, along with a new commentary on the classical motive of the Akedah (the biblical story of the attempted sacrifice of Isaac) and a grotesque scene in which young Israeli lovers passionately court and kiss . . . were themselves among the factors that caused Levin's "Bathtub Queen" to be removed from the stage after only 19 performances.[15]

Soon after, many more voices were to join in with Levin, all carrying anti nationalistic messages that contradicted every theory and practice of nationalism, and rejecting narrow patriotism, militarism and recent myths, telling of bereavement and widowhood.

A quick glance at the "inventory" of productions in the Israeli theatre in the last fifteen years illustrates the tendencies and atmosphere of this brand of satire. In the period that has passed since the "earthquake" that shook the very foundations of Israeli society following the Yom Kippur War (October 1973), and which includes the controversial war in Lebanon — the satiric stage has presented, among other titles, the following plays:

(a) Rami Rosen's "Fash-Cholnik". A review written and performed after the war in 1973. The title is a combination of two words: "Schol" — bereavement, and "Fashla", the colloquial word for a disaster.

(b) "The Last Striptease", by Sobol and Mittelpunkt — a cabaret review offering a glance at Israeli society in the 1980s through the narrow doorway of a cheap and ugly nightclub inhabited by distorted outcasts. (1982).

(c) Kainan's "Friends Talk of Jesus". This is an acute and subjective version of chosen chapters in the Jewish history of torment and redemption. The play was forbidden for public performance by the Israeli censor (1972).

(d) Levin's latest satiric review "The Patriot", which introduces the new type of Israeli character: ready to spit in his mother's face so as to get an immigrant's visa to the US, and ready to kick an Arab boy in the face in order to qualify for land purchase in the West Bank. "The Patriot" was performed in spite of a censorship prohibition, shortly after the main phase of the Lebanon War (1982).

And so, from one war to another, between battles and periods of ceasefire, on the long endless path of continuing armed conflicts, Israel's antinationalist satire has become more bitter, more gruesome, more obscene.

170

At the same time, in a parallel track, the nationalist group of satirists (usually referred to as the "hawkish gang") accordingly adopted a fierce tone in an attempt to defend *their* view of the "original Zionist doctrine". And from time to time these two divisions get busy directing their spears at each other rather than at the social and political institutions surrounding them. They seem to join hands and agree on one issue only: the futility of the satiric comment when it comes time to measure and assess its effectiveness. It does not matter where the satirist stands, nor what ideology he claims to put forward; in the long run each and every one has his followers as well as his adversaries. Political satire in Israel is an expected feature of political life: it changes no opinions and it strengthens predispositions. Or, to put it in the words of Kobi Neev, one of a team that introduced a very successful satirical programme into the national television network, some years ago:

A nation needs satire as babies need calcium. It is good for the bones, yet it does not affect the brain.

NOTES

1. "Lev Hadash", No. 1, September 1921.
2. *Ibid.*
3. *Genazim* archives, Tel Aviv, file no. 119/19.
4. *Do'ar Ha-Yom.* 9 July 1927.
5. Ben-Zion, *Do'ar Ha-Yom,* July 1927.
6. *Genazim, op. cit.*
7. *Ibid.*
8. London, Bezalel. *Teatron,* No. 2, 1962.
9. Keysari, Uri. *Do'ar Ha-Yom.* 24 January 1928.
10. Kishon, E. "Lo Norah", 1957.
11. Gardosh, K. Interview for research, Tel Aviv, 7 July 1976.
12. Kainan, A. "For I Still Believe in Thee", 1974.
13. Gefen, Y. "Starting Anew" (from "The Last War"), 1974.
14. "You, Me and the Next War", 1968.
15. "Bathtub Queen", 1970.

I. Roeh and R. Nir

WHAT? HUMOR? IN THE NEWS? — HOW SERIOUS IS THE NEWS ON ISRAELI RADIO

I. ROEH and R. NIR

Hebrew University, Israel

WHAT? HUMOR? IN THE NEWS?
How Serious is the News on Israeli Radio

A. Introduction: On the Nature of News and Marginality of Humor

News and humor? If you are seriously looking for a playful, amusing experience, you had better look elsewhere. Moreover, analyzing the news may seem fruitless even to one who is trying to gain a better understanding — seriously, intellectually — of what humor is: humor and news?

No definition of humor — neither the one that can be inferred from Aristotle's view that laughter is mainly *at* (another's inferiority, etc.), nor Hegel's point that the highest kind of comedy is when one laughs *with*, not *at* — seems to help us make significant inroads in the study of what news is. At the same time, no definition of news seems to help us gain a better understanding of humor, because — well, because news is all too serious! . . . And if our corpus of Israeli news is representative, then it is deadly serious.

As is widely held by students of Western journalism, news is an institution whose main function is to inform society at large as to whether its basic needs are being satisfied. Basic needs, that is, as they are defined within the limits of a concrete social, cultural and political context. And naturally, an all too crucial question necessarily follows: Who defines these limits? It is beyond the scope of this paper to struggle with this question and with the issues which it implies. To say that news *informs* is not necessarily to suggest that news is not an instrument of control or even of domination. It can well be either, and still our attempt to examine the freedom — though strictly limited — to deviate from the norm of seriousness in the news remains significant. That is our aim in this paper: to analyze how humor infiltrates the territory of serious news.

Whether an instrument of control in the hands of the powerful who define society's needs (and try hard to stay in power), or a medium that authentically reflects the needs of a pluralistic society, the news exists mainly to warn of dangers and threats, to "remind" society of its basic norms and values, of its self-image and so forth. It exists to reproduce (the) dominant belief-system(s) or ideology(ies).

Sociologists who take pains to study news seem obediently to follow Durkheim's dictum as to the morally cohesive function of bad news (cf.

175

Merton and Lazarsfeld, 1971), and this basic assumption is echoed in such different studies of news as Epstein (1973), Tuchman (1978), Gans (1979), Gitlin (1980), Hall (1982), and many others. Each emphasizes different aspects of news and most differ in terms of their theoretical perspectives, but all agree, we would argue, that the news is displayed on the central stage where society's symbols are produced and is therefore immensely obligated to this centrality.

Views may significantly differ, then, as to the power of elites and governments to manage the news; views may vary as to whether news "must" contribute to, or be determined by, the ideological hegemony, or whether it can be seen as a reflection of a pluralistic culture. But there can hardly be disagreement as to its significant role in the process of the production of meaning. Neither Marxists, who assume that meaning is imposed, nor liberals-pluralists, who believe that meaning is continuously negotiable, would deny this role.

It is inconceivable, therefore, that the news would lightly, frivolously or laughingly beat that which is culturally defined as of national importance. It is likewise unthinkable that the news, national news, would treat lightly any (so-defined) legitimate segment of the population, any legitimate institution, any representation of a system of beliefs. The whole nation is present and listening! The situation calls forth dignity and respect. Can the news be anything but a reverent discourse?

But still one may be right to expect some humor to creep in, if only for reasons explained by aesthetic and/or rhetorical need for variation. It can be argued that presentation needs it, form requires it.[1]

The main question becomes, then, what kinds of reality-materials will lend themselves to comic presentation. Jokes, we know from Mary Douglas (1975), debunk established hierarchies. They express community as undifferentiated. It is Victor Turner's "anti-structure" (1978) that can be expressed through a frivolous, irreverent discourse. Turner's "positive structure" which is expressed/reflected in the news, is the highly formalized conventionalized discourse.[2]

Our main hypothesis is that the "permission" to deviate from the reverent (and standardized) presentation is given only: 1) when reality-materials which are defined as irrelevant or unworthy are concerned or 2) when the reality-materials under consideration are deviant social phenomena seen as deserving society's reproach or condemnation.[3]

At this point, the Hobbesian (1870) and particularly the Bergsonian (1956) "culturist" rather than aesthetic definitions of laughter seem to be called on.

176

B. Marginality of Humor as a Main Trait of News

With Hobbes and Bergson, who take the comic to be a social instrument of censorship, even of punishment, one returns to the Durkheimian notion mentioned above. Through punishment, as well as through the very act of publicizing the deviant, social cohesiveness is reinforced. This notion, it is widely held, is exemplified by western news, overrun as it is with warnings, threats, dangers and interruptions — in short, with bad news. And bad news is, after all, not typically comic.

Why, then, take the risks of the researcher's frustration (and not at all the playful frustration suggested by comic incongruities . . .) at realizing, as we did, that traces of humor are so few, so atypical? Why take pains in trying to categorize kinds of humor and generators of humor when all the various types of humor combined are found in only some 3% of the total number of news items in our corpus? It is for a better understanding of the rule through its exception, for a better understanding of what is so serious about 97% of the news. Through an examination of the limits of humor, the limits of what "must" be treated seriously and reverently can be described. The very few news stories which are the focus of this study may help demonstrate:

a)   What the reality-materials are that do permit light-touch presentation in the news, and

b)   What the (digressing) linguistic means and rhetorical devices are that produce the humorous effect.

In contrast to the digressing means that produce humor and to which we will return later, let us stay for a while with what is typical. Roeh (1982) shows how vocabulary, syntax, intonation, patterns of narrative and many other components of presentation in the Israel radio news are strictly constrained. A very limited number of patterns on all levels recur with minimal variation. Moreover, the same study found that the norm of minimal digression is particularly dominant in news stories that represent reality-materials which are more heavily burdened with ideological meanings. Stories related to the political élites or those which directly refer to questions of "national existence" permit the least digression from presentational conventions. It is only in nonélite stories, in those relating to topics considered trivial or inconsequential as far as the established social order is concerned, that some stylistic creativity is found. Similarly, it is argued that the latent message of standardized presentation that forbids direct speech, that excludes first and second persons as well as avoiding other means of *contextualization* is obviously ideological. This decontextualized point of view with its corresponding authoritative intonation implies respect toward, and reaffirmation of what is ideological. Skepticism, ambiguity, light touch, irony — all these digressions may occur where low news value is concerned, and in some cases when society's enemies or its various type of trouble-makers are dealt with.

It follows that humor is bound to occur with the less-than-respectful, less-than-affirmative stories in the news. And, indeed, this tends to be the case in our corpus.

C. Presentation of the Corpus: Three Kinds of Stories that "Permit" Humor

From among some 1,000 stories (or items, as they are called by newspersons) that constitute a random sample from 180 news bulletins broadcast over the last four years, we determined that 31 included an element of humor. Needless to say, our judgment was based on an analysis of the text and on the implied point of view therein, *not* on individually subjective assessments which tend to vary with the observer's perspectives due to differences in location or in time. After all, every proposition, every piece of information may always be taken by somebody at a given point of time to be ridiculous, funny, absurd or whatever. Are the politician's serious statements not always funny to some of his opponents? Over time, do they not seem funny even to some of his supporters?

The largest group of stories consists of those with the lowest news value. It can be argued that the probability for each story in this group to be included in the bulletin is not any higher than for its probability to be excluded. It is, to use Jakobson's terms, for the *poetic function* that they are selected, or, to use another well-recognized literary concept, for the function of comic relief. These are the trivial, that is, the inconsequential stories which bear no relevance "to our lives" (broadcaster's and listener's), and which convey no offense to any group, or are of no value of importance in the specific cultural context. Hence, they "deserve" no respect, no reverence.

The following are a few story subject headings which illustrate this type of low-value news group:

1) Bank robbery in Tucson, Arizona.
2) Car competition in Britain.
3) Beauty contest in Denmark.
4) Football, and rain, in Italy.
5) First woman pilot completes flight around the world and overcomes her fear of flying.

Because they are inconsequential, these stories lend themselves to a kind of presentation which is highly atypical for the news. Here is the very limited province of both stylistic freedom and the freedom to laugh innocently. If irony — which does imply a serious attitude — creeps in, it is very light, as we shall see.

178

In the second group, humor tends to be less amusing and somewhat more problematic. Stories are only marginally consequential, but they are not necessarily trivial. In terms of news value, they are judged to be of higher value as compared to the first group, the actors and plots are "closer" to the societal scene. Here we meet different deviants, outlaws and dropouts for whom, true, there should be no respect, but still, they do "belong" to us in one sense or another. To laugh at them is problematic that their stories may — often do, in fact — contain an element of seriousness. This contrasts with the situation where, for instance, we Israelis can laugh at a bank robber in Tucson. It is, therefore, no longer a case of mere comic relief. The reason stories of this group are included in a newsbulletin cannot be only to satisfy the aesthetic unity. There is some social function fulfilled in addition to the poetic function. To laugh at, to mock deviants is, again, to reinforce social norms, and these stories are consequential at least in this respect.

It is not so simple to make a clear distinction between the ways of storytelling in the first and second groups, and it is likewise difficult to make distinctions as far as kinds of humor are concerned. However, we propose that when the social context *is* involved (when stories do relate to reality-materials of some proximity to broadcaster and recipient), humor will tend to be less amusing, more ironic.

A few illustrations from this second group are:

1) Religious extremists in Jerusalem fight with the police, drawing on arguments from the Talmud.

2) A trial of an ex-political personality who has lost his standing.

3) The police arrest a burglar in a restaurant. He argues: "I was hungry."

The third group, which is smaller than the other two, does suggest a clear distinction between the comic and the ironic — the latter is certainly dominant here. As a rule, bitter and malicious irony seems to be more common here than light irony, even if it is presented with moderation. In this set of stories, the reality-materials are those of serious news, conventional news. They relate to questions of national interests, their protagonists belong to the élite, what is happening and what is said is consequential. This is certainly not what causes liberating, guileless laughter.

As is the case in our corpus, some enemy-élites belong to this group, and other actors are also not the best of Israel's friends. Either way, none of them deserve respect. Irony, we know, is bred on distance. Here are some examples:

1) King Hussein criticizes the PLO.

2) Everybody shoots at everybody in Beirut.

3) Iraq condemns Israel in the UN.

4) The U.S. government is not satisfied with Israeli politics.

5) Millions of Germans support Nazi ideology.

The first item, for instance, is serious stuff, but one may smile at a distance, as one does through a particular linguistic choice, as we will see later. Similarly, number 2 relates to a serious situation, but we Israelis are out of Beirut at this point and there is no danger to any of us any more . . . And, besides, who can make any sense of the absurdities in Lebanon, anyway. Items 3, 4 and 5 are no less serious/consequential and cannot be treated lightly.

Neither the need for comic relief nor an aesthetic/poetic explanation seems of any relevance when this kind of story is under consideration. News value is high. It is a province of serious matter treated ironically, and in a very limited or highly controlled fashion, as we will illustrate later on. The generators of humor are few, and the degree of stylistic creativity is much lower as compared to the first two groups.

As we will show, the first two groups stand together in opposition to the last one, in terms of both representation of social reality and stylistic and rhetorical means. Let us now take a closer look at a number of news items in which the various types of humorous effects can be demonstrated.

D. A Few Illustrations and Analysis*

(1) In Los Angeles the plane of Brook Nass landed this morning. She is the first woman who flew a plane around the world passing over the two poles. Nass, a business woman of thirty-eight, became a pilot only five years ago. Her specific goal was to overcome her fear of flying. Her husband awaited her at the airport, holding a huge bouquet of flowers. President Reagan called her on the phone to congratulate her on the mission. She told him about the present she had brought him — a five-million year-old ice block from Antarctica. The flight lasted 85 hours, 1 minute and 44 seconds. On returning she said she now had just one dream — to take a hot, fragrant bath.

The item is an inconsequential "tail-piece" story. The achievement of a pilot does not, in itself, evoke humor. The comic character of the story is culturally created by the nature of the actor — a woman pilot. The tale is studded with feminine symbols: presents, flowers, dreams, a fragrant bath, the noted "fear of flying." The stereotype of the fair sex is contrasted with her daring act of flying a plane around the globe. This contrast is stressed by the punch line which reminds the listeners: although she performed a manly act, she is still a woman who dreams about a fragrant bath. Another elaborated contrast that contributes to the same effect is suggested by the symmetrical

---

* We have remained as faithful to the Hebrew text as possible, paying only secondary attention to English acceptability.

presentation of the husband (holding a huge bouquet of flowers), President Reagan (congratulating her on the phone), and the pilot (telling them about the presents and the dream . . .).

The reporter throws several numbers at us as if to assign importance to the mission. A detailed enumeration of either objects or adjectives is a recurrent generator of humor in our sample. In this specific story it signifies value and technological achievement, and stands in contrast to "feminine," less-valued symbols of flowers and a bath. In this story one encounters one of the traditional victims of humor — a woman. However, the irony, if at all present, is light and relatively harmless.

(2) Among the arguments that Tel-Aviv policemen heard tonight: "I was hungry and wanted to eat"; so . . . a sixty-year-old man (who was) caught while breaking into a restaurant.
"We were looking for a dentist for urgent treatment" so . . . two suspects (who were) caught while breaking into an apartment.*
Those who provided the excuses will now have to let the ears of the Judge hear them as well.

The reality-materials in this item are taken from the world of crime. The two ministories have low news value since the actors are of no importance (even as deviants), and the actions are of little significance. The aesthetic notion of comic relief — as opposed to the fulfillment of a cultural function — seems to be a better explanation of why it is news. Thus, the reporter can afford to use a rather unconventional and creative style, introducing the item with the topicalized "Among the arguments . . . ." Further, a dramatic effect is achieved by a "showing" rather than "telling"; that is, the suspects are quoted directly, the reporter does not recount their tale.[4] Also, the very combination of two ministories into one narrative frame is noteworthy.

The first story shows a sixty-year-old thief who is caught red-handed. The contrast between the action of breaking into a restaurant and the words he utters about being hungry produce situational irony. This effect is amplified by the topicalized opening sentence, which serves as a lead for both events. Both use similar reality-materials and in both cases the ironic effect is achieved by similar situations — thieves, caught red-handed while committing a crime, utter unreliable, ridiculous excuses.

The ending comment of the item sums up both events. It can be regarded as a punch line, as an intrusion of the narrator, implying: "Now let us wait

---

* Through the mechanism of ellipsis, Hebrew maintains direct speech while deleting the verb "say." Literally the text reads, "I was hungry . . ." so . . . a sixty-year-old man.

181

and see if the suspects will have the nerve to restate their excuses while standing trial in front of a judge."

In the absence of the quoting verb, "say(s)," the Hebrew text emphasizes the root 'hear', *shama,* which occurs in two different forms. The verb (they) 'heard', *sham'u,* opens the item and 'let the ears of the Judge also hear', *yashmiu,* closes it, and twice the word *mipi* (lit.: "from the mouth of") occurs. Thus, an effect of hearing-saying is created, which contrasts with the thieves' actions. The actors — so it appears — try to "repair" their offense through excuses.

The fact that the second story looks almost like a repeat of the preceding one also contributes to the humorous effect. Both events are depicted in a symmetrical manner both lexically and syntactically. Thus, the listener gets the impression that a certain pattern is taking form: time and again the police are engaged in arresting criminals who use ridiculous excuses to explain away their deeds.

(3) The Libyan ambassador to the UN finally agreed to pay taxes to the municipality of Englewood, New Jersey. Ambassador Ali Tariki claimed that he had been harassed by the municipal authorities due to pressure by the Federal Administration. He was pressed to pay unreasonable amounts of taxes. Yesterday the ambassador was ready to compromise and agreed to pay the City treasury the sum of $20,000 — taxes for his 25-room estate.

The actor in this story is a Libyan personality, who belongs to the category of "foe," from an Israeli point of view. However, in this story he does not act in the role of a political opponent of the State of Israel, but rather as a protagonist in a conflict with municipal authorities in the United States. Thus, the event is distant in theme and in location, and enables the reporter to introduce a humorous element.

An ironic overtone is already created by the opening sentence, which includes the colloquial expression, *sof-sof* ("finally"). It stresses the fact that the representative of a rich oil-producing state obstinately refused to pay taxes. The information regarding the size of his residence is withheld until the punch line. The impressive figures — $20,000 and 25 rooms — amplify the irony. The ambassador lives in extravagant luxury, but complains paranoically about being harassed by the Federal Administration and by the municipal authorities.

Formally, the ambassador is quoted indirectly. However, a literary register is also used, thereby creating the effect of "combined speech".[5] The clash of registers between that of the opening expression in the first sentence and the "higher style" in which the actor is quoted — in a somewhat archaic Hebrew — also adds to the humor.

(4) Hussein, king of Jordan, called the heads of the Arab states to take action to stop battles against the Palestinians in northern Lebanon. Without mentioning names, the king of Jordan wrote that certain powers point their weapons against the Arabs in the name of the Arabs, and besiege the Palestinian combatants and their kin.

This item cannot be viewed as presenting "distant" or "irrelevant" reality-material. The actor is the head of a neighboring country which is in a state of war with Israel. Although the battles in Lebanon and Hussein's reaction are of consequential importance to Israel, the reporter maintains a certain distance (the actor is the enemy), thus eliciting irony. He mentions what the king did *not* say.

Hussein is quoted indirectly, and the humorous effect is achieved by an ironic intrusion by the reporter: "without mentioning names." The implicit message is obvious to the informed listener: We all know, only too well, that the king blames the Syrians, but he does not dare be explicit about it. The irony is increased by formulating the reporter's comment as a colloquial expression — 'without mentioning names,' *b'lo lehazkir shemot* — which is a slightly modified and "higher" version of the colloquial *bli lehazkir shemot*. In this way a latent message is conveyed: the king of Jordan behaves in a cowardly manner. He is eager to blame, but at the same time, he shields himself by being vague regarding the identity of the accused.

(5) Minister Itzhak Moda'i blamed Minister Gideon Patt for making his appointment as Minister of Finance fail. He spoke at a meeting of the Liberal Party Council. Gideon Patt told our correspondent that there is no truth to this allegation. Itzhak Moda'i also said at this meeting that he had been finance minister for one night, when Prime Minister Shamir offered him the post. However, the prime minister made the condition that the Liberal Party endorse the appointment, but it objected.

The humor in this item stems from the self-mockery of Minister Moda'i, who is quoted by the newswriter. The quote is presented in a normative and serious style, apparently because of the actor's status. There is no intrusion of the reporter, no digression nor trace of creative usages. The minister is quoted by a "combined speech" technique. His original statement, "I was finance minister for one night," is formally disguised as indirect speech. Thus, the speaker creates an ironic distance between himself and the celebrity. This enables him to convey the latent message: Here are his original words; I am forbidden to comment, so you, dear listeners, can think of it what you like . . . .

Because of the actor's status, the reporter cannot afford any manipulation with the narrative nor any rhetorical devices. The narrative conventions of newsreporting are strictly adhered to. Humor is created solely by the actor's self-ridicule.

E. Generators of Humor: Linguistic Means and Techniques of Presentation

In most cases humor is generated by a combination of several factors which reinforce each other. when involving inconsequential reality-materials, it seems as if the writer is tempted to use stylistic devices in order to amplify the humorous effect. In such cases, the style is marked; i.e., the language draws attention to itself. About two-thirds of the items in our sample possess some kind of rhetorical creativity. This creativity is based on some sort of stylistic incongruity — a deviation from the expected mode of presentation.

The most salient type of stylistic incongruity is a digression from the reverent register of "radio journalese." The digression can be either "upward" (by employing literary, or even Biblical expressions), or "downward" (by inserting colloquialisms). In a story about a forty-year-old thief who has been caught red-handed while attempting to break into an apartment, the suspect is quoted as telling the judge that he was merely taking an innocent walk "in the bosom of Nature." This metaphor is clearly marked in modern Hebrew as belonging to a literary register, and so it is highly unlikely that it would be used by a criminal.

The insertion of colloquialisms is often used in humorous news items by indirectly quoting one of the actors through combined speech. This was illustrated above with respect to Finance-Minister-for-one-night Yitzhak Moda'i. In some cases, the use of such expressions actually serves as an indication of "concealed speech." Another interesting example is a news item about the UN Security Council calling upon Israel to "stop threatening to destroy nuclear reactors." In the Hebrew version, a sequence of infinitives is used (literally, "to stop to threaten to destroy"). This is marked as colloquial in Israeli Hebrew and thus introduces an element of irony directed at the Security Council's decision.

A different illustration of colloquialism can be found in the story about the return of six prisoners of war from their captivity by the PLO. Upon their arrival, one of the soldiers declares that he intends to go home to his family and, literally, "make a crazy life" (a colloquial expression in Hebrew meaning 'to have the time of one's life'). In this case, unlike the preceding one, no irony is involved. The expression sounds quite natural when uttered by a young soldier, although it is incongruous with the reverent style of radio news. By using this expression the writer displays empathy, and the stylistic digression is a sympathetic simulation of soldiers' speech.

184

Insertion of colloquialisms usually involves "showing" rather than "telling," using the technique of direct or combined speech. This is a deviation from the narrative conventions in radio news, which give precedence to "telling" (indirect speech). In the following example, humor is generated through both a presentational deviation and cultural incongruity. First, as a rule, radio news does not present statements of the elite in formal direct speech. Second, the use of colloquialisms by an elite personality is incongruous with our socio-linguistic presuppositions. The two together heighten the humorous effect. We see this when the energy minister says — in combined speech — that it is urgent that the party change its course because the 'nation' is uptight . . . ."

In another item we find the Minister of Finance playing with a slogan which he himself has coined and has been using frequently: "I don't have any (money)." In the news story, he is quoted as saying: "I am willing to change the slogan 'I don't have any' to 'I have.' Indeed, I have distress." The minister is engaged in self-parody, and we laugh *with* him. In fact, the minister changes only the formal expression, but the message remains intact: the nation's treasury is empty.

Another rhetorical device which also generates humor is an unexpected juxtaposition of items. A typical example is the story about a "double achievement" of Ronald Reagan: He has won the support of the Pro-Life Movement and the . . . presidency. The ironic effect is created by the way the narrator presents the facts rather than by situational factors. Such juxtaposition — with "the presidency" following the support of the pro-lifers' — is a clear case of intrusion by the writer by means of a powerful rhetorical strategy.

Let us look at another example which illustrates purely presentational humor — the story about a bank robbery in Tucson, Arizona. There is nothing comic in the situation itself: over 3¼ million dollars in cash has been stolen. The comic effect lies in the punch line: "The robbery in Tucson has been registered in the list of criminal records in the U.S. — the robbers got away with the largest sum of cash in the history of bank robberies in the United States." In the Hebrew version the style is marked by using a chain of five construct-forms: history-bank-robberies-United States. Moreover, in the Hebrew text is was marked by original alliteration and rhyme: *"Betoldot shdidot Habankim."*

In the 31 humorous items we found 9 instances (29%) of presentational humor, as in the last two examples. They are equally divided between stories containing consequential and inconsequential reality-materials. However, stylistic creativity can also be found in cases where the comic effect stems from the situation. Indeed, in only 4 out of 31 items (13%) was no stylistic creativity involved. Other rhetorical devices include alliteration, assonance, repetition and parallelism. Let us illustrate the last of these strategies. One of the news items reports on the amount of support for Nazi ideology in West Germany. Some bitter irony is expressed by the statement that a German weekly finds solace in the fact that the majority of Nazi supporters are over fifty years old and many of them are peasants.... As if to convey the pathetic emotion, stylistic creativity is realized by tripartite constructions: "Five and a half million Germans (1) support Nazi ideology, (2) hate (a) foreigners (b) democracy and (c) pluralism, and (3) see the most important issue in loyalty (a) to the people, (b) to the homeland and (c) to the German family." Thus, a rhythmic pattern is created, reinforcing the ironic attitude of a morally detached, stylistically intrusive writer.

Some of these news-items in our sample end with a punch line, typical of joke-telling. In news bulletins, punch lines are employed in tail-piece stories that lack news value. They can be viewed as a means for ironic presentation: an unexpected development is mentioned (or comment made), contrary to the expectations built up in the story. Again, we have an element of incongruity which creates the humorous effect. For instance, one of the news-items tells about a man who clubbed an old, retired admiral from Santa Barbara, California, on his head. He committed the assault as a protest against the admiral's stand against restrictions on owning weapons by civilians. The story ends with the following words uttered by the assailant: "This kind of weapon is not forbidden even in compliance with my principles."

Another story that ends with a punch line also deals with a criminal offense: Two people rob a dealer at gun point, taking with them a gold chain, a gold watch and two hundred dollars in cash. The story concludes by remarking that when searching the suspects' homes, the police found . . . the gun.

★

In the following table we attempt to indicate connections between the "what" (reality-materials) and the "how" (humor generators). For the sake of simplicity we suggest a binaric distinction between two types of humorous effects: "comic" and "ironic." The "comic" category subsumes touches of amusement and very light irony. The "ironic" category includes effects that are closer to "bitter humor" pole (if arranged on a continuum from the light to the bitter). As was previously discussed, when reality-materials are consequential, humor tends to be of the "ironic" type, whereas lighter comic effects are typical of stories with low news value. Characteristically, the "ironic" and "consequential" stories relate to élites, whereas the "comic," low news value, inconsequential stories — to nonélites.

Finally, the items are grouped according to high or low stylistic creativity (the "low" group includes four cases where no stylistic creativity could be found). The number of linguistic/presentational devices determines the degree of creativity — two or more such strategies per item is considered "high." Again, high creativity tends to be correlated with low news value, while low creativity is more typical of high news value items.

Reality Materials and Generators of Humor*

Reality Materials	Total	Types of Humor		Stylistic Creativity	
		Comic	Ironic	High	Low
Non/Partly Consequential	22 (5)	15 (3)	7 (2)	12 (3)	10 (2)
Consequential	9 (8)	1 (1)	8 (7)	—	9 (8)
Total	31 (13)	16 (4)	15 (9)	12 (3)	19 (10)

* Numbers in brackets indicate number of items in which members of the élite are involved.

NOTES

1. J. Cantor (1976) in a content analysis of TV broadcasts finds elements of humor in 82% of the programs in his sample. Also, an element of humor has been found in 70% of the news programs. The difference between Israeli radio newsbulletins and American TV news programs seems to be huge. But, still, it is noteworthy that when duration is measured (how many minutes of humor out of minutes of programming), in "News Information" the percent of humor is only 1.2%.

2. Adrian Bennett in a paper delivered at the summer meeting of the Linguistic Society of America, 1980, discusses the links between the discourse of frivolity and Turner's "world of becoming" or his concept of "anti-structure."

3. C. Winick (1976) finds an interesting link between a change in the American media in the years 1970-1973 and the number of jokes told on TV. There has been a decrease in communicated jokes when the media became more liberated, and when less taboos were kept. Jokes, humor in general, it is maintained here, are expressions of attitudes that are otherwise hardly encouraged. They "tackle taboo subjects" (p. 126).

4. See W. Booth, *The Rhetoric of Fiction*, 1961, pp. 2–20, 211–240.

5. Literary critics further define the linguistic concept of direct/indirect speech, distinguishing between various kinds of "represented," "combined" or "concealed" speech. By means of combined speech, the author maintains ambiguity as to whose voice is expressed in a given utterance. Various degrees of distance can thereby be controlled between the narrator and his characters. See, J. Even, "Represented Speech" and H. Golomb, "Combined Speech" in *Hasifrut*, 1968.

REFERENCES

Bennett, T., 1982, "Media, 'reality', signification" in Gurevitz et al. (eds.), *Culture, Society and the Media,* London, New York, Methuen.

Bergson, H., 1956, *Laughter,* Garden City, New Jersey, Doubleday.

Booth, W.L., 1961, *The Rhetoric of Fiction,* Chicago and London, University of Chicago Press.

Cantor, J., 1976, "Humor on TV: A Content Analysis", *Journal of Broadcasting,* 20, 4:501–510.

Douglas, M., 1975, "Jokes" in: *Implicit Meanings: Essays in Anthropology,* London, RKP.

Epstein, J., 1973, *News From Nowhere,* New York, Vintage Books.

Even, J., "Represented Speech: A Concept in the Theory of Prose", *Hasifrut* 1/1 1968: 140–153 (Hebrew).

Gans, H., 1979, *Deciding What's News,* New York, Pantheon.

Gitlin, T., 1980, *The Whole World is Watching,* University of California Press, Berkeley.

Glasgow Group, 1976, *Bad News,* London, RKP.

Golomb, H., 1968, "Combined Speech — A Major Technique in the Prose of Agnon", *Hasifrut,* 1/2 1968: 251–262 (Hebrew).

Graham, K. and T. Dean, 1982, "Myth and the Structure of News," *Journal of Communication,* 32/2: 144–161.

Hall, S., 1982, "The Rediscovery of 'Ideology': Return of the Repressed in Media Studies," in Gurevitz et al. (eds.) *op. cit.*

Handelman, Don and B. Kepferner, "Forms of Joking Activity", *American Anthropologist,* 74 (1972): 485–517.

Hobbes, T., 1870, *Human Nature* (Vol. IV, Chap. IX), London.

Lazarsfeld, P., R. Merton, 1971, "Mass Communication, Popular Taste and Organized Social Action" in: Schram and Roberts (eds.), *The Processes and Effects of Mass Communication,* Urbana, University of Illinois.

Roeh, I., 1982, *The Rhetoric of News in the Israel Radio,* Bochum, Germany, Studienverlag.

Shohat-Meiri, H., 1972, *Humor in the Israeli Literature,* Tel Aviv, Sifriat Hapoalim (Hebrew).

Tuchman, G., 1979, *Making News,* New York, Free Press.

Turner, V., 1978, *Dramas, Fields and Metaphors,* Ithaca, Cornell University Press.

Winick, C., 1976, "The Social Context of Humor," *Journal of Communication* 26/3: 124–128.

O. Nevo
DO JEWS IN ISRAEL STILL LAUGH AT THEMSELVES?

O. NEVO
Haifa University, Israel

DO JEWS IN ISRAEL STILL LAUGH AT THEMSELVES?

My interest in the question of self-aimed humor arose while trying to compare Israeli Jewish and Arab responses to humor. Jewish humor has for many years been described as self-aimed. It would be of special interest, therefore, to study whether Jews in Israel still direct humor at themselves.

In the preliminary stage of my study Jewish and Arab students in Haifa University were asked (by advertisement or through friends) "to report as many jokes as they knew about Jews and Arabs." This was done in order to collect jokes for a subsequent more controlled study. The collection itself proved to be of some interest.

The picture that emerged from the collection was intriguing. More jokes were collected with an Arab butt than with a Jewish butt. It could have been attributed to the fact that the author knew more Jews than Arabs; yet even Arabs supplied more jokes against Arabs.

The content of the jokes collected reflected the stereotypes held by Jews and Arabs toward each other. Arabs were portrayed as stupid, dirty and cowardly, while Jews appeared to be courageous, business-minded and stingy. These traits have been found to characterize these groups in studies focusing on stereotypes (Peres & Levi, 1969; Benjamini, 1980). The traits that characterize Israeli Jews were also found in American Jews (Dundes, 1978).

Although the preliminary stage of my study could not lead to definite answers, the impression thus far had been that Israeli Jews tell more jokes about Arabs than about themselves.

My next step was to test this hypothesis in an experimental study.

Study I

SUBJECTS: 50 Jewish and 50 Arab males matched for intelligence by Raven Matrices (Raven, 1960). All were high school seniors, residing in urban areas in Israel.

STIMULI: 35 jokes that had been classified by five Arab and five Jewish psychology students according to one of the following seven categories:

Two non-aggressive categories (1) Denial of frustration; (2) Absurd humor; and five categories of jokes whose butt was respectively (3) Men (4) Women (5) Authority (6) Arabs (7) Jews.

On the basis of these elections, 35 jokes were chosen such that each category of five jokes had on average been rated as equally funny, and such that all ten judges had agreed on the categorization of these 35 jokes.

PROCEDURE: Subjects were asked to rate each joke on a scale of 1-5. This was carried out in their own classrooms and in their native tongue by experimenters of the same nationality and sex. Following the jokes they were given an Intelligence Test and an Attitude Questionnaire about their satisfaction with life in Israel (Hofman, 1972).

Results showed that out of 50 Jews, 34 rated jokes with an Arab butt as funnier, 14 rated them as equally funny, and *only two* rated jokes with a Jewish butt as funnier. Where the Arab subjects were concerned, neither type was preferred over the other. Table 1 shows the same results arrived at in a more sophisticated proper statistical way.

Table 1

Means and Standard Deviations of Jokes Ratings by Israeli and Jews and Arabs

Jokes	Non-aggressive				Aggressive		
Category	Absurd	Denial	Men as butts	Women as butts	Jews as butts	Arabs as butts	Authority as butts
Ethnic Grouping							
Jews	2.800 sd=0.70	2.568 sd=0.64	3.084 sd=0.73	2.912 sd=0.55	3.232 sd=0.65	3.760* sd=0.53	2.964 sd=0.73
Arabs	3.248* sd=0.63	3.306* sd=0.49	2.8255 sd=0.72	3.041 sd=0.59	3.172 sd=0.61	3.172 sd=0.83	2.869 sd=0.70
Total	3.024	2.937	2.937	2.980	3.202	3.464	2.929

$a < .01$

A comparison of Arabs who answered positively to the question "Are you satisfied being an Israeli citizen?" with Arabs who answered negatively, is seen in Table 2. Arabs who feel more favorably toward Israel prefer jokes with an Arab butt as compared to Arabs who feel negatively toward Israel.

CONCLUSIONS: Male Jewish students in Israel prefer jokes about Arabs to jokes about Jews, as do Arabs who feel positively toward Israel.

Table 2

Distribution of Satisfied and Unsatisfied Arabs
According to the Preference of Jokes with Arab-Butt

Preference	Preferred Jokes with Arab butt	Did not Prefer Jokes with Arab butt	Total
Satisfied	17	6	23
Not Satisfied	6	14	20
	23	20	43*

* 7 subjects did not answer the attitude question.
$x^2 = 8.30$ $p < 0.05$
x^2 was used because the basic assumptions needed for Anova were not fulfilled here.

At this stage in my research I asked whether I had the answer to my question "Do Jews in Israel still laugh at themselves?" Does the fact that they prefer jokes about Arabs mean that they do not laugh at themselves? A critical review of literature concerning the subject of self-aimed humor reveals disagreement between researchers as to the meaning and definition of self-aimed humor.

Those who deal with Jewish humor defined self-aimed humor as a preference for a joke with a Jewish butt.

This approach was justifiably criticized by Ben Amos (1973), who claimed that those who enjoy jokes about Jews do not actually laugh at themselves. Rather they laugh at other Jews; the rich laugh at the poor, the poor at the rich, the educated at the ignorant, and so on.

For example, although it was found that Jews preferred jokes with Arab butts to jokes with Jewish butts, the joke that received the highest average rating by Jews was a joke about a Jewish businessman:

A wealthy Jewish businessman is riding downhill in a taxi. All of a sudden the driver says: "The brakes have gone." The Jewish businessman says: "Then at least stop the meter!"

When a Jew prefers this joke he does not necessarily identify with the Jew in the joke. The Jew in the joke might belong to a subgroup that the listener rejects; therefore he is not laughing at himself.

193

La Fave, Haddad and Maesen (1976) argue in the same direction. They claim that people always prefer jokes that enhance their self-esteem. Thus according to this theory, laughing at oneself is an illusion.

They suggest several possible explanations for the illusion of self-aimed humor which can be summarized as follows:

(i) A person who enjoys a joke about his own group (e.g., a Jew laughing at jokes about Jews) might be amused because of humorous components other than those which reduce his self-esteem. This can happen when people misunderstand the joke and do not see it as self-disparaging.

(ii) One may belong, yet not identify with the same group (e.g., the "Uncle Tom" who prefers jokes about blacks to jokes about whites). Once a person does not identify with the group which is the butt of the joke, he does not feel disparaged by the joke. Indeed, La Fave cites Middleton & Moland (1958) who found that blacks report telling more ethnic jokes in general and more antiblack jokes in particular than whites. This was explained as a case in which blacks, while being members of the black group, do not identify with it.

The picture emerging from intergroup humor research is that most of the studies reporting self-aimed humor can be interpreted using La Fave's arguments that humor is not really self-aimed, since it is directed at a membership group which is not one's identification group. (Middleton & Molard, 1958; La Fave, et. al., 1976).

Yet evidence from intragroup humor indicates that self-aimed humor does exist. Observers of group behavior have found that some people direct humorous remarks toward themselves proper.

Pollio & Edgerly (1976) found, for example, that 30% of the humorous remarks in a therapy group were self-aimed. Coser (1960) examined the social functions of humor among the staff of a Boston mental hospital during 20 staff meetings. It was found that 20% of the humorous remarks made were self-aimed, and that lower status members of the group made more self-aimed humorous remarks than higher status members.

Thus we have La Fave's theory that there is no real self-aimed humor, while studies using observations of group-behavior argue for the existence of self-aimed humor. It is clear that these different arguments are based on different definitions of the self and on different modes of the expression of humor. One way to measure self-aimed humor is to present a subject with jokes about his group (i.e., La Fave, as I did in my first study). A completely different way is to observe whether a subject is making humorous remarks about himself. In the first example, "self" is defined as a membership group, while in the second example "self" is defined as the individual himself (self proper). In the first case the subject is asked passively to rate jokes while in the second case he actively produces humor. These examples serve to emphasize the complexity of the concept of self-aimed humor.

At least two dimensions operate in this concept. One is the activity-passivity dimension. Previous humor research (Babad, 1974; McGhee, 1979; Ziv, 1981) stressed the importance of studying the active aspects of humor as well as the passive ones. There may be a difference between hearing a joke about oneself and creating one. Yet both are called self-aimed humor. A second facet of self-aimed humor research is the proximity of the butt of humor to the individual self. Different studies employed different definitions of the self in dealing with self-aimed humor: 1) according to Middleton & Moland, the self is a representative of a membership group; 2) according to La Fave (1976), the self is a representative of a positive identification group; 3) according to researchers of Jewish humor ,the self is a representative of a

Figure 1

A Model for Research in Self-Aimed Humor

Mode of Expression		*Active* ←——→ *Passive*		
	Creative	*Telling Reporting Past Events*	*Memory of Jokes*	*Appreciation*
Butt of humor:				
Self (individual)	Present study Ziv, 1981, Pollio & Edgerly 1976			
Friend				
Representative of sub-group	Present study			La Fave et al. (1976) Present study
Representative of own group		Middleton & Moland 1958		La Fave et al. (1976) Present study
Representative of opposing group	Present study	Middleton & Moland 1959		La Fave et al. (1976) Present study

Jewish group or a Jewish subgroup (Ben Amos, 1973); 4) according to studies observing group behavior, the individual self is the self.

In order to present the important facets involved in research of self-aimed humor, a model is suggested (see Figure 1).

Two dimensions were specified. The first, modes of humor-expression, ranging from active to passive modes: creating, telling, reporting past events, remembering, appreciating. Another dimension is the proximity of the butt of humor to the individual self. This dimension includes the individual self, a friend, a subgroup, one's own group, an opposing group. It could also be conceived as an attitude dimension ranging from positive to negative. The combination of the two proposed dimensions leads to several empirical possibilities.

Study 1 dealt only with two cells. Study 2 attempted to study self-aimed humor using different definitions of self and active modes of humorous expression.

Study 2

SUBJECTS: 139 Jews and 111 Arabs from the same population as Study 1.

STIMULI: 13 cartoon-like drawings depicting an Arab and a Jew involved in a common, mildly frustrating situation. The drawings were based on Rosenzweig 1947 Picture Frustration Study (P-F).

The figure at the left of each picture is saying something that either describes or causes a frustration. The person on the right is always shown with a blank caption box. Subjects were asked to answer as if they were present in the situation, in the most humorous or amusing answer.

Rosenzweig (1950) found that some subjects tended to answer spontaneously with humor to the (P-F) situations. Their humorous answers could be classified according to three main directions of aggression: extrapunitive, impunitive, and intropunitive.

In another study Nevo & Nevo (1983) have shown that when subjects were instructed to respond humorously to P-F like pictures they produced various kinds of humorous responses that could be reliably scored according to the above classification. Some of the answers were relevant to the question of self-aimed humor and I will deal with them here.

PROCEDURE: Half of each nationality group received the test form depicting Arabs as the frustrators, while the other half received the test form depicting Jews as the frustrators. The order of pictures was random. The experiment was run as in Study 1 except for the change in humorous material. Each response was scored on the amount and direction of

Figure 2
Items from the modified Picture-Frustration-test

item i representing the version with an Arab frustrator.
item ii representing the version with Jewish frustrator.

aggression. In the case of self-aimed humor, these stimuli could elicit three types of self-aimed humor.

1) Humor turned against a representative of the subject's own group — when Jews or Arabs produced aggressive humorous responses toward their own representative.

For example:

197

Table 3

Table 3

Means of Extrapunitive Humor Toward
Jewish and Arab Butts by Jews and Arab Subjects

Butts respondents	Jewish butt	Arab butt	Total
Jews	15.73 (N=68)	18.72 (N=71)	17.26 (N=139)
Arabs	15.99 (N=62)	15.97 (N=49)	15.98 (N=111)
Total	15.85 (N=130)	17.59 (N=120)	16.69 (N=250)

"You are dirty Arabs. That's why you want me to be dirty."
"Next time you will be in the mud."

This type of humor relates to self-aimed humor in the case of Jewish respondents who produce aggressive humor toward a Jewish figure and Arab respondents who produce aggressive humor toward an Arab figure. Self is defined here as membership group.

A comparison of extrapunitive humor produced by Jews and Arabs toward Jewish and Arab butts was made by employing ANOVA with repeated measures with covariants. Extrapunitive humor was the dependent variable, and nationality of the respondents and of the butts were independent variables (intelligence and basic aggression were covariants).

As can be seen in Table 3 the main effect is the nationality of the butt of humor.

Both Arabs and Jews produced more extrapunitive humor toward an Arab butt.

2) Another variant of self-aimed humor occurs when Jews or Arabs create humorous answers aimed at a subgroup within their own group.

For example:

"What can you expect from an old Arab like you?" (referring to traditional old Arabs)

Or

"You Rumanians are all the same!"

"You French are all the same!" (referring to Jewish Israelis of different origins).

This response was rare, occurring 17 times in the Jewish sample and 15 times in the Arab sample. It was probably an artifact since there were not enough cues of subgroup identifiers supplied. It can be concluded that there was no difference between Jews and Arabs in this respect.

3) The third possibility occurs when subjects create humorous remarks directed at themselves specifically.

For example:

"It is my fault. I always stand in the way."
"This is the third time it happened to me today."

No significant difference was found between Jews and Arabs in the use of this kind of humor.

Conclusions

One may conclude that Jews in Israel show both by their humor preferences and by their production of humor that they do not laugh at themselves more than Arabs do — that Jewish humor in Israel is not self-aimed. The fact that Jews in Israel belong to the majority may have influenced their approach to humor.

Yet, the answer to the question "Do Jews in Israel still laugh at themselves?" is not simple. In view of the model presented and the arguments against studies equating self-aimed humor with preference for jokes with a butt that represents a membership group (Ben Amos, 1962; La Fave, et al., 1976), one may doubt whether they ever really laughed at themselves in the past; they might have been laughing at other Jews!

As for the present study, it might be said that there is no evidence that Jews in Israel laugh at themselves more than Arabs do, and there is some evidence to the contrary.

Laughing at oneself is a concept that should be studied more carefully giving attention to active and passive modes of expression, and various definitions of self.

199

REFERENCES

Babad, E.Y., A Multi-Method approach to the assessment of Humor: A Critical look at humor tests. *Journal of Personality 42,* 618-631.

Beatie, J. "On Laughter and Ludicrous Compositon," in *Essays,* Edinburgh Creech, 1976.

Ben-Amos, D. "The 'Myth' of Jewish Humor," *Western Folklore, 32.*112–131, 1973.

Benjamini, K. "The Image of the Arab in the Eyes of Israeli Youth," A lecture given in the Levi Eshkol Institute of Research of Economy, Society and Policy in Israel, Jerusalem, May 1979.

Coser, R.L. "Laughter Among Colleagues," *Psychiatry, 23,* 81–95, 1960.

Dundes, A. "A Study of Ethnic Slurs: The Jew and the Polack in the United States," *Journal of American Folklore,* Vol. 84, No. 332, 186–203.

Hofman, J.E., "Readiness for Social Relations Between Arabs and Jews in Israel," *The Journal of Conflict Resolution 16,* 2 241–251, 1972.

La Fave, L., Haddad, I., & Maesen, W.A., "Superiority, Enhanced Self-Esteem and Perceived Incongruity Humor Theory," in: Chapman, A.J., & Foot, H.C. (eds) *Humor and Laughter, Theory, Research and Applications.* Wiley, London, 1976.

McGhee, P., *Humor, its Origin and Development,* W.H. Freeman & co. San-Francisco, 1979.

Middleton, R. & Moland, J. "Humor in Negro and White Subcultures: A Study of Jokes Among University Students," *American Sociological Review 24,* 61–69, 1959.

Nevo, O. "Appreciation and Production of Humor as an Expression of Aggression by Jews & Arabs in Israel," *Journal of Cross-Cultural Psychology 15,* 181–198, 1984.

Nevo, O., & Nevo, B. "What do you do when asked to answer humorously?" *Journal of Personality and Social Psychology,* Vol. 44, 188–194, 1983.

Peres, Y., & Levy, Z. "Jews and Arabs: Ethnic Group Stereotypes in Israel," *Race 10,* 479–494, 1969.

Polio, H.R., & Edgerly, J. "Comedians and Comic Style," in: Chapman, A.J., & Foot, H.C. *Humor and Laughter: Theory, Reserarch and Applications,* Wiley, London, 1976.

Rosenzweig, S., Fleming, E., & Clarke, H. "Revised Scoring Manual for the Rosenzweig picture-frustration study," *Journal of Psychology, 24,* 165–208, 1947.

Rosenzweig, S. "The Treatment of Humorous Responses in the Rosenzweig Picture-Frustration Study: A Note on Revised (1950) instructions," *Journal of Psychology 30,* 39–43, 1950.

Ziv, A., *Psychology of humor,* Tel Aviv, Yahdav, 1981 (Hebrew)

POLITICAL CARICATURE AS A REFLECTION OF ISRAEL'S DEVELOPMENT

KARIEL GARDOSH (DOSH)

POLITICAL CARICATURE AS A REFLECTION OF ISRAEL'S DEVELOPMENT

Beginnings

Since ancient times, people have been in the habit of criticizing their fellow men. The victims of this criticism call it slander. Others, including those expressing these views, prefer to call it by another name — satire. Over the generations, most of the activity in this area has been carried on orally and in writing. But whoever wanted to — and was able to draw — inscribed his views on walls, on clay shards and on parchment.

After the invention of printing, visual satire gained widespread circulation. It attacked the church and its opponents, denounced kings and rebels, slaughtered sacred cows as well as their slaughterers. This popular activity searched for a permanent home. Because of its affinity to current events, it found its natural habitat in newspapers, shortly after these began to appear on a regular basis.

At the end of the 18th Century, a new form of communication took shape in England, known to us as political caricature. Its expressions, which were heavily laced with physical humour, were a bit too simplistic for our more refined modern taste, and their excessive use of words to explain the point seems superfluous to us. However, already in these early creations which were leveled mainly against the wicked Napoleon and his deeds, one can find all the ingredients of modern pictorial satire. They demonstrate the formula underlying their essence, which is political commentary expressed through visual analogy.

Fallacies

The above definition is basically a divisive one. Its purpose is to liberate this unique sphere from any marginal overlapping, which is apt to blur its quintessence. Past experience points to three widespread fallacies in connection with pictorial political satire. One fallacy is that of assigning caricature to the realm of art. In certain countries, a caricaturist is termed an "artist." Regardless of the honor bestowed by this title, it is not relevant. The idea found in the content of the political caricature is far more important than its formal value. It is true to say that an excellent political caricature can be created by someone with minimal graphic ability, while, on the other hand, the most talented pictorial artist cannot turn a weak idea into a significant political caricature.

A second fallacy is that of regarding pictorial satire as a branch of humor, despite the fact that the analogy on which it is based is not necessarily comic. In actual fact, to a considerable extent, the work being done internationally in our time focuses rather on the pathetic level; and there are a great many "sad" caricatures that preach and issue warnings on subjects such as nuclear and ecological dangers, racism, and the like.

The third and most widespread fallacy is that which blurs the distinction between political satire and grotesque portraiture. We will deal more extensively with this fallacy later. It has always been an accepted practice in the art of drawing to depict a person in a distorted manner in order to convey a message about his character. This type of distorted portrait, especially when it took the form of a drawing, defined itself caricature. According to one version of the source of the word, it is derived from the name of a well-known family of 17th century Italian painters who specialised in satirical portraiture. Another interpretation of the term attributes it to the verb which means "to overload". This probably relates to the graphic exaggeration in describing the various parts of the body. At the same time that pictorial political satire began to appear on the pages of newspapers, the status of the grotesque technique as an independent artistic expression diminished. It was integrated into the array of ideas of political caricature. But old notions stay alive long after their original content has undergone a change. Despite the fact that these days the caricaturist deals almost exclusively in political and social commentary, there are still many who think of him as someone who draws "funny faces." In Anglo-American usage, due to an awareness of this confusion, a distinction is made between a cartoon which is mainly a drawing to convey an idea and a caricature which is a grotesque portrait. Other languages, including Hebrew, unfortunately do not differentiate between these two forms.

Pictorial political satire as a unique visual expression, which does not aspire to be either an artistic creation nor a frozen comedy nor a collection of weird portraits, is a distinct form of communication. Its creator is a communicator — a publicist, who expresses his views of events through the language of drawn lines, instead of words. Both the strength as well as the weakness of the "visual statement" lies in the need to forego the use of words. The pictorial commentator loses the semantic flexibility that advances gradually and surely in the direction of his subject, while at the same time keeping open a path of retreat, by means of formulae such as "on the other hand" ... notwithstanding that ... nevertheless.." and the like. Thus, that same "truth" which is supposedly made up of various shades of grey, is caught up in the net of language. The cartoonist works in a setting of black and white, while paring down to a minimum and even totally rejecting the insignificant. He has only one arrow in his quiver and an excellent chance of hitting a bullseye — straight into the heart of the significant point.

The French Connection

Until the middle of the 19th Century Britain kept the lead in this new form of communication. The magazine Punch acquired many devotees of "cartoons" — a specific term for a drawing that conveys an idea, widely used in English speaking countries. (The term originated at an exhibition of enlarged caricatures held in the Parliament building in London in 1842). The newspapers on the European continents also began to regularly publish pictorial satire, and in the United States, the cartoon became an integral and lively part of the election campaigns. Caricature reached new heights in France, thanks to the greatest caricaturist of all time, Honore Daumier (1808-78), a belligerent political man, brimming with ideas and humor, and a first-rate artist. His brilliant drawings which were so disturbing to the "establishment" earned him a prison sentence, a life of deprivation, and a place of honor in the history of art.

Another French contribution to pictorial satire was one of particular importance from the Jewish point of view. This enlightened country gave birth to the modern antisemitic caricature. The iconography of the "ugly Jew", a revolting symbolic figure, depraved and depraving, took shape in the popular Paris press. It was from this source that many years later, the artists of Nazi propaganda in Germany and other European countries draw their inspiration.

Zionism and War

The modest Jewish press in communities throughout the Diaspora and in Palestine, did not hasten to publish caricatures. The absence of pictures and drawings on its pages resulted, among other things, from traditional Jewish objections to all types of portraits and images. This attitude continued to have an influence on the modern Hebrew press. Many of the veteran editors, who had grown up in European townlets, showed a lack of interest in any graphic material, with the exception of printed characters.

The appearance of political Zionism in the Jewish world had its repercussions in the media. The vision of the state seemed a ridiculous idea to many, Jews and non-Jews alike, and it furnished a piquant subject for caricatures. "The ugly Jew" was depicted from a new aspect — he had aspirations of being a hero figure.

Political cartoons began appearing regularly in the Palestinian press, a decade before the outbreak of World War II. The rise of Nazism and the growing crisis between the powers, was given expression in vigorous caricature activity. Most of the darts of Western satire were directed against the fascist tyrants. The latter of course expressed their displeasure, but it in no way made them change their ways. When hostilities broke out, political caricature in both camps was enlisted in active military service. The cartoonists for the Nazi press focussed mainly on the distorted figure of the Jew — a repulsive capitalist and a despicable communist, at one and the same time. There can be no doubt that the brutal and systematic dehumanization of the Jew in caricatures played an important role in creating the psychological conditions for his annihilation. The caricaturists of the Allied camp, on their part, did their best to enlist public opinion in the war effort against fascism.

The greatest satirist of the time appeared in Britain. This was David Low, an excellent artist, of Australian origin, an outspoken anti-Nazi. His caricatures appeared originally in the London Evening Standard and were copied throughout the free world. Low followed the events of the war with his up-to-the-minute, caustic, rousing and exciting commentaries. His work was not merely satire in the narrow sense of the term. He rose to the ranks of a national spokesman-commentator, and wielded a vast amount of influence.

The caricatures of this prominent British artist were very popular with the public in Palestine, and they had an influence on the format of local caricature work. The newspaper editors considered his style the height of professional perfection, and for many long years, local caricaturists were accustomed to hearing the demand: "Try to draw like Low"!

The first Generation and its Exponents

In the short history of Israeli political caricature, three periods can be discerned, during which three generations of creators made their appearance. The most conspicuous difference between the periods is expressed through the change that took place in the public's attitude towards caricature work done in the media. There is naturally a partial overlapping between the generations. Several of the "founding fathers" are still alive and actively creating. along with them, nearly all of the members of the second wave continue to work, and then of course there are the representatives of the young generation.

The pioneers of Israeli pictorial satire, Arye Navon and Yehoshua Ardi, published their first work at the beginning of the '30s. Over the years, they were joined by the other representatives of the first generation: Joseph Bas, Adam Schlein Ross, Mula, Wolff, Noah B. and others. In this first period, it was difficult to make a living from this work, which in this country was a novelty. Most of the caricatures were published in the Saturday editions of the daily newspapers. "Davar", "HaMashkif" and "HaAretz" promised some tenure to Navon, Ardi and Bas, but the drawing of caricatures was still considered a part-time job. The caricaturists found an additional opening for their work in the modest and short-lived satirical magazines, and in the humoristic publications that came out, annually, just before the festival of Purim. In order to earn their livelihood, these creators worked in the field of art (Navon) architecture (Bas) and in graphics and advertising.

206

The content of the satire related to the current events in the pre-state Yishuv. In the "state in the making", there was a lot of brisk political activity, which culminated in a sharp polarization between left and right, following the "Arlozorov affair." The publication of the "White Paper" intensified the old conflict with the administration of the British mandate. The "Yishuv's" participation in the war effort against Nazism and the holocaust that befell European Jewry, caused a temporary relaxation in the tensions within the "Yishuv" society. These tensions were renewed with even greater intensity towards the end of the war. The obstinacy of the Mandate authorities in their attempt to prevent the immigration of the holocaust refugees and the strengthening of the anti-British underground aroused the Yishuv.

This volatile period was expressed only partially and with hesitancy in caricature, but not necessarily because of the weakness or inability of its creators. Throughout all the years, the supremacy of the written word had been preserved in the press. Although some biting and to the point caricatures relating to events were published, it seemed that the newspaper editors, as well as their readers, were not yet fully aware of the potential for communication that lie in visual commentary. The constant censorship on the part of the authorities also made it difficult to work in this area. In the last and decisive stage of the struggle, pictorial satire made its first underground appearance (caricatures by "Shir" — the underground nickname of the cartoonist Dosh, in the Lechi magazine, "HaMa'as.").

The United Nations decision on the establishment of the Jewish state and the British evacuation of the country were reflected in many ebullient cartoons. As is well known, this joy did not last for long. The hostilities that broke out with local Arab forces followed by the invasion of Arab armies led to a hard and bloody war of defense. The pictorial satire in the new country that was struggling for its existence was confronted with a complex conceptual problem. Until that time, the "other side" opposing the Jewish aspirations for independence had taken the form of British imperialism and hostile international interests. These were, from the satirical point of view, "easy prey." For some time now, the national consciousness had been substantially aware of the "Arab danger", but it had repressed it for many weighty reasons. Now it was no longer possible to ignore the fact that the concrete enemy facing us is the Arab, with his weapons and his ideologies. The problem was how to describe him in satire, while sticking to the truth and aiming at strengthening the war effort, but at the same time — without impairing future chances for the so much hoped for co-existence between the two peoples in Palestine.

The cartoonists of the War of Independence tried to meet this challenge, each in his own way and to the best of his understanding. However, the complex question continued to plague Israeli satire over the course of the coming years.

When the War of Independence ended, the Yishuv again turned its attention to internal affairs. The characteristics of the newly gained statehood, the elections to the Knesset, the austerity regime, mass immigration — all these furnished copious subjects for Israeli caricature which was coming of age. The public response was more than encouraging. It turned out that stinging pictorial commentary on current events was popular with newspaper readers. The demand led to a greater supply, and a significant development began in the short history of local work in this field. A "second wave" of creators joined the veteran artists.

This reinforcement: Zev (Yaakov Farkash), Shmulik (Shmuel Katz), Mike (Meir Ronen), Dosh (Kariel Gardosh) and others, came from among the new immigrants. They brought with them boundless energy, a stylistic range, and a fresh look at the Israeli reality.

As part of the absorption of these new forces, the "Maariv" newspaper took a daring step. In this newspaper which had the widest circulation at the time, Dosh began drawing a daily caricature covering current events.

This "section" was very successful and earned itself a place of honor in the newspaper, alongside the main editorial. Other important newspapers followed in the footsteps of this pioneering initiative. Thus, a new fact was created in the field of caricature. The leading creators were given full-time employment and recognized professional status as members of the editorial board. Israeli caricature took its rightful place on the scene.

What was the secret of the success and popularity of pictorial satire? It is a well-known fact that the Israeli public shows an unusual amount of interest in current political events. The newspaper cartoon provided a succinct commentary on events, in an instant, biting and amusing fashion. The public's interest in a visual media experience had not yet found an alternative outlet in television. The daily cartoon brought the background and meaning of events closer to a large segment of the public which had difficulty in reading an editorial in Hebrew. In this way, the idea-conveying drawing of those days played an important role in educating masses to be enlightened citizens with critical faculties.

Against the background of the political caricature's success, a strange phenomenon should be noted. This is the disinterest shown by both the public and the press in the non-political pictorial satire. Visual humor from daily life, which is very popular in most other countries, was published only incidentally, as it were, in the Israeli newspapers, that copied it from the foreign press. Attempts by talented local artists over the years to stimulate activity in this field (Fridel Stern, Yossi Stern, Peri, Shmuel Katz, Dan Gelbart and others) met with disappointment.

This may partly explain the conspicuous absence on the Israeli scene of a specific satirical magazine, in which an open society appreciates stinging criticism in all spheres of life. The first initiatives to set up such a platform were taken a generation ago, but did not endure. ("The Golden Calf", "Pins", "Scarecrow" and others, in which the cartoonists Bos, Zeev, and others were active participants). It is reasonable to assume that another reason is that the most talented creators were already employed by the established and widely-circulated newspapers. During the last decade, an "intermediate area" appears in the Israeli press along with the caricatures: satirical illustration. These were drawings for the purpose of enriching articles and editorials by adding a visual dimension. Those successfully employed at this work were Zeev, Karman, as well as quite a few young artists.

The Product and its Quality

As stated above, during the Sixties the character of Israeli political caricature took on its final shape. Although it is of course difficult to speak in generalizations about this special and variegated sphere, one can discern common lines in the style and mode of thought of the various creators.

It seems that technique is not the strong point of local pictorial satire. Only a few of the Israeli cartoonists received any formal art education. This actually turned out to be an advantage. The typical Israeli caricature concentrates on conveying a message by graphic means that are as economical as possible. It is light and airy in its form, free of the pedantic realism that so encumbers pictorial expressions in many countries. The tendency to add many captions and words of explanation — which was so pronounced in the American cartoon of the '50s and '60s — never caught on in Israel. The use of graphic symbols is widespread and popular, and their development constitutes a succinct focal point for the message. Among foreign influences, one can note the approach of the outstanding European caricaturists of the period: the French Effel and Sennep and the British Vicky.

The expression of opinion in Israeli caricature is free and unrestricted. Most of the activity in this field is in the independent press, and the leading caricaturists made sure that they were given an autonomous status, protected from interference by the establishment. Despite their different outlooks and opinions, there was consensus among the artists regarding the basic values of Zionism. Until recently, the pictorial satire was never violent. The social and political criticism, as harsh as it may be, is expressed without hate or personal denigration.

The unique situation of the State of Israel, which is under a constant state of siege, is obviously a permanent motif in caricature. The Arab hostility that frequently leads to the breakout of bloody wars, naturally resulted in an understandable human tendency to describe the Arab enemy as a stereotype, an object of contempt and hostility. Israeli caricature did not succumb to this temptation, even in the midst of war. The hostile Arab leadership and the terrorist organizations are, as might be expected, the objects of caustic satirical condemnation, but the image of the Arab as a person does not appear in a distorted manner. The self-restraint which is considered obligatory in this area, as well as qualms about expressing "visual racism", create an instructive contrast between Israeli caricature and that of the West. During periods of confrontation with the Islamic countries — due to oil crises or acts of terror — European and American satirists do not exhibit excessive "ethnic sensitivity." They show ugly Arab-semitic types, that no Israeli caricaturist would dare to put on paper. Local veteran caricaturists recall the time when the first contacts were set up with African countries that had just achieved independence. Then as well they hesitated to depict Negro figures in "full black", lest they be accused of racism.

Another obstacle on the path of local caricature was the absence of a "code of symbols", which generally characterizes homogenous societies. The Western artist has at his disposal a host of figures from Greek mythology, from folk tales, nursery rhymes, and popular literary works. The Israeli caricaturist, who also had all these tools in his kit, was forced to forego their use when he came into contact with a multi-cultural population. The natural source to fill this lack is the Bible. Biblical images are used very frequently in Israeli caricatures, but the feeling is that this national common denominator has not yet been fully exploited. In this context, it is worth citing an original view that the prophets of Israel who employed a "picturesque" Jewish style, were the first political caricaturists in the world. (See the words of Jeremiah about Egypt as a "broken reed", about Syria as a "boiling pot" — perfect visual messages).

Intensive caricatural activity creates symbolic figures that represent nations and countries. The American Uncle Sam, the French Marianne, the Russian bear, and the like, are extremely important and useful "words" in the language of pictorial satire. The first attempt to create a figure to symbolize Israel was made by Arye Navon, a veteran caricaturist, back in the days of the War of Liberation. His solution was a natural and simple one — a small boy wearing a Palmach "stocking cap." The most enduring national symbol was designed by Dosh. His "Israeli" a young boy with a "Tembel hat" (one of the very few objects that has a distinctly local flavor). His clothing is well defined as that of a typical Sabra. The appearance of this symbol in the center of thousands of caricatures, over the course of many years, accorded him a "unique" personality. The maturing youth represents the typical features of the "Israeli entity", with all of its complexity and contradictions. Arrogance and shyness, an exaggerated sense of self-assurance alongside a lack of confidence, tolerance and aggressiveness, naivete and sophistication — all worked together to create a sense of identification with and support for the "little Israel" within the wider community of nations.

The nature of the outstanding personalities in the political arena had a considerable influence on satirical expression. A leader who is "charismatic" both in his character and physical appearance adds a great deal of interest to the pictorial message. This is, of course, a two-way process. Caricature imprints the leader in the public consciousness more effectively than the written word and the photograph.

Israeli caricature was lucky in that it had, during the decisive stages of its development, a particularly "picturesque" personality on which to focus. This was David Ben Gurion, the dominant "presence" in public life during the course of an entire generation. His famous crest of hair, the build of his head and body, made his immediate visual identification possible. His vigorous and energetic conduct of affairs, which was so often the object of controversy, was an unending source of enthralling commentary. His physical vitality created choice moments for satirical images, such as his custom of "standing on his head." His complex and "juicy" personality kept caricaturists occupied for many years.

At the end of Ben-Gurion's "heroic" period, a strange "recurring principle" began to manifest itself. His successor, Levi Eshkol, conciliatory and modest by nature, had a grey appearance, which did not easily adapt to graphic depiction. The correlation between the style in which a man functioned in his office and his external appearance proved itself throughout. Figures that lacked leadership qualities also were difficult subjects for caricatures, both from the graphic and the conceptual point of view. On the other hand, the brilliant and volatile Moshe Dayan, with his black eye patch, was a caricaturist's "dream." The same was true of Golda Meir, and of Menahem Begin. This rule also held for foreign leaders. Egypt's Nasser, the Arab "star" of Israeli caricatures during the fifties and sixties, stood out not only for his leadership qualities, but because of his impressive appearance and facial features.

From the standpoint of the quality and originality of ideas, Israeli caricature achieved reputable international standards, and its creations are quite frequently published in newspapers throughout the world. The Israeli political artist is deeply engrossed in local topics. Only a small portion of his output relates to events not directly connected with the affairs of the State and the region. In this connection, mention should be made of Raanan Lurie, the only native-born Israeli among the second generation of Israeli caricaturists. After working very actively for the local press, Raanan took up residence abroad. He has been very successful and his work is published, through a syndicate, in many newspapers throughout the world.

Extremist Tendencies

The Six Day War brought about many important changes in all walks of Israeli life. At its end, Israel was confronted by a frustrated Arab world, extreme in its hostility and supported by the communist bloc and most of the countries of the Third World. In the friendly countries of the West, the image of the country, which had refused to fulfill its "natural" role as a victim of aggression, underwent a change. The "era of forebearance" towards her had come to an end. Within Israeli society, the first signs of a deep ideological split appeared. Large segments of the public regarded the achievements of the war as a guarantee of security and the realization of a vision. On the other hand, there were influential circles that opposed the "occupation" and launched a re-examination of national mores. A new front was opened against Israel — a campaign of terror, under the flag of the "Palestinian national movement." These tensions were faithfully expressed in pictorial satire, and its creators took on one or the other of the opposing stands adopted by the public. The style of expression became more extreme. Another contributing factor was the encounter with the new anti-Israel political drawings, in which clearly antisemitic motifs began to appear. No one expected self-restraint from the Arab visual propaganda, but the rabidity of the caricatures, that were created under communist inspiration, caused surprise and dismay. The "ugly Jew", well known from the Nazi period, returned to the scene as the "typical Israeli."

The Third Generation and its Problems

A new school of creators appeared in the local press. The outstanding representatives of this "third generation" of Israeli caricaturists, Yakov Shilo, Moshik Lin, Dudu Geva, and others, are native-born, whereas Yakov Kirshen and Maris Bishop are new immigrants. The last two tried to introduce to the Israeli press satirical approaches to which it was unaccustomed. Kirshen, who came from the United States, developed a political comic "strip." The message is conveyed by means of a series of drawings, with a dominant text. This innovation, known by the name "Dry Bones" was very well received in the local English newspaper, but attempts to transplant it into the Hebrew press were not successful. Bishop brought with him from Russia "philosophical" caricatures, with a social sting of the sort popular in Eastern Europe. The conservative Israeli reader preferred to regard these as works of art.

The Israeli society underwent a difficult traumatic experience in the Yom Kippur War, and the "black winter" of its aftermath gave birth to irate protest movements. The drama of the settlements in the administered territories which was to arouse so much controversy began. A political reversal took place, peace "broke out" between Israel and Egypt. These events were accompanied by

212

spirited caricature activity. At the same time, there was a feeling that the visual-news-commentary focus had moved over to television. Attempts were made to merge the two areas and to broadcast caricatures on the TV screen. It very quickly turned out that the two means of expression, which at first glance seemed so similar, work on different habits of observation that cannot be bridged. Caricature also was forced to pit itself against written political satire, which in its new aggressive style, gained wide circulation during the last decade. One of the signs of this period is the fact that more political satire is published in the Israeli media than in most other countries.

In Summary — Humor

The war in Lebanon and its ramifications created an unprecedented conflict in the media both within and outside of Israel. Most of the communications media in Israel took a firm stand against the government, whereas the foreign press and television carried on an enormous campaign of vilification of Israel. In this assault, all of the boundary lines were blurred between journalism and propaganda, between legitimate criticism and prejudice, between factual reporting and vicious lies. International caricature enlisted itself at the head of the anti-Israeli front. Any disparity between the Arab and communist expressions, on the one hand, and satire in the free world — differences in level, in style and standards of decency which until then had manifested themselves — now completely disappeared. In a rare communality of ideas, the same fallacious motif appeared in both worlds: the identification of Israel with Nazi Germany. Israeli leaders and soldiers were depicted in many caricatures with a Hitleresque image, and a drawing of this type even gained international recognition when it was awarded first prize at the "1983 Montreal Salon". One can only hope that the blurring of moral lines and the lapse of international justice that infected the profession — and which were apparently motivated by non-rational impulses — will turn out to be temporary and fleeting. At the moment, there is only one way to relate to this depressing phenomenon, and that is by means of that proven Jewish defense mechanism, which is of course humor. To what extent is humor an ingredient in Israeli caricature and what is the quality of this humor?

Humor is a basic essential of pictorial satire. There is an immediate comic effect in translating a situation or a political event into banal visual terms. At the same time, it may be possible to detect a certain "national" trait in the degree of sophistication, the level of analogy, and in the subtlety of allusion. In terms of this criterion, Israeli caricature rates a "good place in the middle" between the dry sophistication which is the hallmark of caricature in the West and "folksy" simplicity. The question that arises is whether the local creation has a specifically Jewish-Israeli intonation. It seems this is in fact the case. A meticulous examination of Israeli pictorial satire is likely to turn up a trace of "typical" self-castigation. The motif of the nation and its citizens as the victims of machination, so frequently and flagrantly depicted in local caricature, with almost a sense of pleasure, in which there is a far-off echo of "classic" Jewish humor, is offset by the Israeli component in the picture which is revealed through expressions of somewhat boastful national pride.

One can sum up by stating that Israeli caricature, from the standpoint of its humor, is in keeping with the worldwide trend: the comic ingredient in political caricature is diminishing. The Israeli caricaturist may possibly exhibit more professional "seriousness" than his foreign colleagues. Drawings that convey ideas are taken more seriously in Israel by their creators and their audience. Is this a favorable characteristic from the standpoint of satire? Time and those passing judgement will tell.

In the meantime, the Israeli cartoonist gives up on getting laughs. He is content with a lean smile of satisfaction and appreciation, which original and apt visual commentary deserves. And that same strange vocation, based on contradictions, also deserves the creative flash, that is routinely born, under the harsh deadlines imposed by the media.

Scholarly Bibliography on Jewish Humor

Abramson, G. "Mightier than the Sword: Jewish Cartoons and Cartoonists in South Africa," *Humor: International Journal of Humor Research* 4, 2 (1991): 149–164.

Adler, R. "Shalom Aleichem's 'On Account of a Hat.'" In A. Ziv, ed., *Jewish Humor.* Tel Aviv: Papyrus, 1986, 19–28.

Afek, Y., ed. *Israeli Humor and Satire.* Tel Aviv: Sadan Publishing House, 1974.

Alexander, D. "Political Satire in the Israeli Theatre: Another Outlook on Zionism." In A. Ziv, ed., *Jewish Humor.* Tel Aviv: Papyrus, 1986, 165–174.

Alter, R. "Jewish Humor and the Domestication of Myth." In S. Cohen, ed., *Jewish Wry.* Detroit: Wayne State University Press, 1987, 25–36.

Altman, S. *Comic Image of the Jew: Explorations of a Pop Culture Phenomenon.* Rutherford: Fairleigh Dickinson University Press, 1971.

Anderson, Gary A. *A Time to Mourn, A Time to Dance: The Expression of Grief and Joy in Israelite Religion.* University Park: Pennsylvania State University Press, 1991.

Baruch, Miri. "The Development of Humor in Israeli Children's Literature in the Twentieth Century." In Avner Ziv and Anat Zajdman, eds., *Semites and Stereotypes: Characteristics of Jewish Humor.* Westport, CT: Greenwood, 1993, 177–184.

Ben-Amotz, D. "Myth of Jewish Humor." *Western Folklore* 32, 2 (1973): 112–131.

Berger, Arthur Asa. "Jewish Humor." *An Anatomy of Humor.* New Brunswick, NJ: Transaction Publishers, 1993, 75–96.

Berghahn, K. L. "Comedy Without Laughter: Jewish Characters in Comedies from Shylock to Nathan." In R. Grimm and J. Herman, *Laughter Unlimited: Essays on Humor, Satire, and the Comic.* University of Wisconsin Press, Madison, 1991, 3–26.

Bermant, C. *What's the Joke? A Study of Jewish Humour Through the Ages.* London: Weidenfeld and Nicolson, 1986.

Bloch, R. H., Fabiaux. "Fetishism and Freud's Jewish Jokes." *Representations* 4 (1983): 1–26.

Bodkin, J. "Beyond Kvetching and Jiving: The Thrust of Jewish and Black Folk Humor." In S. Cohen, ed., *Jewish Wry.* Bloomington: Indiana University Press, Bloomington, 1987, 53–79.

Boyer, J. "Schlemiezel: Black Humor and the Shtetl Tradition." *Humor: International Journal of Humor Research* 4, 2 (1991): 165–176.

Brandes, S. "Jewish-American Dialect Jokes and Jewish-American Identity." *Jewish Social Studies* 45, 3–4 (1983): 233–240.

215

Chard-Hutchinson, Martine. "The Functions of Humor in Bernard Malamud's Fiction." *Humor: International Journal of Humor Research* 4, 2 (1991): 177–88.

Charney, Maurice. "Stanley Elkin and Jewish Black Humor." In Sarah Blacher Cohen, ed., *Jewish Wry*. Detroit: Wayne State University Press, 1987, 178–95.

Cohen, Sarah Blacher, ed. *From Hester Street to Hollywood: The Jewish-American Stage and Screen*. Bloomington: Indiana University Press, 1986.

———. *Jewish Wry: Essays on Jewish Humor*. Detroit: Wayne State University Press, 1990.

———. "Jewish Literary Comedians." In S. B. Cohen, ed., *Comic Relief: Humor in Contemporary American Literature*. Detroit: Wayne State University Press, 1978, 172–186.

———. "Unkosher Comediennes: From Sophie Tucker to Joan Rivers." In S. B. Cohen, ed., *Jewish Wry*. Detroit: Wayne State University Press, 1987, 105–124.

Cooper, A. "Jewish Sit-Down Comedy of Philip Roth." In S. B. Cohen, ed., *Jewish Wry*. Detroit: Wayne State University Press, 1987, 158–177.

Cray, E. "Rabbi Trickster." *Journal of American Folklore* 77 (1964): 331–345.

Davies, C. "An Explanation of Jewish Jokes about Jewish Women." *Humor: International Journal of Humor Research* 3, 4 (1990): 363–378.

———. "Exploring the Thesis of the Self-Deprecating Jewish Sense of Humor." *Humor: International Journal of Humor Research* 4, 2 (1991): 189–210.

———. "Jewish Jokes, Anti-Semitic Jokes and Hebredonian Jokes." In A. Ziv, ed., *Jewish Humor*. Tel Aviv: Papyrus, 1986, 75–96.

Dorinson, J. "Jew as Comic: Lenny Bruce, Mel Brooks, Woody Allen." In A. Ziv, ed., *Jewish Humor*. Tel Aviv: Papyrus, 1986, 29–46.

———. "Jewish Humor: Mechanism for Defense, Weapon for Cultural Affirmation." *Journal of Psychohistory* 8 (1981): 447–464.

Eilbirt, H. *What is a Jewish Joke? An Excursion into Jewish Humor*. Northvale: Jason Aronson, 1991.

Eisen, George. *Children and Play in the Holocaust*. Amherst: University of Massachusetts Press, 1988.

Freadman, Richard. "Love among the Stereotypes, or Why Woody's Women Leave." In Avner Ziv and Anat Zajdman, eds., *Semites and Stereotypes: Characteristics of Jewish Humor*. Westport, CT: Greenwood, 1993, 107–120.

Friedlander, Y. "Halachic Issues as Satirical Elements in Nineteenth Century Hebrew Literature." in Avner Ziv, ed., *Jewish Humor*. Tel Aviv: Papyrus, 1986.

Fuchs, E. "Is There Humor in Israeli Literature and If Not, Why Are We Laughing?" In S. B. Cohen, ed., *Jewish Wry*. Detroit: Wayne State University Press, Detroit, 1987, 216–233.

Gardosh, K. "Political Caricature as a Reflection of Israel's Development." In A. Ziv, ed., *Jewish Humor*. Tel Aviv: Papyrus, 1986.

Goldberg, J. N. *Laughter Through Tears: The Yiddish Cinema*. Rutherford: Fairleigh Dickinson University, 1983.

Goldberg, M. H. *Jewish Connection: The Incredible, Ironic, Bizarre, Funny, and Provocative in the Story of the Jews*. Lanham: Scarborough House, 1993.

Goldman, A. "Laughtermakers." In S. B. Cohen, ed. *Jewish Wry*. Detroit: Wayne State University Press, 1987, 80–88.

Goldsmith, Emanuel S. "Sholom Aleichem's Humor of Affirmation and Survival." In Avner Ziv and Anat Zajdman, eds. *Semites and Stereotypes: Characteristics of Jewish Humor*. Westport, CT: Greenwood, 1993, 13–28.

Good, Edwin. *Irony in the Old Testament*. Philadelphia, PA: Westminster, 1965.

Gotjhan, M. "Dynamics of Jewish Jokes." *American Behavioural Scientist* 30, 3 (1986): 96–98.

Greenstein, M. "Mordecai Richler and Jewish-Canadian Humor." In S. B. Cohen, ed., *Jewish Wry*. Detroit: Wayne State University Press, 1987, 196–215.

Guttman, A. "Jewish Humor." In L. D. Rubin, *The Comic Imagination in American Literature*. New Brunswick, NJ: Rutgers University Press, 1983, 329–338.

Harap, L. *Dramatic Encounters: The Jewish Presence in Twentieth Century American Drama, Poetry, and Humor and the Black-Jewish Literary Relationship*. New York: Greenwood Press, 1987.

Harris, D. A. *Jokes of Oppression: The Humor of Soviet Jews*. Northvale: J. Aronson, 1988.

Hes, J. P. and J. Levine. "Kibbuts Humor." *Journal of Nervous and Mental Disorders* 135 (1962): 135, 327–331.

Howe, I. "Nature of Jewish Laughter." In S. B. Cohen, ed., *Jewish Wry*. Detroit: Wayne State University Press, 1987, 16–24.

Knox, I. "Traditional Roots of Jewish Humor." *Judaism* 12, 3 (1963): 330–331.

Landmann, S. "On Jewish Humor." *Jewish Journal of Sociology* 4 (1962): 193–194.

Lewis, Anthony. "The Jew in Stand-up Comedy." In Sarah Blacher Cohen, ed., *From Hester Street to Hollywood*. Bloomington: Indiana University Press, 1986, 58–70.

Lipman, S. *Laughter in Hell: The Use of Humor During the Holocaust*. Northvale: J. Aronson, 1991.

Mast, G. "Woody Allen: The Neurotic Jew as American Clown." In S. B. Cohen, ed., *Jewish Wry*. Bloomington: Indiana University Press, 1987, 125–140.

Miller, Carolyn. "Are Jews *Funnier than Non-Jews?*" In Avner Ziv and Anat Zajdman, eds., *Semites and Stereotypes: Characteristics of Jewish Humor*. Westport, CT: Greenwood, 1993, 59–70.

Mindess, H. *Chosen People? A Testament, Both Old and New, to the Therapeutic Power of Jewish Wit and Humor*. Los Angeles: Nash Pub., 1972.

Mintz, L.E. "Devil and Angel: Philip Roth's Humor." *Studies in American Jewish Literature* 8, 2 (1989): 154–167.

———. "Rabbi versus the Priest and Other Jewish Stories." In A. Ziv, ed., *Jewish Humor*. Tel Aviv: Papyrus, 1986, 125–134.

Morris, C. "Woody Allen Comic Irony." *Literature-Film Quarterly*. 15, 3 (1987): 175–180.

Nevo, O. "Do Jews in Israel Still Laugh at Themselves?" In A. Ziv, ed., *Jewish Humor.* Tel Aviv: Papyrus, 1986, 191–202.

———. "Does One Ever Laugh at One's Own Expense? The Case of Jew and Arabs in Israel." *Journal of Personality and Social Psychology* 49, 3 (1985): 799–807.

———. "Humor Diaries of Israeli Jews and Arabs." *Journal of Social Psychology* 126, 3 (1986): 411–413.

———. "Jewish Humor in the Service of an Israeli Political Leader: The Case of Levi Eshkol." In Avner Ziv and Anat Zajdman, eds., *Semites and Stereotypes: Characteristics of Jewish Humor.* Westport, CT: Greenwood, 1993, 165–176.

———. "What's in a Jewish Joke?" *Humor: International Journal of Humor Research* 4,2 (1991): 251–260.

Nilsen, Alleen Pace. "We Should Laugh So Long? The Influence of Jewish Humor on Contemporary Books for Young Readers." *School Library Journal* (November 1986): 30–34.

Nilsen, Don L. F. "Israeli and Jewish Humor." *Humor Scholarship: A Research Bibliography.* Westport, CT: Greenwood, 1993, 200–207.

Oring, E. *Israeli Humor: The Content and Structure of the Chizbat of the Palmah.* Albany: State University of New York Press, 1981.

———. *Jokes of Sigmund Freud: A Study in Humor and Jewish Identity.* Philadelphia: University of Pennsylvania Press, 1984.

———. "Jokes and Their Relation to Sigmund Freud." *Western Folklore* 43 (1984): 37–48.

———. "People of the Joke: On the Conceptualization of Jewish Humor." *Western Folklore* 42, 4 (1983): 261–271.

Ornstein-Galicia, J. L. "Linguistic Patterns and Devices in American Jewish Humorous Discourse." *META: Journal des Traducteurs* 34, 1 (1989): 125–127.

Pauwels de la Ronciere, Marie-Christine. "Visual and Intellectual Humor in Saul Bellow's Fiction." *Humor: International Journal of Humor Research* 4, 2 (1991): 241–50.

Perlmutter, R. "Woody Allen's *Zelig*: An American Jewish Parody." In A. S. Horton, ed., *Comedy: Cinema, Theory.* Berkeley: University of California Press, 1991, 206–221.

Pinsker, S. "Lenny Bruce: Shpritzing the Goyim/Shocking the Jews." In S. B. Cohen, ed., *Jewish Wry.* Detroit: Wayne State University Press, 1987, 89–104.

———. "Instruments of American Jewish Humor: Henny Youngman on Violin, Mel Brooks on Drums, Woody Allen on Clarinet." *Massachusetts Review* 22 (1981): 739–750.

———. "Mel Brooks and the Cinema of Exhaustion." In Sarah Blacher Cohen, ed. *From Hester Street to Hollywood.* Bloomington: Indiana University Press, 1986, 245–56.

Raskin, R. *Life is Like a Glass of Tea: Studies of Classic Jewish Jokes.* Aarhus: Aarhus University Press, 1992.

218

————. "The Origins and Evolution of a Classic Jewish Joke." Avner Ziv and Anat Zajdman, eds., *Semites and Stereotypes: Characteristics of Jewish Humor.* Westport, CT: Greenwood, 1993, 870–106.

————. "God versus Man in a Classic Jewish Joke." *Judaism* 40, 1 (1991): 39–51.

Reik, T. *Jewish Wit.* New York: Gamut Press, 1962.

————. "Freud and Jewish Wit." *Psychoanalysis* 2 (1954): 12–20.

Rosenberg, B., and G. Shapiro. "Marginality and Jewish Humor." *Midstream* 4, 1 (1959): 70–80.

Rovit, E. "Jewish Humor and American Life." *American Scholar* 36 (1967): 237.

Saper, B. "A Cognitive Behavioral Formulation of the Relation between the Jewish Joke and Anti-Semitism." *Humor: International Journal of Humor Research* 4,1 (1991): 41–60.

————. "The JAP Joke Controversy: An Excruciating Psychosocial Analysis." *Humor: International Journal of Humor Research* 4,2 (1991): 223–240.

Saposnik, I. "Yiddish Are Coming! The Yiddish Are Coming! Some Thoughts on Yiddish Comedy." In R. Grimm and J. Herman, eds., *Laughter Unlimited: Essays on Humor, Satire, and the Comic.* Madison: University of Wisconsin, 1991, 99–105.

Schechner, M. "Dear Mr Einstein: Jewish Comedy and the Contradictions of Culture." In S. B. Cohen, ed., *Jewish Wry.* Detroit: Wayne State University Press, 1987, 141–157.

Spencer, Gary. "An Analysis of JAP-Baiting Humor on the College Campus." *Humor: International Journal of Humor Research* 2, 4 (1989): 329–48.

Stora-Sandor, Judith. "From Eve to the Jewish American Princess: The Comic Representation of Women in Jewish Literature." In Avner Ziv and Anat Zajdman, eds., *Semites and Stereotypes: Characteristics of Jewish Humor.* Westport, CT: Greenwood, 1993, 131–142.

————. "Stylistic Metamorphosis of Jewish Humor." *Humor: International Journal of Humor Research* 4, 2 (1991): 211–222.

Telushkin, J. *Jewish Humor: What the Best Jewish Jokes Say About the Jews.* New York: W. Morrow, 1991.

Walden, Daniel. "Neil Simon's Jewish-style Comedies." In Sarah Blacher Cohen, ed., *From Hester Street to Hollywood.* Bloomington: Indiana University Press, 12–66, 1986.

Whitfield, Stephen J. "Jules Feiffer and the Comedy of Disenchantment." In Sarah Blacher Cohen, ed., *From Hester Street to Hollywood.* Bloomington: Indiana University Press, 1986, 167–82.

Wiener, M. "On Sholom Aleichem's Humor." In S. B. Cohen, ed., *Jewish Wry.* Detroit: Wayne State University Press, 1997, 37–52.

Wisse, R. R. *The Schlemiel as Modern Hero.* Chicago: University of Chicago Press, 1980.

Zajdman, A.. "The Transactional Implications of the Jewish Marriage Jokes." In Avner

Ziv and Anat Zajdman, eds., *Semites and Stereotypes: Characteristics of Jewish Humor.* Westport, CT: Greenwood, 1993, 143–64.

Ziv, A. "Humor in Israel." In A. Ziv, ed., *National Styles of Humor.* New York: Greenwood, 1988, 113–132.

———. "Psycho-Social Aspects of Jewish Humor in Israel and in the Diaspora." In A. Ziv, ed., *Jewish Humor.* Tel Aviv: Papyrus, 1986, 47–71.

———, ed., *First and Second International Conferences on Jewish Humor.* Tel Aviv: Tel Aviv University, 1986.

———, ed., *Jewish Humor.* Tel Aviv: Papyrus, 1986.

———, guest ed. "Jewish Humor." Special issue of *Humor: International Journal of Humor Research* 4, 2 (1991): 1–288.

Ziv, A., and A. Zajdman, eds., *Semites and Stereotypes: Characteristics of Jewish Humor*, Greenwood Press, Westport, 1993.

Index